About the Author

Paul A. Tucci is a writer, researcher, and author of the books *Traveling Everywhere* (2001) and *The Handy Geography Answer Book* (2008), as well as numerous articles on the information industry. He is a frequent guest lecturer in man agement, marketing, and strategy at various universities, including New York University, Northwestern University, the University of Michigan, and Oakland University. An amateur investor for over thirty years, and a former global information/publishing manager, he is also a business owner and partner of an innovative IT services and software development firm, a consultant to and investor in small private equity funded businesses, and board of directors member of the Rislov Foundation, a charitable foundation dedicated to providing funding for classical music education, instruction, and programming. He resides in Michigan.

Also from Visible Ink Press

The Handy Anatomy Answer Book
by James Bobick and Naomi Balaban
ISBN: 978–1–57859–190–9

The Handy Answer Book for Kids (and Parents),
2nd edition
by Gina Misiroglu
ISBN: 978–1–57859–219–7

The Handy Astronomy Answer Book
by Charles Liu
ISBN: 978–1–57859–193–0

The Handy Dinosaur Answer Book, 2nd edition
by Patricia Barnes–Svarney and Thomas E.
Svarney
ISBN: 978–1–57859–218–0

The Handy Geography Answer Book, 2nd edition
by Paul A. Tucci
ISBN: 978–1–57859–215–9

The Handy Geology Answer Book
by Patricia Barnes–Svarney and Thomas E.
Svarney
ISBN: 978–1–57859–156–5

The Handy History Answer Book, 2nd edition
by Rebecca Nelson Ferguson
ISBN: 978–1–57859–170–1

The Handy Law Answer Book
by David L. Hudson Jr.
ISBN: 978–1–57859–217–3

The Handy Math Answer Book
by Patricia Barnes–Svarney and Thomas E.
Svarney
ISBN: 978–1–57859–171–8

The Handy Ocean Answer Book
by Patricia Barnes–Svarney and Thomas E.
Svarney
ISBN: 978–1–57859–063–6

The Handy Philosophy Answer Book
by Naomi Zack
ISBN: 978–1–57859–226–5

The Handy Physics Answer Book, 2nd edition
By Paul W. Zitzewitz, Ph.D.
ISBN: 978–1–57859–305–7

The Handy Politics Answer Book
by Gina Misiroglu
ISBN: 978–1–57859–139–8

The Handy Presidents Answer Book, 2nd edition
By David L. Hudson, Jr.
ISBN: 978–1–57859–371–0

The Handy Psychology Answer Book
by Lisa J. Cohen
ISBN: 978–1–57859–223–4

The Handy Religion Answer Book
by John Renard
ISBN: 978–1–57859–125–1

The Handy Science Answer Book®, 4th edition
by The Science and Technology Department Carnegie Library of Pittsburgh, James
E. Bobick, and Naomi E. Balaban
ISBN: 978–1–57859–140–4

The Handy Sports Answer Book
by Kevin Hillstrom, Laurie Hillstrom, and
Roger Matuz
ISBN: 978–1–57859–075–9

The Handy Supreme Court Answer Book
by David L Hudson, Jr.
ISBN: 978–1–57859–196–1

The Handy Weather Answer Book, 2nd edition
by Kevin S. Hile
ISBN: 978–1–57859–221–0

Please visit the Handy series website at handyanswers.com

THE
HANDY
PERSONAL
FINANCE
ANSWER
BOOK

THE HANDY PERSONAL FINANCE ANSWER BOOK

Visible Ink Press®
43311 Joy Rd., #414
Canton, MI 48187-2075

Visible Ink Press is a registered trademark of Visible Ink Press LLC.

Most Visible Ink Press books are available at special quantity discounts when purchased in bulk by corporations, organizations, or groups. Customized printings, special imprints, messages, and excerpts can be produced to meet your needs. For more information, contact Special Markets Director, Visible Ink Press, www.visibleinkpress.com, or 734-667-3211.

Managing Editor: Kevin S. Hile
Art Director: Mary Claire Krzewinski
Typesetting: Marco Di Vita
Proofreaders: Sharon Malinowski
Cover images: iStock.

Library of Congress Cataloguing-in-Publication Data

Tucci, Paul A., 1962—
The handy personal finance answer book / by Paul A. Tucci.
    p. cm.
Includes bibliographical references and index.
  ISBN 978-1-57859-322-4 M— ISBN 978-1-57859-389-7 — ISBN 978-1-57859-390-3 — ISBN 978-1-57859-391-0
  1. Finance, Personal. I. Title.
HG179.T817 2012
332.024—dc23   2011027529

Printed in the United States of America

10 9 8 7 6 5 4 3 2 1

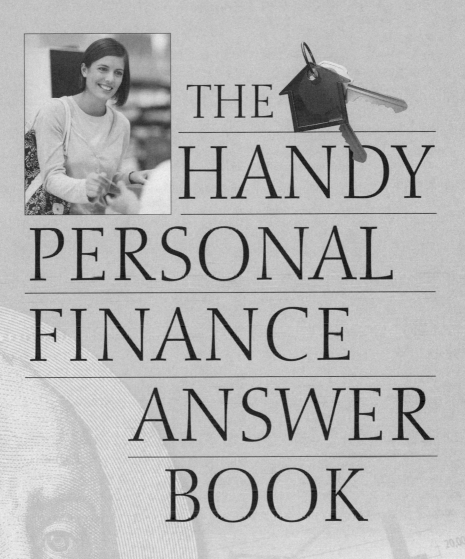

THE HANDY PERSONAL FINANCE ANSWER BOOK

Paul A. Tucci

VISIBLE INK PRESS

Detroit

Contents

INTRODUCTION ... 1

History of Money, Banks, and Saving ... History of Credit Cards ... Our Financial Mindset ... Blogs

BASIC BANKING ... 15

Banks ... Credit Unions ... Managing Your Account ... Online Banking ... Paying Bills Online ... Phishing and Other Online Scams ... Personal Finance Software

SAVINGS AND INVESTMENTS ... 33

Overview ... Stocks ... Investors ... Investing for Retirement ... Market Timing, Technical Analysis, and Fundamental Analysis ... Buying Stocks ... Protecting Yourself from Fraud ... Analyzing Stocks ... Helpful Financial Websites ... Bonds ... Mutual Funds ... Individual Retirement Accounts ... Investing in Gold ... Investing in Real Estate ... Selling Your House ... Financial Planners and Investment Advisors

INSURANCE ... 105

Home Insurance ... Insurance for Renters ... Automobile Insurance ... Health Insurance ... Life Insurance ... Small Business Insurance

TAXES ... 131

Federal Taxes ... Accountants and Tax Payers ... IRS Audits ... State Taxes ... Local and City Taxes

Acknowledgements

I wish to thank my parents, for their encouragement to open my first bank account when I was about five years old, to save at such a young age, and for letting me begin to work when I was nine years old; my big sister, Michele, who was my accountant for my paper route, as well as a model to me of financial responsibility when I was young and impressionable.

This book is also for Leo, who helped me to learn about what a money market fund was when I was sixteen, when interest rates were at historic highs. Also, from back in the days when I working as an intern in Washington, D.C., I wish to acknowledge the guy from the brokerage house on "K" Street, who advertised a free seminar that I attended when I was eighteen that taught me what a mutual fund was. John Riedel, former CFO of Proquest, taught me a lot about corporate finance over many years, and Zach Savas, with whom I had conversations over the years on the markets and private equity investing. I also spoke with Nick Demopoulos about global markets and currency trading over the years. Ray and Brad Berk taught me about tax issues. In addition, I would like to thank the following people who assisted with ideas and questions for the book; all of them are masters in their respective fields:

- Michele Tucci-Berube, J.D.: legal questions

- Amy Randazzo: personal tax questions

- Nick Demopoulos: stocks and mutual funds questions

- Sarah Butterfield, a tax professional, in the area of high net worth family and individual accounting: on tax questions

- John O'Brien, marketing/advertising professional: on all questions, specifically on financial advisors

- Isabella Tucci, Realtor™, thirty-five-year-real estate professional, Cranbrook Real Living, Inc.: real estate questions

- Michael Garcia, an automotive industry and logistics executive and entrepreneur who is experienced in issues about health and the subsequent loss of his beloved parents: caring for the elderly

- Dr. Evelyn Katz, cognitive therapist extraordinaire: financial mindset

I would also like to acknowledge the team at Visible Ink Press, who make this and so many other consumer reference works possible and accessible to so many people: Roger Jänecke, Publisher; Kevin Hile, Managing Editor; Mary Claire Krzewinski, for cover art and page design.

And, of course, my family....

This manuscript was entirely created and managed using Google Documents.

Photo Credits

All photos are courtesy of iStock.com, except for the following, provided by the author, Paul Tucci: pages 3, 6, 20, 42, 60, 106, 118, 120, 122, 127, 167, 194, and 266.

Introduction

The Handy Personal Finance Answer Book takes the reader through each of what we feel are major themes in personal finance. There are so many variables that affect our ability to manage our money; we decided to look at factors that may not be found in other personal finance reference books and present our information in a way that surprises, assists, and enables readers to change the way they feel about and view money. The questions and answers include broad statistical references that demonstrate how many people are affected by some aspect of finances, as well as broad macroeconomic data to support trends and allow the reader to draw his/her own conclusions. The line of questions also takes a subject and moves from broad to specific—but never too specific—answers that are never "over the heads" of the audience. Some answers are definitions, while others are explanations.

My journey into personal finance began when I was about eight or nine, after I responded to an ad in the back of my Superman comic book to sell vegetable seeds door to door. I had to buy a box of seeds and sell them to the neighboring houses. I ended up selling most of them, and I even planted the carrot seeds that I couldn't sell near a stump at my house, but they didn't grow. It was my first job, and I was so proud to begin earning money. My parents encouraged me to work, and soon I was painting the interiors of houses and managing a 150-house paper route at 4:00 in the morning in order to save for the future. I had already opened a bank account some years before, and I have been continuously employed ever since.

When interest rates were in the double digits in the late 1970s, I managed to open a money market account comprised of U.S. Government Treasury Bills and T Bills in order to take advantage of the returns while working and attending university. It was pretty rewarding to see how fast this money grew at the historically high rates, and so it was relatively easy for me to save even while in school.

If we value money and what financial security can bring to us, why are we so bad at managing it? It is most likely that we neglect a few key elements. We express little enthusiasm and interest in understanding personal finance until it is too late; we are late or errant in developing, over time, the discipline to use what we have learned; and we do not change the way that we view money.

You should know that you can change your views and behaviors, and over time you can make little changes that will contribute to your ability to permanently manage your finances.

Our mindset is key to our success in managing our money.

A friend of mine who was a currency trader in Tokyo noticed that his fellow traders would always reach a certain level of income in a day, and then somehow trade it down, so that they could never climb over their self-imposed wall. I thought about this and wondered how it is related to how we view money. People like predictability. If they are used to having a certain amount of money in savings—say $500—the idea of having $10,000 would be pretty stressful. They would have to decide what to do with it, how to spend it, what to pay off, who to give some to, etc. Eventually, and with sad predictability, the person would manage to spend his newfound cash right back down to the level of $500, the amount of money he or she was used to having.

If we just change what we feel is an acceptable amount to have, we begin to act a bit differently. Perhaps, if we are given $10,000, we might say to ourselves, "This is my new zero." We will start with this amount and pretend we do not have it, and just keep our expenses where they have always been. We can now be comfortable that we can use this money to invest and, hopefully, grow it.

This is but one change in mindset that leads to the creation of wealth. If we just changed our view on what is an acceptable amount of money to have in our checking account, for example, we would then do those things that help us get to that goal. So, if you can convince yourself that you prefer the feeling of having $10,000 in the checking account, you will begin to do things that will get you to that goal.

We might want to think about expensive purchases a little differently, too. If you think about buying a new $1,000 television because the other two-year-old that you own is smaller than your neighbors', imagine how much that money could have grown if you had not tried to compete with the Joneses and invested it instead? You have to have $10,000 earning ten percent per year in order to make enough interest to buy that television. In today's banks, you would need about $100,000 earning one percent to make enough extra money in interest to buy it. You begin to appreciate what each purchase means when you look at the expense in terms of investment earnings or income.

We have to simplify our financial lives by living beneath our means and saving and investing the extra income that we might get from raises, commissions, bonuses, and job changes. This means staying focused on keeping expenses low. The difference between what we manage to make and what we save plants the seeds of future wealth.

Take just one expense that you may have and see if there is a way to lower it. Maybe you never use your home phone anymore, but you still keep it at a cost of $80 per month, which is nearly $1,000 a year. See if there is a way for you to control and cut one expense per month. You may find many thousands of dollars available to you to save by the end of the year. Practice with just a small item before taking on an entire year of expense budgeting.

The world of personal finance seems like a difficult subject to take on, but it actually is not. It is just like a tree, and in many ways, just as this book has been organized, it enables us to distill the general areas of the subject one branch at a time, going neither too shallow nor too deep in any one area. Our quest for information on the subject can begin by delving into popular magazines like *Money* and *Kipplinger's*. We look at interesting news articles that relate to something that we have heard about and read the article to try to learn, and think, how it is related to our situation. Can we use this information in some way? Are the conclusions or suggestions useful or valuable? Have we heard or read reports from other people making the same claims or drawing the same conclusions? Are these people all reading from the same material, or are they drawing these conclusions from a variety of sources? This is what enables us to learn.

How do we know when to stop exploring a certain subject? It is probably good to stop when the subject gets too complex or too specific for your interests. Remember where you left off, and move on until you are ready for more in-depth reading.

The Internet provides a wealth of information on personal finance, so sifting through it can appear to be difficult, but it really is not. As you read an article that cites a U.S. Census Bureau study, you can easily click on the underlying research and see the exact report that the writer describes, deciding for yourself the material to explore. After a while, you can become well trained in surfing around to explore a subject. If you search Google news on a subject like income tax deductions, you may find many articles that describe ways of saving money on your taxes, spending only a few minutes doing so. Blog information is also valuable if you are interested in the articles that appear every day on the subject covered. But there is no one "good" source of information. In order to really understand personal finance, to learn about personal finance, and to develop a broad perspective on personal finance, you need to pull information from many different sources.

Personal finance is an area of our lives over which we probably can exert the most control. You make a certain amount of money every month, and you can spend it (or save it) any way that you like. Spenders will find novel ways to spend it down to zero. Savers will think of ways of turning one dollar into three. It is truly your choice. Sometimes people let their emotions run wild, and this impacts their ability to make proper financial decisions.

As we learn more about what is happening in the area of personal finance, choosing to focus our attention on this area of one's personal life can help you learn to make better financial decisions. We can easily make the "right" decision about whether or not to buy a used car, a leased car, or a brand new car. The decision should not be emotional. It should be straight analysis informing us as to which option helps to improve our current financial state. If you believe that debt is bad in almost all cases, then the option of getting a car, and getting a loan to do so, does not even come up. The idea of leasing an expensive car also is not considered because you have to have a lot of money invested in order to pay for the lease. It seems that paying cash for a used car is probably the option that makes the best financial sense. This is in contrast to the emotional, feel good option that says: "My friends all drive new cars, so I want one too," or "I should be driving a brand new car because everyone else does." Sorry to tell you, but most millionaires, including one of the most famous and wealthiest men in the world, Warren Buffet, drive cars that are paid for, often purchased used, and that are anywhere from ten to twenty years old. The reason why they are so wealthy, aside from a good deal of luck, is that they are able to make these kinds of decisions, time and time again, without letting their egos or emotions enter into the equations.

The goal of *The Handy Personal Finance Book* is to help you get a better handle on your saving and spending attitudes so that you, too, can build a more financially secure future for yourself and your family. While you might not be the next Warren Buffet, there is no reason why you cannot save a tidy nest egg, retire comfortably, and have enough left over to help your family. All it takes is some planning and discipline. Good luck!

Disclaimer

The material in *The Handy Personal Finance Book* and its affiliate sites has no regard to the specific investment objectives, financial situations, or particular needs of any audience. This book is published solely for informational purposes and the information contained within it is not to be construed as a solicitation or an offer to buy or sell any securities or related financial instruments. Your access and use of this book or affiliate sites is subject to the following terms and conditions and all applicable laws. By accessing and browsing this book or its affiliate sites, you accept these terms and conditions without limitation or qualification. This information is provided "as is" without warranty of any kind, and Visible Ink Press makes no representation, expressed or implied, as to the accuracy, reliability, or completeness of this information, or the timeliness of any information in this book or its affiliate sites.

References made to third parties are based on information obtained from sources believed to be reliable, but are not guaranteed as being accurate. Visitors should not regard *The Handy Personal Finance Book* as a substitute for the exercise of their own judgment. Any opinions expressed in this book are subject to change without notice, and Visible Ink Press is not under any obligation to update or keep current the information contained herein.

Under no circumstances shall Visible Ink Press have any liability to any person or entity for (1) any loss or damage in whole or part caused by, resulting from, or relating to any error (neglect or otherwise) or other circumstances involved in procuring, collecting, compiling, interpreting, analyzing, editing, transcribing, communicating or delivering any information in this book or its affiliate sites, or (2) any direct, indirect, special, consequential or incidental damages whatsoever, resulting from the use of, or inability to use, any such information.

Visible Ink Press accepts no liability whatsoever for any loss or damage of any kind arising out of the use of all or any part of this material. Our comments are an expression of opinion. While we believe our statements to be true, they always depend on the reliability of our own credible sources. We recommend that you consult a licensed, qualified professional before making any investment decisions.

INTRODUCTION

What is **personal finance**?

Personal finance is the management of our income, expenses, and investments in order for us to realize our personal financial goals. It is the study of, and attention to, the management of our money in order for us to create wealth and ultimately, independence. It focuses on establishing short and long-term goals; and, by making incremental steps in our present, we are able to realize our financial goals in the future. Through the study of personal finance, we learn possible strategies to take and choices to make in our decisions in order realize our financial goals.

Why do we **care** about **personal finance**?

There are many reasons that we care about personal finance. We wish to be able to have a certain level of income, which when properly managed, gives us more options for how we wish to spend, save, and invest the money. Many people wish to eliminate their current worries about their financial situation by having a good plan in place to save and invest a portion of their income. Others' primary personal financial focus may be on doing whatever it takes to save for their retirement, so that they may live a life near the same financial level that they were at when they were working. And millions of others care about personal finance so that they realize very specific goals such

Who said, "He who knows when enough is enough, will always have enough"?

Chinese philosopher Lao Tzu wrote this in the *Tao Te Ching,* sometime around 600 B.C.E.

1

as saving for their children's university education. Ultimately, people wish to feel secure. It is our pursuit of feelings of security that we focus our attention on when creating strategies that help us become financially secure.

HISTORY OF MONEY, BANKS, AND SAVING

When did the **word "money"** first **appear**?

The word "money" first appeared in the thirteenth century. It was derived from the Latin word "monete," a name given to the Roman goddess Juno, at or near whose temple the Romans first began minting coins around 300 B.C.E.

Who said, "A **penny saved is a penny earned**"?

This quote is often attributed to Benjamin Franklin, but he never actually wrote this. In his *Poor Richard's Almanack,* which he wrote under the pseudonym Richard Saunders, published from 1733 to 1758, Franklin actually said, "A penny saved is twopence dear."

How old is the concept of saving?

The concept of saving may go back as far as the Neolithic Period (around 10,000 B.C.E.) when early man began settling in villages and engaged in agricultural production and animal husbandry. The very fact that they were producing more food than each farm could consume means that they had to save and, later, trade the surplus.

When did the first banks come into existence?

Around 3000 B.C.E., according to many scholars, some of the first banks may have been inside of temples, used for both religious ceremonies and the storage of agricultural products, like wheat and other grains. Farmers would deposit their

One of America's Founding Fathers, Benjamin Franklin published many wise sayings in his *Poor Richard's Almanack*, but is misquoted in the saying "A penny saved is a penny earned.'

Money in paper form is a fairly recent development. Currency has typically been in the form of coins made of precious metals.

supply at the temple and were given a receipt for the amount of product that they deposited. It is thought that this receipt was of value, and would most likely be the earliest form of money used in trade.

When was the **earliest written evidence** of the **use of money**?

We began to see laws mentioning the use of money as payment for restitution in the *Code of Ur-Nammu*. It was written in Sumerian by the King Ur Nammu of Ur, who ruled from 2112 to 2095 B.C.E.. In law 22, it is written, "If a man knocks out a tooth of another man, he shall pay two shekels of silver."

When did we begin to see **laws that regulated commerce**?

Around 1790 B.C.E., Hammurabi, the sixth king of Babylon, created a code of 282 laws for his kingdom, some of which covered such subjects as the leasing of land, the payment of debt, banking, real estate, and trade.

When did the use of **money** first **begin**?

As early as 5000 B.C.E., the Sumerians, in modern-day Iraq, began to produce silver ingots to be used as a standard measurement and currency. They also invented the wheel and arithmetic. The Egyptians began using gold as a form of currency around 4000 B.C.E.

3

The history of credit cards dates back to 1908. Early credit cards acted almost like bank accounts, and customers had to carry a balance to make a purchase. Today, Americans use credit cards to pay for large or small purchases on time, and the average household carried over $14,000 in credit card debt in 2011, according to CreditCards.com.

When did the **first coins appear**?

The first coins, imprinted with a turtle in relief, appeared around 700 B.C.E., in Aegina Island, in modern-day Greece.

HISTORY OF CREDIT CARDS

Who popularized the **phrase "credit card"**?

A nineteenth century author named Edward Bellamy (1850–1898), writing in his Utopian sci-fi novel *Looking Backward,* used the word credit card 11 times. His book, which describes a society in the year 2000, sold more than one million copies.

When did the first **credit cards appear**?

In the late 1800s, business owners used charge plates in order to advance credit for the purchase of items in their stores. By the 1900s, oil companies and retail stores began issuing paper cards that allowed the bearer to purchase goods and pay at a later date. They could only be used at the particular business that issued the card or at limited locations. In 1950, Diners Club began, and was the first card used for general travel and entertainment. Both American Express and BankAmericard (now Visa) began issuing their own competitive credit cards in 1958.

When did the **first bank card** appear?

The first bank card, called Charg-it, was issued in 1946 by a man named Paul Biggins. Cardholders had to have an account at his bank in order to use the card.

How has the **use of credit changed** over the past century?

In a 1908 advertisement appearing in the *New York Times,* Macy's department store advertised its first credit cards to potential clients by setting up a credit account at its stores, where customers could deposit money, earn 4% interest on their deposits, and use the money to buy whatever they wanted. Customers never had to pay interest on anything; and when they wanted their money back, they could withdraw it at any time, plus their interest earned.

OUR FINANCIAL MINDSET

What are some **basic steps** in our **personal finance journey**?

There are several steps that we must all take in our pursuit of personal financial management. We have to begin by really thinking of, and assessing our attitudes toward, money and focus on what thoughts or attitudes seem to be blocking our ability to attain our financial goals. Many of these concepts started at an early age by observing how our parents dealt with financial issues. The good thing is that all of the beliefs and attitudes about money that are blocking us can easily be changed. We have to begin to read and learn about personal finance, by using all the information available to us, like searching the Internet, reading magazines on personal finance, paying attention to the business and financial section of the newspaper, and watching personal financial shows on television and online.

It may seem a bit intimidating at first, but after a while the information begins to make sense. You begin to see how small economic changes affect things like today's stock price, but not next year's stock price. You begin to see what economic variables affect each other, why the price of oil, or the interest rate in a far-away capital like Tokyo or London, is so critical to the economy. We have to assess our financial picture and have a truthful and open view of where we are in terms of our income and expenses. Can I improve my income this year? Am I even trying to improve my skills, work better than others, and ask for the raise? We have to look at our expenses and see where the overages are. Do we make enough money to go out for dinner three nights a week? We have to see if we have at least six months' of emergency funds that we never touch,

5

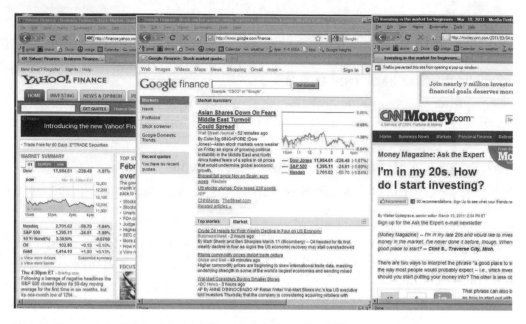

Many Americans go to the Web to get the latest financial news. Sites such as CNNMoney.com, Google Finance, and Yahoo! Finance offer updated stock market information, international news, and helpful columns.

in case of a job change, or costly personal event, so that we can ride through it before we settle again. And we must consider paying ourselves first a certain percentage of our income each pay period, never touching these funds unless they are in support of some financial goal, like education, retirement like education, retirement, etc.

We have to design attainable goals, both short- and long-term. This allows us to build our confidence that we can actually attain a goal before moving on to the next. It allows us to visualize a long-term goal and not let our current desire to buy that new thing get in the way of attaining our long-term goal. Once we have our goals in mind, it's time to execute our strategies to attain our goals. By this point, we have some ideas or strategies in place that help us reach our short-term goals and long-term goals. We may decide to begin taking money out of our paycheck and directing it to a retirement fund. We may decide to sell the leased car and buy a cheaper used car, and begin saving the monthly payment that we used to make, each month. All of a sudden, after 12 months, we find that we have an additional $2,400 available to invest. Our personal finance journey also involves learning how to analyze our performance and how good we are at meeting our short and long-term goals:

- Should we cut out the investments that are doing poorly in the short-term?
- Do we have too much money tied into our real estate?
- Should we now move from keeping cash to investing in mutual funds?

It's important to look at the performance of our portfolio in order to make sure that it is helping us meet our goals, or make the necessary changes. And finally, per-

Average family income in the United States has taken a downward turn in the twenty-first century. Some economists fear that the next generation of Americans will be the first in over a century that actually earns less than the preceding generation.

sonal finance teaches us to have the flexibility to occasionally re-adjust our goals and strategies along the way, and make adjustments in both our spending habits and savings habits, depending on what events life throws at us. We learn how to make the right choices at the right times, and see opportunity to improve our methods and strategies as we reach different stages in our lives.

Mean Household Income Averages, 1980–2009

Year	Mean Income*	Median Income
1980	$52,202	43,892
1981	$51,565	43,163
1982	$51,879	43,048
1983	$51,990	42,747
1984	$54,002	44,074
1985	$55,255	44,898
1986	$57,434	46,488
1987	$58,539	47,071
1988	$59,266	47,433
1989	$60,996	48,279
1990	$59,505	47,637
1991	$58,242	46,269
1992	$58,177	45,888
1993	$60,556	45,665

Year	Mean Income*	Median Income
1994	$61,731	46,175
1995	$62,802	47,622
1996	$64,148	48,315
1997	$66,214	49,309
1998	$68,145	51,100
1999	$70,462	52,388
2000	$71,165	52,301
2001	$70,521	51,161
2002	$68,976	50,563
2003	$68,886	50,519
2004	$68,662	50,343
2005	$69,597	50,899
2006	$70,819	51,278
2007	$69,940	51,965
2008	$68,164	50,112
2009	$67,976	49,777

* Source: U.S. Census Bureau. All figures have been adjusted to equal 2009 dollars and include all family members who earned income in the household.

What is the **median income** of **typical American families**?

The median income is $72,000 for families where both spouses are in the work force.

How many **households** have **credit cards**?

There are 54 million households with credit cards.

How much **credit card debt** is there?

There is roughly $866 billion dollars in credit card debt in the United States today.

What is the **average** amount of **credit card debt** for U.S. card holders?

The average card holder has $15,788 in credit card debt. This could be debt related to everything from everyday purchases of food and gas, to clothes, large household items like TVs or washing machines, to monthly utility bills.

What is the **mindset** that helps us to become **financially successful**?

We have to begin to think that we live in an abundant world, a place where earning money is unlimited, smart work is rewarded, and financial goals are always attained. Think of how you feel, for example, when you do not have to worry about making a mortgage or rent payment, or what it feels like to create a budget, and actually stick to it, each month. It is very important to believe that you can control your finances, and create wealth. No matter what our back ground is, whether we were struggling to make ends meet, or in a relatively more affluent family, or somewhere in between, we want to have a clear picture in our minds of where we want to be, in terms of our personal finances.

How do we **attract wealth** in our life?

We have to look first at our attitudes toward money, and understand how these attitudes contribute to our financial situation today. By recognizing these attitudes we can see which ones are helping us, and which ones are blocking our goals. We simply have to change some of our beliefs about money and finances in order to begin to attract wealth. Our imagination is very important. In fact, it is our imagination that drives our desire to buy things, since we have a mental picture of the new car or cell phone that we want, we see images of it in commercials, our friends talk about it, and then we buy it. The trouble is, it's a little more difficult to imagine a pile of money 20 years from now that we will use to pay for our kids' tuition. So we have to teach ourselves how to imagine personal financial goals, and actually visualize them. We have to give ourselves permission to be wealthy, that it's not something reserved for some other people, that it includes all of us. By having a vision of what it feels like to have wealth, it makes us more able to use behaviors and see opportunities that create wealth. Some people think of wealth like water, something that flows to you. If you begin to act as if you already have financial security and have the discipline to meet your goals, financial security will happen.

How do I know if I am **out of control** of my **finances**?

Everyone is in control of their finances, to a certain degree. We all choose every day whether or not to purchase something. If we were to rent an apartment, or buy a car, we make the decision based upon how much income we have, and if it is affordable or not. A person who cannot tell the difference between an apartment that is too expensive, versus one that is within his or her budget, would be more out of control with regards to spending. People who spend more of their income than they make, would be closer to out of control. A person who has learned to consistently make the right spending decisions over time, someone who manages to have a large net worth, on a relatively meager income, but understands and practices personal finance each day, is very much in control of his or her finances.

If I just **make more money**, will I still have to **worry about my personal finances**?

No, just because you may have a high income does not ensure that you will be secure. There are millions of Americans who make much more than average and yet are still

9

one paycheck away from disaster, because they spend nearly all of what they make, and have no short-term or long-term financial plan. It is easy to see evidence of this by looking at the number of foreclosures of very expensive houses, condominiums, and vacation properties that came on the market after 2008. Many of these people were making well over $100,000 per year, yet, did not have emergency funds available to ride through a job change, or other life change, because they spent everything that they made and more.

Why is attaining great **financial goals easier** than we think?

Great financial goals are actually a series of small financial goals. If you make saving and investing and the general management of your money a priority, like your date with your favorite television show, over a long period of time, each of your financial goals is attained. If you do anything in small incremental steps, the largest goals are attained over time. And because the changes can be small steps, it's actually very easy to attain our large financial goals.

How much would my **savings grow** at different interest rates if I invested just **$25 a week**?

Savings Earned on Investing $25 per Week

Interest Rate	10 Years	30 Years	40 Years
5%	$16,850	$90,300	$165,580
7%	$18,775	$132,000	$283,700
10%	$22,280	$246,510	$690,650

How would my **savings increase** on an initial $10,000 investment, depending on the **interest rate**?

The following table shows how an initial investment of $10,000 can grow dramatically, depending on the rate of return over time.

Money Earned Over Time at Different Rates

Interest Rate	0 years	25 Years	40 Years
4%	$10,000	$26,658	$48,010
5%	$10,000	$33,863	$70,400
10%	$10,000	$108,347	$452,592

We can do a lot to control our finances and prevent money crises at home, but some things, such as unexpected medical bills or being fired from a job, are beyond our control. A financial plan for such emergencies is important. The old adage "save for a rainy day" still applies in modern times.

Why do people **spend down** their **savings**?

People are comfortable with predictability, and have a hard time getting used to new situations. So, if they grew up in an environment where there was never enough, and suddenly have a lot, no matter how painful, people will spend themselves down to the level that they are most comfortable with. If you never had more than $500 in your checking account, and all of a sudden are given a bonus of $1,000, people without financial goals will find a way to spend that $1,000 down to zero, because they are more familiar with having $500 at the most in their checking accounts. A person committed to attaining a financial goal will get the money, and put it away in a safe place, and pretend as if it didn't exist, and not change his/her spending behavior at all. Goal-oriented people will change the way they view their checking account, and decide that having $1,500 is the minimum to keep for a balance than the previous $500. While the spender is spending all of the excess, the saver has changed his minimum view to $10,000 and is setting aside this extra income to reach that new goal.

So **wealth creation** is really **about our thoughts**?

Yes, it doesn't really matter what your background is, if you decide that it actually feels better to be independent and live debt free, you will begin to take the proper steps to make this happen. You will resist the urges to spend, in favor of a longer term goal. If you tell yourself that it's okay to have $500 in your account, you will take steps to

11

Coffee drinkers in American drink an average of 3.1 cups of coffee a day. According to CoffeeResearch.org, that came to about $165 a year per coffee drinker in 1999, or almost $19 billion.

make this happen. If you tell yourself that it's okay to have $100,000 in your account, you will take steps to make that happen as well.

How much does our ability to **delay present gratification** in favor of future gratification play in **personal financial success**?

The belief that it is okay to do without something now, and save for something in the future, is the core to financial success. We have to make the decision every day that it is okay to delay our rewards today in favor of rewards in the future. This is something that we can learn to do, each day, so that we may become comfortable getting rewarded for our work many years later, instead of today.

Isn't it **easier** for me to just have a **financial adviser**, so that I don't have to spend the **time learning about personal finance**?

No, in order to make the best use of anyone's advice, you must take the time to be well informed, so that you can understand the different options or strategies. Millions of people feel that a financial adviser can make decisions for them, or that they can pay someone to "manage" their finances, so that they need not learn about it. People often fail to learn enough about personal finance, and cannot tell the difference between bad advice and good advice. If we are not well informed about the myriad of choices available to us and our advisers, it is very difficult to know what option is best for us.

DELAYED GRATIFICATION WORKSHEET

A major hurdle in disciplining oneself to stop spending so much is that many of us seek immediate gratification. Consider the following:

- ❑ Do you really *need* it? List below items or services you purchased over the last three months that you really did not need. How much money would you have saved if you had not purchased them?

- ❑ Can you pay cash for it, rather than putting a purchase on your charge card? If you wish to be debt free, use your charge card as little as possible. Pay for items as you go.

- ❑ Do you need it right now? To avoid impulse purchases, pause a moment before you buy something and decide if it is something you really need or if it is just simply a treat, whether it is a box of doughnuts or a big screen television. Delay gratification as much as possible.

Over the course of a week, write down items and services you have purchased using the worksheet below. Categorize each item as either a "Need" or a "Want" and list the price. Total up the columns and compare how much you spent that week on needs versus wants.

Need	Cost	Want	Cost
_____	_____	_____	_____
_____	_____	_____	_____
_____	_____	_____	_____
_____	_____	_____	_____
_____	_____	_____	_____
_____	_____	_____	_____
_____	_____	_____	_____
_____	_____	_____	_____
_____	_____	_____	_____

BLOGS

What are some of the good **personal finance blogs**?

According to Technorati, some of the top personal finance blogs include:

- Free from Broke (http://freefrombroke.com/);
- Digerati Life (http://www.thedigeratilife.com/blog/);
- Oblivious Investor (http://www.obliviousinvestor.com/);
- Cash Money Life (http://cashmoneylife.com/);
- and Get Rich Slowly (http://www.getrichslowly.org/blog/).

There is **so much information** on the **Internet**, how do I **choose what to read**?

It is important to use the Internet to search for broad topics, beginning first at various financial sites, and then digging deeper into the subject, and then moving on to the next subject. If you study this information in small increments, over time, you will learn a considerable amount about each of the areas of personal finance that are of interest to you. When you feel that the subject matter is getting too technical for you, stop and move on, until you are ready for more details. Websites are developed and produced in the same manner as newspapers and magazines. Editors and writers cover many topics, from basics on personal finance to very advanced technical analysis of individual stocks and trading strategies. Find Websites that are at your level and just dive in. If the story or topic is too deep, try Googling that word or phrase, and read a definition of it, before continuing. After doing this daily or weekly, you begin to see similar stories covered many times, and are able to develop an opinion on that idea from reading so many different perspectives. This is how you begin to build your knowledge on personal finance and keep current on what is happening with your money.

BASIC BANKING

BANKS

What is a **bank**?

A bank is a financial institution, which is licensed by the government, that provides a variety of financial services, such as: accounts in which to save, including savings accounts, retirement accounts like IRAs and 401Ks, certificates of deposit, and spending accounts, like checking accounts, and debit and ATM cards to make transactions. These institutions are profit-making entities that seek to give the highest possible return on the investment to its investors, which can be both those who initially created the bank, and in the case of those publicly traded banks, those who invest in ownership of the banks by purchasing the stock or shares of the bank.

What other **services** do **banks** provide?

Banks are also a great source of capital for account holders or those who have a relationship with the bank by taking out loans for significant capital purchases like house mortgages, automobile loans, home equity loans, small business loans, and large commercial loans of corporations. Banks also manage the transactions of credit and debit cards. In short, banks provide for us the place to save money, the means to spend that money, and wholly new sources of money by way of loans, which provides the fuel of our economy.

Can **banks** sell **stocks** and **mutual funds**?

Yes, many banks also provide financial stock exchange trading services, enabling account holders to purchase stocks on all major exchanges, as well as providing portfolio management and advice.

Banks are more than just places to maintain a checking or savings account. Today, they can provide a wide array of retirement savings options, provide loans for everything from a house to a college education to small business loans, and issue credit cards.

How many Americans **do not** have a **bank account**?

According to a survey by the Federal Deposit Insurance Corporation (FDIC), 7.7% of all U.S. households do not have any kind of bank account, representing nearly 17 million Americans.

Where do people **without bank accounts** get their **cash**?

According to the same FDIC survey, 18% of all U.S. households rely on pawn shops and paycheck cashing businesses to provide themselves with cash.

Why **use** a **bank**?

A bank gives us a secure place to hold our cash. It allows us to keep track of the growth of our most important assets, the product of all of our work, and gives us a means to make this asset grow. Bank use also contributes to our credit history, and may open up many financial opportunities, from the ability to seek advice, to managing our retirement plans, to helping us secure a loan for a significant purchase like a house or car. Banks also give us the means to write checks against our cash in the form of a checking account, so that we may easily make purchases without the need to carry cash. And banks pay interest on our deposits, both in our savings accounts and certain types of checking and money market accounts, and certificates of deposits, as well.

What **percentage** of **banks** offer **mutual funds** to their customers?

According to the Federal Reserve Bank of St. Louis, nearly one-third of all banks in the United States offer mutual funds to their clients. This amounts to approximately 3,500 banks in the United States. Some banks may refer customers to other brokerages, while others offer the funds directly to clients.

What is the **FDIC**?

The FDIC, or Federal Deposit Insurance Corporation, was set up during the Great Depression in 1933, to fight the effects of the thousands of bank failures that happened in the years preceding. It protects depositors up to $250,000 per account holder at each institution, and guarantees this amount for every depositor at every FDIC-insured institution in the United States. In the event that a bank fails, the FDIC is the receiver, and is entrusted to pay all eligible depositors up to this amount, as well as handle the liquidation of all assets owned by the failed institution, combining them with other healthier banks, when possible, or selling them off entirely. This ensures that all Americans have complete trust in the banking system, since most Americans have substantially less money on deposit, and know that the deposits are backed by the U.S. government.

What else does the **FDIC do**?

The FDIC also examines the health of the banking system by analyzing 5,160 banks, more than half of all banks in the banking system, to make sure that they have enough cash on deposit, and assessing the quality of assets and loan repayments. Whenever a bank is having difficulty, the FDIC may intervene to help the bank move toward a healthier state. If this doesn't work, the FDIC may take over the bank or merge the bank with another healthier bank.

How is the **FDIC funded**?

Although an independent agency of the federal government, in fact the FDIC is not funded by any congressional appropriation. It is funded entirely by insurance premiums charged to member institutions and from earnings by investing in U.S. treasury securities.

How much money does the **FDIC protect**?

The FDIC protects $4 trillion in deposits of every bank and savings institution in the United States.

Will my **money** always be **protected** by the **FDIC** up to $250,000?

The amount of coverage of each account holder will change back to $100,000 per account holder on January 1, 2014.

The headquarters of the FDIC in Arlington, Virginia.

What doesn't the FDIC insure?

If your bank offers stocks and mutual funds, these are not insured by the FDIC. Your bank must disclose to you everything that is insured and not insured when you open up an account.

What is the success record of the FDIC?

Since the start of FDIC insurance protection of consumers on January 1, 1934, no depositors have lost any of their insured funds as a result of a bank failure.

CREDIT UNIONS

What is a credit union?

A credit union is a not-for-profit institution that provides many financial services of traditional banks, including allowing members to hold deposits, clear checks against checking account deposits, and obtain credit in the form of loans. In order to become a member, a prospective client should belong to the group in which the credit union is chartered to service. Many credit unions are organized by professions, employers, geographic location, or associations to which one may belong. Prospective members are then allowed to make a nominal deposit, which then gives them access to all of the other services available at the credit union, including obtaining home loans, car loans, short-term construction loans, etc.

When did the **first credit union** appear?

During the Great Depression, President Roosevelt signed into law the Fair Credit Union Act, which enabled the creation of available credit to members all over the United States, in order to stimulate savings, and prevent usury (charging exorbitant fees for loans) by making reasonable interest rate loans to its members. This enabled the United States to set up a nationwide network of nonprofit, cooperative, member-owned credit unions.

Why use a **credit union**?

Credit unions have very low or no fees, since they are not profit-making entities. Whatever profits that are made during the course of the year are paid back to members in the form of interest on their savings and/or checking accounts, as well as better terms and conditions on loans.

What are some **other reasons** to use **credit unions**?

Credit unions have lower interest rates for loans than banks, lower or no fees for using ATMs, lower overdraft charges, low or no fee checking accounts, low or no minimum balance accounts, as well as personal and local services.

How big of a **difference** is there between **interest rates** for loans and savings accounts at **credit unions versus banks**?

In a study by the National Credit Union Association, using interest rate data from Datatrac, loans are from 0.66% to nearly 2% better at credit unions than at banks. And interest rates on savings accounts are between 0.09% and 0.72% higher at credit unions than at banks.

What's the **difference** between **fees** charged by **credit unions** and **banks**?

Credit unions charge $25 for each overdraft versus $30 for banks. And credit unions charge $20 for credit card late fees, versus $35 at banks. On mortgage closing costs, credit unions charge about 1% less than banks.

How much do America's **credit union members benefit** from higher savings interest rates, lower interest rates on loans, and lower fees?

Member benefits total $9 billion per year.

Credit unions differ from banks in that people using their services must become members and, in effect, become a stakeholder in the credit union.

How do I **join a credit union**?

Check with your employer to see if your company belongs to a group covered by a credit union. You may also ask other family members, check the Internet for credit unions near where you live, or visit the National Credit Union Association on the Internet, to find a credit union near you. After you have decided on one, after comparing fees, interest rates, services provided and benefits to members, you may fill out an application and make a small initial deposit.

What is the **minimum amount** that one needs to **open an account** at a credit union?

Some credit unions require a $5 share deposit to initiate an account.

Is my **money safe** in a **credit union**?

Yes, through the protection of the federal government's National Credit Union Share Insurance Fund, each depositor is insured up to $250,000 for individual accounts and $500,000 per joint account holders. This fund protects all depositors across the United States, and ensures that every depositor will be paid up to the maximum, in case the credit union ever becomes insolvent.

How many people have money saved in credit unions?

82 million people regularly use credit unions to save.

How much money do Americans save at **credit unions**?

More than $520 billion is saved in credit unions today.

How many credit unions are there in the United States?

There are 9,500 federally insured credit unions.

How much **money** in loans are **credit unions responsible for**?

Credit unions lend $355 billion to members.

MANAGING YOUR ACCOUNT

What is an **overdraft**?

An overdraft occurs when we write a check or make a withdrawal from our account for an amount in excess of what our current balance is, and a fee is charged.

How many people overdraw their accounts?

Over 50 million people overdraw their accounts each year, and 27 million overdraw their accounts more than five times each year.

How much money do banks and credit unions **earn from overdraft fees**?

They earn more than $24 billion per year.

Do people spend more money on **overdraft fees, or vegetables** during the course of a year?

According to the Center for Responsible Lending, American families spend only $22.8 billion on vegetables, versus $24 billion every year on overdraft fees.

How much have the **overdraft fees** been **growing** over the past few years?

From 2006 to 2009, overdraft fees charged by both banks and credit unions have grown 35% per year.

Why do account holders put their accounts in an **overdraft situation**?

Because of the wide availability of debit cards and their usage, people are becoming accustomed to making many small purchases instead of using cash. Even one pur-

Don't go too long without balancing your check book or you are probably going to give yourself a headache! The best approach is to balance your account each month when your financial institution issues you a statement.

chase for a few dollars, when it arrives at an account too short of cash, will cause the account holder to be charged upwards of $35 at some institutions.

How can I **prevent being overdrawn** on my account?

Its very important to properly balance your check book or savings book.

What is **balancing your check book**?

To balance your check book is to go through your statement on a monthly or even weekly basis, comparing it against your check or savings book register.

How do I **balance** my **check book**?

It's really quite simple. Each month you are sent a statement. And each time you have used your ATM/debit card or written a check, or made a withdrawal, you have been writing down every single deduction from your account and every single deposit, and all fees. Start by circling the amount of the current balance on the statement. You will need this number later. Next, go through each line of the statement, and write a little mark next to the same corresponding item in your register. Circle anything that is in your register, but not on your statement. Some of them are checks written, but not yet presented to your bank, deposits not yet credited, etc. Now, remember the number you circled above, your current balance?

Take this number, and subtract from it all of the checks and debits in your register that did not show up on your statement. Add all deposits that also have not yet shown up on your statement. The final number should equal what you have in your account.

ONLINE BANKING

Why use an **online bank**?

Online banks compete intensively for new customers, by offering some of the highest interest rates for savings accounts. They do this in part because some banks are Internet-only banks, without physical locations and the thousands of employees needed to staff the branches of traditional brick-and-mortar banks. They pass on these savings to the customers in the form of very competitive interest rates, and better than normal loan rates, like mortgages and home equity loans. They can be completely paperless, and send you your monthly statements by email.

Why else should we **use an online bank**?

Increasingly, we are turning into a cashless society. We pay our bills online, get our entertainment online, and pay for things that we buy on the Internet, so it's only natural that we also wish to have a virtual bank account. Maybe we are tired of having to drive to a branch location, park, and wait in line, just to make a deposit. In an online bank, making a deposit is as easy as making a few clicks with your mouse. The time savings alone is enough to make people switch to an online bank, since you can do all of the same things with an online bank that you do with your local bank, but in a much faster way.

What is a **virtual bank**?

A virtual bank is an online bank with no physical branch locations. It exists completely on the Internet.

How can I get **comparisons of interest rates** of different banks?

The Website Bankrate.com offers many tools to compare banks, from savings interest rates to loan interest rates. You can select from a variety of criteria and compare fees to determine the best bank for you.

How do I know if a prospective **online bank** is **legitimate** or not?

The FDIC has a bank locator tool that allows users to go online and put the name of the bank into the database to see if the bank is covered by the FDIC. If the bank that

23

you are interested in does not show up with the exact name and address of the bank in question, do not complete an application. You may also read reviews of the banks on the Internet, and ask family or friends if they have used the bank. Most people will know someone who uses an online bank.

How do I **open an online account**?

In order to open an account, you go to one of the online banks and complete an application. This takes only a few minutes. Then you associate or tie one of your checking accounts with your new account, and your Internet bank makes two small transactions into your new account. Once you receive these, you go back online and tell them the date and amounts of the two transactions, and your account is then opened. You now may make your first initial deposit, and then may move money in and out to your tied account with a click of a mouse.

Online banking has become a convenient resource for businesses and private individuals alike. You can accomplish almost any transaction with most online banks, including making deposits and withdrawals, transferring funds, and paying bills. However, online banking still has not managed to completely replace human interaction for prompt attention during those times when there is a problem you wish to resolve quickly.

Is my **money available** when I want it?

Your money is not immediately available, so when you make a deposit, there is a hold of three business days before the money appears in your account. If you make the request on a Friday, you may have to wait until Wednesday before your money actually appears in your linked account. At the same time, this forces customers to become savers, as their money is just a bit more inaccessible and therefore less prone to impulse withdrawals or purchases.

Is my **money protected** the same way in an **online bank**?

Absolutely. The FDIC (Federal Deposit Insurance Corporation) coverage is the same for virtual or online banks, protecting each account holder to up to $250,000 and $500,000 for joint account holders.

Can I **open** an **online checking account**?

Yes. Online banks offer checking accounts, which are truly paperless. Your statements are all available online, and your check register is entirely online. You can set up each of the companies that you normally pay paper checks each month, and can easily transfer money to them in the form of an electronic check. You can even write checks

25

for people locally in the same way. The money is either automatically transferred into their accounts or a paper check is printed and sent, whatever you choose to do. Since so much of what we do today is centered around the Internet, it is a natural decision to begin using online banking.

Why do people **like online banks**?

Your online bank is always open. You can see all of your transactions updated every second. Online banks also allow users to manage many different types of accounts, including savings and checking, as well as IRAs, CDs, mutual fund accounts, and even individual stock transactions. Your money is readily available, either by using your ATM/debit card, or by electronically transferring your money to your associated checking account. Your accounts are truly paperless, with no need to have to file statements in folders and less mail to manage at your home.

Why do people **dislike online banks**?

Sometimes, depending on the bank that you choose, you may have trouble communicating with foreign customer service operations. To cut costs, online banks tend to use call centers located in countries where English is not the native language, therefore making communications sometimes more difficult. You have to find the online bank that has excellent customer service, with highly trained representatives that will always be there to help you should you have any questions. Online banks tend to put a hold on online deposits and withdrawals from three to five days. Online banks may have an easy to use or more complex user interface that may be changed with each new version of the Website, so it may require the user to learn how to navigate more easily. Users of online banks no longer have the local human presence of the teller that greets you, and for some, the human touch and trust factor are important considerations. These are just some of the variables that users must consider when deciding which bank to choose.

How **popular** is the use of **online banks**?

According to a survey by the Gartner Group, more than 47% of all adults in the United States are using online banking. More than 50% of all adults with incomes higher than $30,000 are using online banking, and only 25% of adults with incomes less than $30,000 are online bankers.

How fast is **online banking growing**?

In another survey by Forrester Research, the use of online banking is growing at an annual rate of 5.4%, with 48 million users today, growing to over 63 million users by 2014.

PAYING BILLS ONLINE

What is **online bill paying**?

Online bill paying enables users to pay many of their bills that would otherwise be paid by physical check writing completely online.

How do people **pay bills online**?

There are a myriad of options for online bill paying. Users can pay bills through services offered by their local banks, credit card companies, the vendor's own Website (like your electric utility or phone company), or through online banks. Users can also pay bills through the use of home banking software, which allows one to set up bill payments, and record the transactions in their check registry on their local computers at home. The payments to the vendor can be transmitted from both the user's bank or directly from the user's credit card.

What are the **advantages** of using **online bill paying**?

Most often, the reason for using online bill payments is time and convenience. Users no longer have to spend time sifting through paper bills, writing checks, getting and using stamps, and sending the checks in the mail. Online bill paying also helps reduce late fees, as the transactions, when posted before the due date online, are immediate. The funds are withdrawn at the click of the mouse.

How do people use **online bill payments**?

Some people set reminders on a virtual calendar, which remind them when bills are due, and then pay the bill before the due date. Other people prefer the convenience of automatically deducting the bill amount from their bank account each month. Either way, users find that the time savings alone makes it worthwhile.

Does it **cost** anything for a user **to pay bills online**?

No, in fact it may cost less to pay bills online, as one does not need to buy stamps and envelopes. Also, you can easily avoid late fees because the money is instantly available when you click your mouse.

What are the **disadvantages** of using **online bill paying**?

Security can be a big factor for some people. There is some risk of users getting trapped into a phishing scam, where a spammer may send to you a fake Website that looks as if it has originated from your vendor, like your phone company or credit card company,

27

Identity theft is a huge problem in the electronic age. With a few choice bits of information, such as your name, social security number, mother's maiden name, or an important password, criminals can open charge accounts and make transactions without your knowledge. This is why checking phone statements, bank statements, and credit reports on a regular basis is essential.

asking you for your log in identification number and password. The user sends that information to the spammer, who then can access other accounts that they may have, or make fraudulent purchases.

PHISHING AND OTHER ONLINE SCAMS

What is **phishing**?

Phishing is when a spammer sends out an email, with content that makes the recipient think that it is a legitimate site, in hopes of obtaining personal information. Phishing emails ask for personal information, especially credit card numbers and social security numbers. They may merely ask you to click on a link, which then installs a file on your computer that mines your computer for passwords and other important numbers, in hopes of catching the right combination of log in IDs and passwords. The spammer may sell lists of thousands, perhaps millions of these numbers to other spammers, who then continue to make charges on the credit card numbers that they have stolen.

Who are these **spammers**, and where are they located?

According to the Spamhaus Project, 80% of all spam to North America and Europe is perpetrated by about 100 companies. Spammers hijack servers, and then use these servers located in many countries, including the United States, Russia, China, and Europe.

How do we **protect** ourselves from phishing scams and other **fraudulent Internet related crimes**?

Make sure that you use long, not easily identifiable passwords, using a mixture of different characters, including upper and lower case. And never reply to an email asking for a password or log in ID from any company that you do business with. In fact, most, if not all of the companies that offer online bill paying state on their sites that they will never ask for any personal information from you by way of email.

How do you know if an **online transaction** is **secure**?

Make sure the site that you enter is a "secure site," as indicated by the tiny icon at the bottom of your browser that resembles a padlock. This means the site is encrypting the data of your transaction, and that the information that you are sending is secure.

What if someone **steals my identity** and **charges** my credit card for purchases?

Most card companies and banks protect clients against fraudulent purchases, if they are reported in a timely manner. Check with your bank or credit card company to see what protections they offer for online transactions. Card holders are not responsible for fraudulent transactions on their credit cards.

PERSONAL FINANCE SOFTWARE

What is **personal finance software**?

It is financial software for home use that enables users to manage all aspects of their financial activities.

What **types of activities** does personal financial **software help manage**?

Personal financial software helps manage your budget, payment of your bills, your savings accounts, and tracks your investments. It also includes online check registers, credit card expense statements, net worth analyses, graphing and reporting, tax management and hundreds of financial calculators.

Do I have to **use everything** that comes with a personal financial **software package**?

No, you can start by using just one element of the software at a time, until you get comfortable using the software. Try using just the budgeting aspect of the software first, and then move on to using the net worth application of the software. Once you become familiar with how the software works, you can easily set it up to do electronic bill paying and banking by tying the software to the log in ID and password information of your banks and bills. You can use the software to help manage as much of your financial life as you want.

29

What if I already use **financial software** and wish to **switch**?

Most software allows you to import all of your data from one software to another, so that you can actually switch to more desirable software packages with a click of the mouse.

How much does personal finance **software cost**?

The price of personal finance software can be as little as free, on software download sites like CNET, to about $60.

What are some of the most **popular personal financial software** packages?

Some of the most popular packages include Quicken, Ace Money, Money Dance, Banktree Personal, Rich or Poor, iCash, Budget Express, Turbo Tax, H+R Block at Home, and iBank.

There are so many **choices of software**, how can I choose one?

Do your research. Go on the Internet and read as many reviews as you can find. Find out what your friends and family use. Most software publishers offer free trials. Find out which ones are easiest to use, integrate well with your bank accounts and credit card companies, and are easiest to import and export data to and from. Do a search on personal finance software at your favorite online stores, like Amazon.com, and sort the results by which ones sell the most (best sellers) or which have the highest reviews. This will give you an idea of which ones to compare and test drive.

Is my financial **information safe** using such software?

Yes, the software is written in such a way that your information as it travels to and from your associated accounts is encrypted, which makes it very difficult for someone to steal this information. Data on your computer, where you will store all of your information, is only as safe as your computer is, so make sure you always back up copies of your financial information to ensure that you will never lose the information.

Must I have **personal financial software** in order to be **financially successful**?

No, you do not need software in order to become financially successful. Your money can be easily managed on everything from the back of a napkin to an Excel spreadsheet. What you do need to focus on first is changing behaviors, which will allow for you to begin to accumulate wealth, keep spending in check, and be sensitive to your financial goals. Software merely helps you keep track of most of your sources of spending and saving in one place and imports data automatically from your banks and investment accounts, saving you time that would be spent doing everything on paper.

What **types of financial management** can I set up without using personal financial software?

Using such programs as Excel or Google spreadsheets, you can create specific files that help you manage all aspects of your personal life. Both have templates of such documents as expense budgets and net worth calculators, which help you keep track of your expenses and the growth in your savings portfolio, without having to learn any software. You can do this virtually by using Google documents, as the information will always be available to you, whether you are accessing it from home or at work, or even from your phone, which is an added convenience. As long as you keep up with entering the information into your spreadsheets you can easily use your own, rather than having to buy and learn how to use personal finance software.

SAVINGS AND INVESTMENTS

OVERVIEW

What is **investing**?

Investing is the act of using money to buy a financial product, with the expectation of making more money than what you used to buy the financial product, over a period of time.

How long should we **hold** an **investment**?

Some people who trade stocks can make a return on their investment in a few seconds, others a few months or even years. If you keep your money in a bank, you might make anywhere from 0% interest to a small percentage of return on the investment over a few years.

What must you **consider before investing**?

You must decide what type of investment to buy, how much money to put into the investment, how long you will hold it, how much of a return you wish to make, how much risk there is of losing money on the investment over time, how much could you potentially make, and how much you can afford to lose.

What is a **return on an investment**?

A return on the investment means how much more money will you make or earn over a period of time, as a result of buying the investment, expressed as a percentage.

33

What is **total return**?

Total return means how much income or money did your investment grow, over time, including all interest, dividends, and capital appreciation, less any fees or commissions.

How do you **compute** your **return on investment**?

You can figure your return by taking how much money you originally put in when you purchased it, and subtracting it from the value of your investment when you sell it, less any fees/commissions or taxes, and then divide this number by the amount that you originally invested, multiply by 100, and this is your return on the investment, expressed as a percentage.

Can you give us a **simple example**?

If you bought a stock for $5,000 on January 1st, and sold it one year later for $5,500, your return would be 10%. You can compute this by subtracting 5,000 from 5,500 and dividing this number (500) by 5,000 and multiplying by 100.

Why is **patience** important?

Patience is important in investing, because one must have the patience to ride out what may be temporary short-term storms or declines in the market, and keep a long-term view.

What are some of the **biggest mistakes** that individual **investors make**?

People investing in the markets sell when the price is low, like during or at the end of a significant decline, out of panic. And they buy at the highest price, once they have discovered a new investment that they heard of from their friends, who heard it from their friends, and so on. By the time the news reaches you, it's probably long past the time to have invested.

What are some **other mistakes** that investors make?

Making emotional decisions about owning investments, perhaps refusing to sell a stock of a company, because your father worked there, or being afraid to sell a stock, because you lost a certain amount. If you sold it, you may lose less than if you had kept it, but because of emotions, you hold on to it in hopes that it will go back up.

Why are people **afraid of investing**?

Most people fear investing because of a lack of knowledge about investing, not knowing about how to manage the risks, and hearing and reading about various crashes

> ## What does the saying
> ## "Don't put all of your eggs in one basket" mean?
>
> It demonstrates the principle of the need for diversification. If you put all of your investments in one stock, and if the stock price falls, you lose a significant amount of money. If you had put your money in three different stocks, and two of three go up, and only one goes down, you could still have made money, or perhaps lose less money than if your investment was concentrated in one stock.

in the markets that have happened periodically, which can cause people to lose lots of money.

What types of **investment** or **financial products** are there?

There are many different financial products, most divided into one of these broad categories: stocks, bonds and cash. In addition to this, there may also be real estate, insurance policies, private equity ownership, currency trading and hybrid investment products which combine the benefits of a mixture of these and other investments.

What are some of the **most important investment types**?

Emerging market stocks, foreign stocks, U.S. stocks, precious metals, commodities, high yield corporate bonds, municipal bonds, cash, treasury bills, money market funds, U.S. high quality bonds, European bonds, global bonds, and long-term U.S. government bonds are some of the more significant types of investments.

What is a **portfolio**?

A portfolio is a mixture of investments of different types and risks that individuals or institutions may own, in hopes of making more money over time.

What is **diversification**?

Diversification is the act of making investments in different categories with the hope and expectation that the risk of losing money is spread out or diversified within the portfolio, thus reducing the overall risk of losing money in the whole portfolio.

How does **diversification reduce your risk**?

By having a variety of investments in your portfolio, the fluctuations in the value of any one investment has less of an effect and minimizes the risk of losing money.

35

What is a **ticker symbol**?

A ticker symbol is a unique series of characters, sometimes as many as four or more characters long, which identifies the name of the investment actively traded on an exchange. For example, Google is known as "goog" on the NASDAQ exchange and Ford is known as "F" on the New York Stock Exchange.

STOCKS

What are **stocks**?

Stocks are a way of owning the assets and earnings of a company. Companies that offer the opportunity for investors to own stock in the company place a value in the shares or pieces of the company based upon the value of all of the assets of the company and the value of the past, current, and future earnings of the company. A stock can be traded, purchased, or sold.

What else is a **stock**?

A stock may also be created and then marketed and sold when a company wishes to raise capital—cash to use to help fuel the development of the business, and to pay off loans and other debt, and perhaps to buy back shares from other investors at attractive prices. A stock in a company is originally valued when the company first begins, based upon the amount of capital or cash and other assets that are brought to the table when the company is first formed.

What is a **stock market**?

It is a place, whether a physical building or an online virtual environment, where stocks are bought and sold. Stock markets or exchanges, as they are also known, can trade not only stocks, but bonds, and derivatives of stocks and bonds.

Does the **stock market ever close**?

Because of the fact that there are stock markets in many parts of the world, investors are able to trade 24 hours a day.

Which market **opens first**?

As the day begins in each part of the world, there is a flow of stock trading. Of the major markets in the world, the first to open are the countries nearest the International Date Line. This means New Zealand's market opens first, followed by Sydney

Stocks are typically traded at a stock exchange in a brick-and-mortar building, though increasingly they are being traded in virtual environments.

(Australia), Tokyo, Hong Kong, Singapore, Mumbai (India), and Moscow. Europe then follows, with Switzerland, Europe Xetra, France, Germany's Frankfurt and London, followed by Toronto, New York and finally Chicago.

How do **stocks** perform **versus bonds**?

Over the long-term, stocks are more likely to outperform bonds. The table below summarizes the odds of doing better with stocks versus bonds if you are able to keep the money invested and not withdraw it.

Stocks vs. Bonds

Number of Years Invested	Likelihood Stocks Will Earn More
1	80%
5	70%
10	80%
20	91%
30	99%

What are the **largest stock markets** in the world?

By far the largest is the New York Stock Exchange, which trades $30 trillion worth of stock, followed by NASDAQ in New York ($15 trillion), London ($10 trillion), Tokyo

Stock Exchange ($6.4 trillion), Euronext, which is in Belgium, France, Holland, Portugal (5.6 trillion), Frankfurt ($4.3 trillion) and Shanghai, China ($4.1 trillion).

How many **countries** have **stock markets**?

Stock markets are found in 77 countries, on all continents of the world.

What **affects the price** of a stock?

Because stocks are traded in a market, where buyers and sellers meet, the market price is determined by how many shares are available to buy, and how many buyers are willing to pay, and at what price. Because of the demand or lack of demand for a particular stock at a particular moment during the day, the price may change.

What are **assets** of a company?

Assets are any tangible or intangible economic resource, which when given a monetary value, has the potential to produce value for the company.

What are **tangible assets**?

Tangible assets might be physical buildings, property, factories, products sitting in a warehouse, stocks, or cash sitting in a bank.

What are **intangible assets**?

Intangible assets are non-physical, and could be patents that have been applied for, the name of the company and its brand identity, and logos, trademarks, or experience of the people.

Can you **pay too much** for stocks?

Yes, like anything that you buy, if you are first in line to buy a stock, you may get a very good deal, because the company may have thought that there is less demand for the stock than there really is. So, if there is a lot of demand for a stock, in an instant, the price of the stock may increase quickly in a few minutes or even seconds, from the initial offering price, until all buyers and sellers of the stock have been satisfied during the trading day. If you arrive at the sale late, the price could be many percentage points higher than in the morning, and you may end up paying more than the person who bought the stock first thing in the morning.

What is an **initial public offering** or IPO?

This is when a company wishes to offer to the public shares in the company in hopes of raising capital for the first time.

How many **initial public offerings** are there **in a year**?

In the 1990s, due to the onset of the Internet era, there were an average 193 IPOs per year. After the economic crashes in the 2000s, IPO activity fell to an average of 48 per year.

Why should I **care about IPOs**?

An IPO can give investors the opportunity to invest in a company at an early stage in the company's development. Individual investors may be able to buy up those shares that large institutional investors haven't purchased, giving the small investor the opportunity to profit or not from the sale of the shares.

How long has a **company** been in business before it **issues shares** for the **first time** to the **public**?

Most companies have been around an average of seven to eight years by the time they "go public." At this time, after the IPO is made, the original investors in the company may be paid back money owed to them.

INVESTORS

What is an **individual investor**?

An individual investor is each individual person who directly or indirectly purchases stocks or bonds and invests in the market on his or her own account.

How many **individual investors** are there in United States?

It is very difficult to estimate the number, because so many people are investing in the markets in some way, either by having retirement funds, buying individual shares of stock in a company, by keeping money in a money market fund, which in turn invests the money, by owning mutual funds, or by paying insurance premiums. All told, there are most likely more than 200 million Americans with some exposure to the markets.

Being your own investor without the help of a financial advisor is a real challenge. To do it correctly, you need to invest considerable time in following markets and financial news.

What is an **institutional investor**?

Institutional investors are large organizations that pool money together from other large organizations, and individuals, and invest this money in companies, both private and public.

Who are these **institutional investors**?

They can be commercial banks, investment banks, mutual funds, pension companies, retirement fund companies, and hedge fund companies.

Why is it **good** to be an **institutional investor**?

Because of their size, they are able to get a better price for the shares that they buy. They trade in huge volumes of stock, both buying and selling, and their effect can swing stock prices at any moment during the day. They also can command the best price when they are interested in selling their positions because they hold so much of particular stock.

What other **benefits** do **institutional investors** have?

Because of the magnitude of the number of shares that they own, their positions can allow them to have management say in the direction of the company, and are occasionally given a seat on the boards of both private and public companies that they may own.

What is the **Dow Jones Industrial Average**?

It is a price-weighted average of 30 blue chip stocks that are traded on the New York Stock Exchange, and is often seen as a barometer of the health of the our stock markets.

How **important** is the **Dow** to investors?

It is widely regarded as the most important index to follow in the world, and indicates stock prices and investor confidence in a broad manner.

Who **picks stocks** that are **components** of the **Dow**?

The editors of the *Wall Street Journal* in New York decide which companies should make up the Dow, looking for a balance of companies that reflect the U.S. economy as a whole.

When was the Dow **started**?

Charles Dow selected 11 stocks in 1896, thus founding the Dow index.

How else do we **use the Dow**?

We use the Dow in order to compare the performance of our stocks, bonds, or mutual funds, and ask ourselves the question whether or not we are out-performing the Dow, or under-performing the Dow. It helps to see this comparison over different periods of time, in order to assess the success of our investment choices.

What is the **oldest company** in the **Dow**?

General Electric has been a component of the Dow since 1907.

Who are the **newest entries** in the **Dow**?

Cisco Systems and Travelers were added to the Dow in 2009.

How many **times** has the list of **Dow** companies **changed** since its inception?

The Dow components have changed 48 times, since 1896.

Why are companies **removed** from the **Dow list**?

Companies are removed because of economic and managerial trouble, while others no longer offer a good representation of components reflective of the American economy at large, and must be replaced by healthier, more representative companies.

Which **companies** have been more **recently removed** from the index?

General Motors, Citigroup, AIG, Altria Group and Honeywell have all been removed.

What is **volatility**?

Volatility is the relative rate that the price of a stock or market index moves both up and down. If a price moves up and down over short periods of time, it is said to be highly volatile. If the price doesn't move very much it has low volatility.

What are some of the **largest percentage moves** of the Dow?

In March 1933, the Dow gained 5.34% in one day. In October of 1987, the Dow declined by 22.61% in a single day.

General Motors was recently removed from the Dow Jones index, along with Citygroup, AIG, and other large corporations.

How well has the **Dow performed** since it began?

Through 2009, the Dow has risen 64% of the time and declined 36% of the time.

What is a **bear market**?

A bear market is a period of time in which the prevailing stock prices are trending downward by more than 20% for two months or more.

Why does this **happen**?

It happens because investors are pessimistic about where the economy is headed, and this causes the declines to sustain themselves over a long period of time. Investors sell their shares, anticipating losses, and other investors see more losses in their portfolios so they sell also, and so on.

The bull and the bear have become symbols of the financial markets. A bull market comes in good financial times when stocks and other indicators such as employment rates are up, while a slump is called a bear market.

What is a **correction**?

A correction occurs in the stock markets when the trends of indexes show a decline in the prices of 10%–20% over a short period of time, from one day to less than two months.

Are **corrections good**?

Some investors look at corrections as buying opportunities, as often overvalued stock prices are reset to a lower level, representing their true value, and giving investors an opportunity to buy at a lower price.

What are some of the **greatest declines** of the Dow during a **bear market**?

In October 2007, the Dow entered into a bear market that lasted 517 days, and saw the Dow average decline by 53.8%. By contrast, the initial crash, which heralded the Great Depression, saw a decline in the Dow of only 47.9% and lasted 71 days.

What is a **bull market**?

It is a period of time in which there are more buyers than sellers of stocks, causing overall stock prices to rise, and where investor confidence is trending higher in anticipation of rising prices, increasing their investments over time.

How long does a **bull market last**?

Through the year 2009, and 113 years since the inception of the Dow, the average length of a bull market has been 2.7 years.

43

INVESTING FOR RETIREMENT

What is a **401k** Plan?

It is a corporate retirement plan which allows employees to set aside a certain percentage of their income, tax deferred up to a limit, and withdraw from this account when they retire. It also allows companies to match a certain percentage of the employees' income up to a limit, and also contribute to the account.

Do I have to pay **taxes** on my **401k investments**?

All earnings on these investments in your 401k are not taxed. You pay taxes only when you retire.

When did **401k plans start**?

They began in 1978, when Congress revised a section of the Internal Revenue Code by adding a section called 401(k), whereby employees would not be taxed on income that they direct as deferred, but only on their direct income they receive today. In effect, we could set aside a portion of our income and not pay any taxes on it until we retire. The law went into effect in 1980.

How much should I **save for retirement**?

If your portfolio has an annual growth rate of 8% per year, and for 30 years you put away 5% of your income into your retirement savings, you may retire with almost half the income that you were making before retirement. If you save 10% per year of your income per year, you will be very comfortable in retirement. But if the portfolio's inflation adjusted annual return is only 2%–3% per year, you would need to put away almost 40% of your current annual income, just to have half the income you are currently earning in retirement.

What is the **limit** to the amount that we can **contribute** into our **401k** plan?

The limit may change each year, and is currently $16,500 per year.

Why are **401k plans great**?

Because of the compounding of investment returns over time, you have the ability to grow your account tax free, over the long-term. You don't have to pay taxes on the amount of income earned that you contribute into your 401k, so it is a way of shielding your income from taxes. Since you will most likely be making more money now, and paying more in taxes now, than when you retire, when you do begin to withdraw from your 401k, it will be taxed at the rates that your income bracket will be when you are earning much less, thus allowing you to pay less taxes on that money in the future than you would be paying on it today, if you didn't invest in your 401k. So you get retirement savings, company matches, tax deferrals, and tax free earnings just by deducting a small percentage of your income each year.

Can you **withdraw money** from your 401k **before your retirement**?

Yes, you can but you will pay rather severe penalties to do so, if you are younger than age 59 1/2. Although the penalties may include employer penalties in addition to IRS penalties, you will most likely have to pay 10% additional taxes on this money withdrawn.

Can you make **loans against your 401k**?

Yes, you can, as long as the balance and interest is paid back into the account according to the IRS rules and the rules of your employer.

What sorts of **rules** are there regarding **loans from 401k**?

Typical rules are that payments must be made regularly, at least every quarter, that interest rates on the loan are "reasonable," and that the loan must be paid off within a certain time frame (say, five years), unless it is used for the purchase of your principal residence, and in that case the payoff may be extended considerably.

What is a **participant-directed 401k** plan?

It is when the employers give the employees a myriad of investment choices allowing the employees to choose how they wish to invest their retirement savings through investment vehicles such as stocks and mutual funds, bonds and bond funds, and even the purchase of their employer's stock.

Why is **purchasing** your **employer's stock risky**?

Like all investments, you may get great benefit or loss from investing in your own company's stock. But in a bad economic year, you may lose both your job and your retirement savings, if you have it all tied up in the stock of your company.

When can I **begin withdrawing** money from **my 401k**?

You may begin withdrawing from your account by April 1 of the calendar year after turning age 70 1/2 or April 1 of the calendar year after retiring, whichever is later.

You should always try to keep your nest eggs safe and not access money that you should be saving for a rainy day. Once you turn 70 and one half years old—or April 1 of the year after you retire—you can start withdrawing money from your 401k without a penalty.

What **percentage** of people **do not invest** in their **company's 401k program**?

More than 30% of all employees do not invest in their company-sponsored retirement programs.

What **percentage** of Americans **don't diversify** their **retirement portfolios**?

27% of all Americans who have retirement plans keep more than 50% in their employer's stock.

What **percentage of employees** actively trade or **manage their retirement funds**?

According to a study, only 17% of employees made transfers within their funds; 83% showed no activity.

What is a **matching program**?

An Employer matching program is the opportunity for millions of Americans to get free money from their employer, deposited directly into their 401k. Employers will match a percentage of what you put in, as long as you set aside a certain minimum amount each year, with a limit on the amount per year. So when a company matches 5% of what you put in, this means for every $100 that you contribute to your retirement account, they give you $5 for free.

What **percentage of employees** who learn of their employers matching program actually **take out** of their paycheck each week **enough** money to be able **to get the matching funds** from their employer?

Only about 15% of all employees, which is pretty surprising, considering the match is free, take advantage of employer-matching programs.

What **percentage** of employees are **knowledgeable about** investing in their **401k program** at work?

About 66% of employees know what choices of investments their company offers, but one third of employees have no idea. Another 25% are very knowledgeable, and actively manage their own investments.

Do **people in their twenties** manage their **401k portfolios** the same way as **people in their sixties**?

No, they are quite different. People in their twenties have a much longer view of the market, and have many years to make great financial moves, and mistakes as well. People in their sixties tend to have a shorter investment horizon, and wish to have more security and less risk.

So how does this translate to **their investment behavior**?

When it comes to our 401k retirement plans, twenty-somethings invest nearly 46% of their total portfolio in equity mutual funds and company stock and only about 23% in stable fixed income, bond or cash funds. People in their sixties tend to invest only about 36% in equities or stock funds, and 47% in stable fixed income funds or guaranteed investment contracts (GICs).

What **else** can we **see** from these two **groups** of investors?

53% of all twenty-somethings have more than 80% of their 401k portfolios in equities, while the majority of sixty-somethings only have about 23% of their portfolios in equities.

What **percentage** of **401k assets** are in **mutual funds**?

55% are invested in mutual funds.

PLANNING FOR RETIREMENT CHECKLIST

The following checklist can help you make sure you don't rush into retirement without a plan.

❑ Choose a date when you wish to retire.

❑ Before you retire (and as soon as possible) put as much into your company retirement plan as possible, taking advantage of any corporate matching (a few companies still contribute a percentage of your contributions to your retirement package).

❑ After age 50, evaluate government programs that allow you to save more for retirement. The 2001 Economic Growth and Tax Relief and Reconciliation Act allows those 50 and up to put an additional $4,000 a year into their company's retirement plan.

❑ Set goals for your lifestyle at retirement. Do you wish to live modestly, or do you plan on traveling, taking exotic vacations, and building a dream retirement home? You will likely need to have an income of at least 80% of your current earnings to live comfortably.

❑ Create a retirement budget and stick to it. Create a balance sheet, listing expected income sources and expected outgo on a monthly basis.

❑ Review your retirement benefits so you understand what you may need in order to close the gap between these benefits and what you actually need to get by.

❑ Review your social security benefits. The government sends out annual reports to future beneficiaries with estimates as to how much you will draw monthly.

❑ Evaluate your current and potential health care needs. This is easier to assess if you already have a chronic medical condition, but you should also consider the possibility of other medical issues arising and plan accordingly.

What is a **403b** plan?

It is similar to a 401k retirement plan, except that it is open to public education employees and employees of certain types of nonprofit organizations.

How much **personal wealth** was **lost** during the **crash of 2008**?

$11 trillion of Americans' personal wealth, whether in the form of stocks, bonds, cash, or real estate, was wiped out in a very short period of time.

What **percentage** of Americans saw their **portfolios decline** during the period of economic decline 2008–2010?

35% of all Americans saw a decline in their personal investments.

FINANCIAL RISKS OF RETIREMENT

There are several notable factors you need to consider when planning for retirement. Awareness of these potential risks, and planning for them, can help you avoid financial crises during your retirement years.

❑ People are living longer, which is good news in one way, but also puts a strain on your savings. According to the U.S. Census Bureau, men born in 1970 can expect to live to be about 67 years old, while women on average can expect to live to be 74. Men born in 2010 can expect to live 76 years and women 81. These are just averages, of course. Many people live well into their 80s and 90s or more.

❑ Rising health care costs. In the last couple of years, health care has risen over 10% annually, or about four hundred percent that of the rate that people's Incomes are rising.

❑ Don't forget overall inflation. While not as bad as health care, with the possible exception of gas prices, costs for food and other necessities are steadily going up and you need to factor that in as you plan for retirement.

❑ Be wary of withdrawing funds too quickly from your savings.

❑ And, while you should invest more conservatively in your later years, don't be too conservative to the point where your investments earn a rate lower than that of inflation.

Americans are living longer these days, so make sure you plan accordingly when preparing for retirement.

49

What are seven things to **consider before investing**?

According to the U.S. Securities and Exchange Commission (SEC), every investor should:

1. Evaluate your current financial plan.
2. Evaluate how much risk you are comfortable taking.
3. Diversify your investments.
4. Create and maintain an emergency fund.
5. Consider using dollar cost averaging when making an investment.
6. Re-balance your portfolio when necessary.
7. Avoid circumstances that may lead to fraudulent investments.

MARKET TIMING, TECHNICAL ANALYSIS, AND FUNDAMENTAL ANALYSIS

What is **dollar cost averaging**?

Dollar cost averaging is a simple timing strategy of investing, where an investor buys the same dollar amount of a stock at regular intervals (say, $100 per month of a certain stock). By doing so, the investor may acquire more stock as the price goes down, and less stock if the price rises. This lowers the total average price per share of an investment, meaning the investor is able to invest more profitably than if he or she were to "time the market."

What is **timing the market**?

It is the act of using economic, fundamental, and technical indicators to predict future performance and time one's decisions to enter or exit a stock position based upon this information.

Why is **timing** the **market controversial**?

Some believe that the markets are random and yet efficient, so that there are exactly the right number of buyers and sellers at any given point during the day and the most efficient price is realized. Because of the randomness of market movements, it cannot be accurately timed. Others who trade every day, rely on technical and fundamental analysis to determine their trading positions, and believe that, given certain clues, the markets can be timed, allowing the investor to make profit because of it.

What is **technical analysis**?

Technical analysis is a method of understanding the patterns and trends of the price of stocks, and using this information to profit in the future from those trends.

How does **technical analysis work**?

People who use technical analysis may observe certain trends in the movement of the price of a stock, as seen on a graph, that would indicate a buying or selling opportunity. The model doesn't necessarily consider how "good" the company is, or whether or not its products are of a high quality, or whether the unemployment rate just went up. The primary focus is on analyzing the mathematical variables that may influence the trend in a price of a stock.

What is **fundamental analysis**?

It is the analysis of the effects of various economic indicators and financial statements that have influenced and may influence the prices of stocks in financial markets.

How does **fundamental analysis work**?

Investors employing fundamental analysis may look at the company's financial information and other economic data to gain an understanding of the company's ability to use capital wisely and to create products and services in what is considered to be the most productive way.

What does a **fundamental investor** look for?

The fundamental investor may analyze the company's ability to generate profit growth, sales growth, and cost-cutting measures, which can influence a company's profits, as well as macroeconomic variables like jobs report, trade data, oil prices, and interest rates to predict what the future price of a stock may be.

What is a **price earnings ratio**?

A PE ratio is the current price of a stock divided by the amount of earnings per share. The earnings number used could be several past quarters of reported earnings, or even include a forecast of future quarterly earnings. Different industries have different growth prospects, and companies with high PE Ratios are expected to grow very quickly.

What is a **multiple**?

In the example of a company with a PE ratio of 15, it is also called "trading at a multiple of 15," meaning that someone who buys this stock is willing to pay $15 for every dollar of earnings, or a multiple of earnings. The PE ratio may be used to see how a company compares to its peers, and whether a stock price is too expensive or trading at a discount relative to its peers. Stocks with very high PE ratios are very highly in demand, as investors have bid up the price of a stock in order to profit on expected earnings in the future.

You should occasionally check your portfolio to make sure that your investments are diversified in the percentages that you wish. Over time, for instance, some investments may increase or decrease to total an undesirable percentage of your total investments. At such times, you should shift your money as needed to either more aggressive or more conservative investments, depending on your goals.

When should you **rebalance** your **portfolio**?

This is a personal decision based upon many factors, including how averse to risk you are, what return goal you have, after what period of time are you willing to wait for the return that you expect, what industries or sectors comprise your portfolio, and how they are weighted. A professional portfolio manager may choose to rebalance a portfolio when a single holding becomes a higher percentage than a certain percentage of the total portfolio, determined in advance.

How many people **use the Internet** to find economic or **financial information**?

Of the approximate 220 million online users in the United States, according to the Pew Research Center, nearly 70% or 154 million people seek some form of economic information while surfing the Internet.

What is a **more popular source** of **financial information**: the **television** or the **Internet**?

Of people who use broadband as a means to connect to the Internet, 52% of all Americans get their financial and economic information from the Web versus 43% for television and 46% for newspapers.

How do Americans **find economic information**?

Americans use a variety of sources, from talking to people, to using the Internet, to hearing some financial information on television or radio, to reading a newspaper.

How active are Americans in **using the Web** to find **financial and economic information**?

Only 18% of Americans actively use the Internet every day to find such information. About half of all Internet users get this information every few days.

What **percentage** of **online** economic users **receive alerts or feeds about news** and information pertaining to their investments**?**

About 13% of these users are using rich site summary (RSS) feeds and other alerting tools, which allow them to automatically receive information from a Website, blog, financial company, or news source that is relevant to their investments or investing ideas.

What **percentage** of economic users on the Internet **use the Internet** to find information to **protect** their **personal finances**?

Twenty-seven percent of all users use the Internet in some form to seek information in order to protect and grow their investments. Seventeen percent use the Web to compare financial companies and professionals who work in financial services.

Does **access to so much information** come at another **hidden price**?

According to research at the Pew Research Center, 37% of all economic users of the Internet feel more worried about our nation's economic future, versus 10% who feel more confident about it. The access to so much information both good and bad shapes how we feel about our investments and future financial picture.

What **percentage** of all **online economic users** think they have **learned something** about our **financial crisis**?

Thirty-nine percent of these users feel that they have increased their own understanding of the situation by using the Web.

53

What **percentage** of all Americans have **contributed** to content about the **recession** on the **Internet**?

About 23% of all adult Americans have contributed something online about the recession, through blogs, social media sites, comments on news sites, or discussion boards.

Who are the **financial information seekers** on the **Internet**?

The majority of users of the Internet seeking financial information are older than 30. In fact, 14% are aged 30–49, 13% are 50–64, and 15% are 65 and older. Only 6% of these users are aged 18–29.

BUYING STOCKS

How do you **buy individual stocks**?

You can buy stocks through a stockbroker, a stock brokerage firm, banks that offer stock investments, online brokerage firms, and directly from some companies which offer stocks directly to consumers.

Does a **stockbroker make money** on what stocks he directs me to buy?

Yes. Stockbrokers are compensated in many ways to direct clients to purchase stocks by being paid commissions, bonuses, and even gifts and vacation travel as incentives to purchase and sell the stocks. It is best to ask exactly how your potential broker is being compensated for your trades.

Do **brokers** have any obligation to **monitor** the performance of the **investments** that they sell to you?

No, as long as the investment they sold to you was good at the time you purchased it, they are under no legal obligation to follow that investment and plot the course for you, although many do advise the best time to buy or sell. You have to determine when to buy and sell, even if you use a broker or adviser.

What should I do if I wish to **invest** in an area that my **broker is unfamiliar with**?

Ask him for a referral to another broker who is an expert in this area and has the necessary credentials and education, as well as training, to help you invest.

Stockbrokers are compensated in various ways—typically, on commission—for the work they do. Talk to your broker to make sure you understand how much of your investment goes to pay for the services you receive.

What should I do if my **broker suggests an exotic investment**?

If the investment is too difficult to understand, do not invest your money.

Do **brokers know all about the investments** that they are telling me to buy?

Some brokers are well informed on the investments that they are selling, and are well trained in investment analysis. Sometimes, brokers may sell clients exotic investments, investments inappropriate for the age of the client, or investments that are far too risky, without knowing the difference. To avoid this, the client must do research and understand what it is that they are investing in, and what the risks are.

What should I **consider** when **choosing a broker** or firm in which to invest my money?

Some of the most important considerations are training and education of the broker, the fees or commissions on trades, both buying and selling, the broker's track record of performance, especially how well he or she does during both down markets and when the markets are doing very well, the firm's reputation, whether or not there have been any official complaints against the firm, whether the firm is solvent, whether or not they trade directly in the markets, and whether the firm is legitimate.

55

How can we find **information** on the **legitimacy** of a **stock brokerage firm** or complaints against them?

You can check on the legitimacy of a firm by visiting www.finra.org, created by the Financial Industry Regulatory Authority. The site allows users to look up the names of individual firms to see what actions have been taken against them. The U.S. Securities and Exchange Commission (SEC) maintains a great source of investing information designed to protect investors at www.investor.gov, which is a portal site to many tools and information that potential investors need to use before making an investment.

How many **complaints does the SEC receive** each year?

The SEC receives 82,000 complaints each year, growing at 2.7% per year.

What are the **top complaints** that individual investors make to the SEC?

The top complaints are liquidation/accounting closing issues, short selling, theft of funds/securities, manipulation of securities/prices/markets, advance fee fraud, inaccurate or incomplete disclosure of information, retirement/401k plan issues, bankruptcy/issuer reorganization, delivery of funds/proceeds, and failure to disclose relevant information about investments.

PROTECTING YOURSELF FROM FRAUD

How can I **protect myself** from **fraud**?

Never invest any money in a stock based purely on a tip or advice from a friend, colleague, family member, or trusted source. You must do all of the research first, with a very skeptical eye, in order to find a relatively safe place to invest a portion of your portfolio of investments.

Why should I **avoid investments** with "**guaranteed returns**"?

According to the SEC, promises of high returns, with little or no risk, are classic warning signs of fraud.

What does the saying, "**If it sounds too good to be true, it probably is,**" mean?

It means that when someone tells you of a guaranteed investment, that will give you incredible returns, with little risk, it is not true. The higher the return, the greater the risks. This should alert you that there could be fraud, and you should run away from this opportunity.

ANALYZING STOCKS

What kind of **research** do I need to do **before investing**?

There are hundreds of ways of analyzing stocks, but looking at very basic information about a company in several areas is a good way to start. These areas include analyzing the company's financial picture, especially its ability to consistently generate profits, its assets, and its debt and obligations. You may also look at external factors, like the market that the company is in, how does the company compare to its competitors, past stock performance, and its ability to create products or services that are in high demand.

What are some **general factors** that might be interesting to **evaluate a stock**?

Whether or not it is a company that you know and understand, has a stable management team, is diverse geographically or concentrated in any region or country, and if it is a great place to work.

What are some **macro factors** that might **influence** the **growth of a stock**?

Questioning which economic trends might affect the stock price helps place the stock in the context of which aspects of the economy may suppress or grow its earnings. The company could be dependent on oil prices, employment rates, currency values, prices of commodities, etc.

How important are **market forces** on the **long-term growth** of a stock?

They can be very influential. Find out how great the market potential is for its products, the threats to the company's products or profits, and whether the market in which the company is engaged is growing or declining.

What types of **financial signs** should I look for?

You want to find companies with strong quarterly earnings growth over a long

Stocks fluctuate in value constantly, and their values can be difficult to track, especially in volatile times.

period of time, the size of the company's debt load, the diversity or concentration of the company's income streams, its annual sales growth over time, its ability to make great products year in and year out, the ability of the company in controlling expenses, and whether the company uses capital wisely. You may also want to see if the company spends money appropriately on (people, equipment, marketing, research and development, etc.).

What about the **analysis of the stock** itself?

It's good to see if the company's stock is doing better than that of its peers, if the price of the stock is too high or too low, and the reasons why. You may also want to know if there is a large percentage of the stock owned by any single individuals or entities, which could influence the price both up and down. It's also good to know if the company regularly pays a dividend back to its shareholders.

What is **insider trading**?

It is when corporate insiders—officers, directors, and employees—buy and sell stock in their own companies. When corporate insiders trade in their own securities, they must report their trades to the SEC, which makes this information available to the public.

What does **insider trading tell us** as investors?

This indicates something is changing in the market, company, or its products and services. It may also indicate whether or not the price of the shares is too high or low, depending on whether the management is buying or selling its own shares. You may also want to pay special attention to when they are buying.

Are there any **other factors** to consider?

You may want to know if the company was recently in bankruptcy, or merged with another company, or if the company is for sale, as all of these could affect the share price, both short and long-term.

Where can I find **information** in order to **analyze a company**?

There are thousands of sources for information that answer many questions about a stock. Some notable places include the finance sections of Google and Yahoo, to the use of EDGAR database on the SEC Website, financial pages of such sites as the *Wall Street Journal, Investor's Business Daily,* MSNBC, the *Economist, The New York Times, Forbes, Fortune,* local newspaper sites, and financial blogs, among many others.

HELPFUL FINANCIAL WEBSITES

What are the **top financial sites** that can help individual investors **learn about investing**?

Some of the top sites include Yahoo Finance, MSN Money Central, Google Finance, marketwatch.com, CNBC, CNN Money, Bloomberg, and fool.com.

What are some great **financial sites that investment insiders use**?

Some of the best sites for insiders include: gurufocus (www.gurufocus,com); Mish's Global Economic Trend Analysis (http://globaleconomicanalysis.blogspot.com); King World News (www.kingworldnews.com); Mauldin (www.johnmauldin.com); The Street (www.thestreet.com); Minyanville (http://www.minyanville.com/); Zero Hedge (http://www.zerohedge.com/); Financial Times Alphaville (http://ftalphaville.ft.com/); Business Insider (http://www.businessinsider.com/); The Financial Times (www.ft.com/home/uk); Wall Street Journal (http://online.wsj.com/home-page); and Bloomberg (http://www.bloomberg.com/).

Can I **learn anything from** going to the **Websites of the stock exchanges** themselves?

Yes, each stock exchange Website disseminates an incredible amount of information, including trading models, activity of share trading, which stocks are increasing the most, which ones are declining the most, which stocks are hitting new highs, etc.

How does the **Dow Jones Industrial Average** indicate **movement** in my **stock**?

The Dow, as it is known, is the indicator of share prices, which is based upon a basket of 30 stocks traded on the New York Stock Exchange, representative of the stock market as a whole. It is used to indicate whether or not the broader market share prices are moving higher or lower.

What is a "**blue chip**" stock?

The expression "blue chip," borrowed from the lexicon of card games, refers to the most valuable chips to use when betting and means stocks that are nationally recognized as stable, growing companies capable of weathering financial downturns. These companies have very broad based appeal in the industries they represent because they are financially sound, managed well, and provide high quality goods and services.

59

What are the major **stock exchange sites**?

By putting the name of an exchange in your favorite search engine, you can go to such sites as Nasdaq, NYSE (New York), American Stock Exchange, London Stock Exchange, and TMX (Toronto).

BONDS

What is a **bond**?

A bond is a financial instrument or debt security, issued by governments, both local, state and federal, as well as corporations, large and small, that offer fixed interest payments over a period of time greater than a year.

What **types of bonds** are there?

There are three main types of fixed-income securities: government bonds, municipal bonds, and corporate bonds.

Municipal bonds are used by cities and local governments to make local improvements, such as water towers or sewer systems. They are not glamorous investments, but they are generally safe ones.

What are **government bonds**?

Government bonds fall into three categories: treasury bills, which mature in less than one year; treasury notes, which mature in one to ten years; and treasury bonds, which mature in more than ten years.

Are U.S. **government bonds safe**?

Because they are backed by the U.S. government, they are extremely safe, as there is very little risk that the U.S. government will default on the loans.

Are **all government bonds safe**?

No, in fact some foreign government bonds may not be safe investments at all, as the debt of those countries can cause economic collapse. So one must consider the region and the country before investing in foreign government bonds.

What **countries** are having **significant debt problems**, making investments there relatively more risky?

Some notable European countries, including Greece, Ireland, Portugal, Spain, and Italy, have been having economic problems.

What are **municipal bonds**?

When a city government needs capital to fund the building of a water system, or improve roads, or build a new school, they fund this activity through the issuance of a bond.

Are **municipal bonds** a **safe** form of investing?

Yes, they are, as the chances of an entire city going bankrupt is pretty remote. But there are interest rate risks and risks of default, and one must consider the economic prospects for the city before investing in the bonds issued by that city.

What **cities are at risk** of going under?

Some very large cities are running very high budget deficits, meaning they spend more than they actually collect in taxes. Some of those cities include San Diego, Norfolk, San Jose, Las Vegas, Phoenix, Reno, Chicago, Baltimore, Yonkers, Honolulu, New York, San Francisco, Los Angeles, Detroit, and Harrisburg.

What if the **municipal bond issuer defaults** on the bond?

If you happen to invest in bonds for a city that goes under, you may lose all of your investment plus any interest payments due to you.

What **percentage** of **municipal bond holders** are **individual people and mutual fund investors**?

About 80% of all municipal bonds are held by individual household investors either directly or through mutual funds that invest in those bonds.

What is the average five-year cumulative **default rate** for **investment-grade municipal bonds**?

According to Moody's, the bond rating agency, it is less than half a percent, making municipal bonds a very safe investment.

Are municipal bond **defaults rising**?

Yes, in 2009 there were more than 183 borrowers who defaulted on the loans, many in Florida. By contrast, in 2007 there were only 31 defaults, according to *Fortune* magazine.

Why would a municipality default on the loans?

There are a variety of reasons that affect a municipality's ability to repay the bonds, including high unemployment, which affects tax receipts, low consumer spending, underfunded municipal pensions, labor costs, or a gross mismanagement of the municipal government's finances.

What are **corporate bonds**?

Corporate bonds come in several forms, depending on the maturity, short-term (less than five years), intermediate term (five to twelve years), and long-term (over twelve years). Corporations issue bonds in order to raise capital to fund projects, instead of issuing new stock to raise capital.

What do **companies** do with the **money they make from selling bonds**?

The proceeds of the sale of the bonds may help fund new plants and factories, new equipment, upgrade old facilities, or retire more expensive debt, which ultimately makes the company able to compete and thrive in the future.

Are **corporate bonds risky**?

They are the most risky forms of bond investment because of the possibility that the company might default and go under.

Why are the **yields higher** for **corporate bonds** than for **government or municipal bonds**?

The yields tend to be higher because of the risk. The higher the risk, the higher the return must be in order to make the investment attractive to investors.

Is **owning a bond** like owning a **stock**?

No, when you own a stock, you actually own a piece of the company, its assets, and profits. But when you own a bond, you are in effect giving the issuer a loan, for which they pay you interest on the loan and your principal back when it is due.

Is a **bond** like an **IOU**?

Yes, a bond is another word for an IOU, with the added advantage of paying you interest on the IOU.

What is **principal**?

Principal is the face value of the loan or bond—the original loan amount is what is used to calculate interest payments. The principal and the interest is what an investor receives when a bond is due or matures.

What performs better, **stocks or bonds**?

For many years in the period of 1870–1940, bonds performed better than stocks. Since then, stocks have performed better during most economic cycles.

What affects **bond prices**?

Bond prices move in the opposite direction of interest rates. So when interest

A bond is just like an IOU, except that it also pays interest. Bonds can be safer than stocks for investors, but they usually pay lower interest rates, as well.

rates rise, bond prices fall, and vice versa. If you buy the bond at a discount and hold the bond for the full term, you will get all of your money back plus interest.

Is your money **safe with bonds**?

As long as the issuer is financially sound, there is little risk of default on the bonds. But if the company or government that issues the bonds has a major economic catastrophe, there is a risk, like all other forms of investments, of losing your money.

How do we **buy bonds**?

We can buy bonds through a full service broker or discount broker. Some large banks also can provide clients access to bonds. You may also buy bonds directly from the U.S. government at www.treasurydirect.gov.

Can you invest in **bonds through mutual funds**?

Yes, you may invest in all types of bonds, and even mixtures of different types of bonds by buying bond mutual funds.

If you buy bonds through a **broker**, is there a **commission**?

They may not call it a commission, and may in fact say it is commission free, but in fact they nearly always charge some sort of transaction fee. Check with your broker to discuss all fees, both when buying and selling, to make sure that you are aware of any fees associated.

What are tax free or **tax exempt bonds**?

These are bonds issued by a municipal, county or state government, with interest payments that are not subject to any state, local, or sometimes federal taxes. These rules depend on what bonds you buy and what state or municipality in which you reside.

MUTUAL FUNDS

What is a **mutual fund**?

It is a professionally managed investment vehicle, which pools the funds from many investors and collectively invests these funds in stocks, bonds, cash instruments, commodities, other mutual funds, real estate, and many other types of investment instruments, which enables the investors to gain or lose from the performance of the fund.

Why should I **read a prospectus** of a **mutual fund**?

By reading a prospectus, we see how the fund is managed, its portfolio, its sectors, percent of portfolio for each holding, the fees, and past performance history. You can begin to understand how a mutual fund manages risk in order to get high returns on invested capital.

What is a **portfolio**?

A portfolio is the collection of investments held by an individual, investment company, or mutual fund.

How is the **mutual fund priced**?

The price of a mutual is its net asset value. The individual share price of an open-ended mutual fund is determined by the value of the net assets of the fund, minus any liabilities held by the fund, divided by the number of shares outstanding. If a mutual fund had assets of $100 million, and liabilities of $10 million, its net assets are $90 million. If there are 9 million shares of the stock outstanding, then the net asset value is $10.

How does a **mutual fund work**?

A management team of the fund seeks to invest in specific industries or ideas that they think will grow over the short, medium, or long-term. They create a portfolio of investments in individual shares of many companies, and intensively follow every nuance of the financial, marketing, product development, and competitive threats of the companies in their portfolio.

How does a **mutual fund make money**?

The collective investments of the mutual fund may earn dividends on the shares they own, and capital gains on shares that they purchased and then sold, as well as capital losses, if they have sold shares at less than the purchase price. The fund also charges a management fee to all shareholders. After we subtract the expenses from the gains, the earnings of the fund are distributed to each investor in proportion to the amount of shares invested. Investors believe that, although any one stock or group of stocks in the fund's portfolio may go up or down, the total gains of the portfolio will be positive over time.

What are a **mutual fund's expenses**?

The mutual fund's expenses may be the management fees, offices and staff, and taxes on the business.

Why buy **mutual funds**?

We buy into a mutual fund in order to have instant diversification of our money. Since buying one share of a mutual fund gives individual investors access to a large, diverse portfolio of other shares, the exposure to risk that the investment will go down is diminished.

Is there such a thing as a **risk-free mutual fund**?

No. The risk of loss never entirely goes away, no matter how diverse a portfolio is, but it may be less risky than investing in any single share of a company directly.

When did **mutual funds begin**?

Many people believe that the first mutual funds were organized in Northern Europe, specifically in The Netherlands, by King William I (1772–1843) in 1822. Others believe that it was in 1774, when another Dutch merchant named Adriann van Ketwich created Eendragt Maakt Magt, which means "unity creates strength." He may have influenced King William I to create his fund some years later.

65

Some historians hold that the concept of mutual funds was originated back in Holland in 1822 by King William I.

When did **mutual funds begin** to be created in the **United States**?

Some believe that the first mutual funds in the United States began in the 1890s, with the advent of the Boston Personal Property Trust (1893). The Alexander Fund in Philadelphia, founded in 1907, was one of the first funds that allowed its investors to make withdrawals or redeem shares on demand.

What are two of the **oldest mutual funds**?

In 1924, a private investment fund was started in Boston, calling itself the Massachusetts Investors Trust. It later offered its shares to the public in 1928, and today it still exists as MFS Investment Management. Putnam Investors Fund began in 1925, and also still exists today.

How many **people own mutual funds**?

Of the 78 million households in the United States, 44% of them invest in mutual funds, or more than 90 million people.

How much **money** is **managed** by **mutual funds**?

About $12.2 trillion is managed. This number fluctuates every moment, as share prices change.

How many mutual funds are there?

There are 8,624 mutual funds. If you add in closed ended funds, exchange traded funds, and unit investment trusts, the number reaches 16,120.

What is a turnover rate?

This is a measurement of the fund's trading activity, what percentage of the total portfolio is traded each period. Low turnover rates suggest that the portfolio is holding onto assets, expecting higher returns, whereas a higher turnover means that the fund is trading very actively, trying also to realize positive returns, minimize losses, or manage the inflow and outflow of cash into the fund effectively.

What has been the average turnover rate of an equity mutual fund?

An equity or stock mutual fund during the period 1974 to 2009 averages 58%.

What types of mutual funds are there?

Mutual funds can be divided into three broad categories: equity funds (stocks); fixed income funds (bonds); and money market funds (cash/cash equivalents).

What other subdivisions of mutual funds are there?

Mutual funds are then broadly divided into three classes of investment types—value, blend, and growth.

What are value funds?

Value funds attempt to find stocks in companies that are trading below their inherent value, because they are out of favor in the markets, but still have great products and services, so that over time the stock will appreciate faster.

What are growth funds?

Growth funds identify stocks that have high potential for growth in their profits and share price.

What are blended funds?

Blended funds seek to combine value stocks and growth stocks, which reduces the investors risk over time.

67

What **other types** of **mutual funds** are there?

There are also international funds, which invest purely in companies that are outside the United States, global funds, which invest in companies both outside and inside the United States if they have strong sales and operations located worldwide, and regional funds, which invest in a portfolio of companies in various regions of the world, like Europe, Asia, South America, and Asia.

What about **sector/specialty funds**?

Sector funds seek to invest in companies that are in various specific sectors of our economy like health care, manufacturing, oil and gas, financial services, information technology, bioengineering, and Internet. Because of their specificity, these funds tend to have higher risks, but also higher rewards, if the mutual fund company finds the right basket of winners.

Do **socially responsible funds** exist?

Yes, socially responsible funds seek to invest in stocks of companies that do no harm to the world, the environment, or its people. These funds may find companies that are involved in recycling, energy efficiency or contributing to education. As an example, a socially responsible fund would not invest in tobacco companies, or companies that genetically alter seeds for agriculture, or companies that are big polluters.

What is the **final category of funds**?

The last category of funds are index funds. Index funds purchase a share in each of the stocks that comprise a certain index, like the S&P 500 or Dow Jones Industrials, and seek to mimic the returns that the index may obtain. These funds have the lowest management fees, since there is very little management needed to maintain the portfolio, as the managers are merely buying shares weighted exactly as the index. This enables investors to minimize their risks by having the volatility of the portfolio distributed over dozens, if not hundreds or thousands of stocks. Ultimately, the return that you get is the same as whatever the return of that index is in any given period of time.

Does **size** really matter when deciding what type of **mutual fund** to purchase?

Yes, size does matter. In each broad category, we have the choice of buying mutual funds that invest in small companies, which may have a higher potential return, but more risk. Medium sized companies may reduce the risk over time since they are not as small and are more established than small companies, but have the ability to generate profit growth over time. Large company stock funds may have fewer risks, as these are very established companies that have proven track records, dividends, and growth, and are thought to be less risky than small company funds.

What is the **median age** of owners of **mutual fund shares**?

The median age is 50.

Who invests in **mutual funds** the **most**?

People aged 35–64 are using mutual funds more than other age groups.

What is the **median** number of **mutual funds** that an **individual owns**?

In 1958, the median number was one. Today, it is four.

How much money does the **typical investor** in today's market have in **mutual fund accounts**?

The typical investor has about $80,000 in his or her accounts.

What **percentage** of a household's **financial assets** are in the form of **mutual funds**?

Twenty-one percent of a household's financial assets are in the form of mutual funds.

What **percentage** of a typical person's **retirement plans** are in the form of **mutual funds**?

For 401k and related plans, 51%, and for IRAs, 46% are in the form of mutual funds.

How do we **buy** a **mutual fund**?

We can buy mutual funds in many ways. We can go directly to the mutual fund company, through a broker, a full service bank, or through the company that manages our 401k or retirement plans.

What **financial goal** does the **typical investor in mutual funds** have in mind when making an investment?

Seventy-six percent of mutual fund investors are investing and saving for retirement.

69

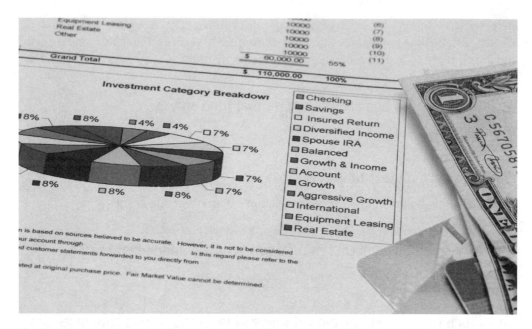

Equipment Leasing
Real Estate
Other

10000	(6)	
10000	(7)	
10000	(8)	
10000	(9)	
10000	(10)	

Grand Total $ 60,000.00 55% (11)

$ 110,000.00 100%

Investment Category Breakdown

8% 8% 4% 4% 7%

7%

7%

8% 8% 8% 7%

- Checking
- Savings
- Insured Return
- Diversified Income
- Spouse IRA
- Balanced
- Growth & Income
- Account
- Growth
- Aggressive Growth
- International
- Equipment Leasing
- Real Estate

n is based on sources believed to be accurate. However, it is not to be considered
ur account through
d customer statements forwarded to you directly from
in this regard please refer to the

sted at original purchase price. Fair Market Value cannot be determined

"Don't put all your eggs in one basket" is a wise adage when it comes to your portfolio. Always try to diversify your investments. That way, if one investment goes sour and loses money, you won't lose everything.

What is the **trend** in mutual fund **expenses and fees**?

Since 1990, the fees that mutual funds charge their investors has fallen by half, according to the Investment Company Institute.

How many **people are employed** in the **investment company business**?

In 2009, there were 157,000 people working in the business.

Why are **fees and costs** of **mutual funds** so **important** in deciding which fund to choose?

Because the size of the expenses or fees that a mutual fund charges may lower your annual return. Mutual funds with the highest returns and lowest fees over time will give investors very good returns on the investments. Funds that have average returns and high expenses may perform much worse over time.

How do mutual funds **justify high fees and expenses**?

Some mutual funds justify their high fees because of the costs of employing the many hundreds of managers and analysts who work to bring the high returns that investors wish to have. But these same managers may be of the same quality as managers of funds with fewer expenses. So all things being equal, it is best to find the funds with the highest returns, fewest risks, and lowest fees.

How do we **decide which funds** to choose?

This is a very complex question because it involves so many different variables. We have to analyze the performance of many periods, say, one year, three years, five years, ten years, and life of the fund.

What does the phrase "**past performance is no indication of future performance**" mean?

Most mutual funds advertise a disclaimer that essentially means that just because a mutual fund was number one last year does not necessarily mean that it will be number one this year.

What **other considerations** are there in **choosing the right mutual fund**?

Another consideration is how well the fund does compared to its peers. Is it the best of all of its peers or is it among the worst?

Consider also the actual manager, and the time that the manager has been managing this portfolio, since it is his/her stock picks that will create the returns that you will realize. Has the manager been in the job for a few months, years, or decades. Does the manager have a great track record over time?

What are some **other considerations**?

Try to find out how well or poorly the mutual fund does in the best of times and the worst of times. Ask yourself, if the fund loses 25% in the worst decline, but its peers lose 50% in the worst decline, can I live with that decline?

What are **no-load mutual funds**?

These are funds that do not charge any fee for either purchasing or selling shares of that fund.

What are **loaded funds**?

These are mutual funds that charge a fee for purchasing (front load) or selling (back end load) shares in the fund. They have the highest expenses associated with them, and are offered by brokers, who may then get paid commissions on your transactions. Because of the fees associated, an investor in loaded mutual funds may experience lower returns as a result.

71

How do we **compare expenses** of mutual funds?

The SEC Website provides a mutual fund expense calculator that allows the user to compare expenses related to mutual funds. Many Websites provide the expense ratios so the investors may compare expenses, so that they may make a more well-informed decision before purchasing.

What is an **expense ratio**?

The expense ratio is the amount of expenses divided by the average net asset value of the portfolio of stocks, expressed as a percentage. A mutual fund with 1% expense ratio means that 1% of the value of the entire portfolio is used to actually operate the mutual fund.

Why does and **expense ratio matter?**

It matters because if your fund has an annual return of 5% this year, and it has a 2% expense ratio, your annual return could have been 7%, but because of high expenses, it is actually lower. The same type of fund with a lower expense ratio would in effect put more money in your pocket over time, since it spends less of your money administering the funds. This is why expenses matter.

What is an **open-ended fund**?

It is a mutual fund that has no restrictions on the number of shares it issues to the public, and is continuously buying and selling shares of its portfolio of stocks to both new and current investors. Most mutual funds are open to investors.

What is a **closed-ended mutual fund**?

The managers of a closed-ended mutual fund may decide that the number of investors and portfolio value is of a certain size, and they wish to limit the inflow of new capital into the fund. In this case, the fund may be closed to new investors, but current investors may continue to invest or sell shares.

What is a **closed ended mutual fund**?

This is a type of mutual fund that offers a fixed number shares on a public exchange during its initial public offering, and then is listed on an exchange with the price of the shares determined by the supply and demand for shares in that fund, as well as the underlying value of the stocks in the portfolio of the fund. These tend to be sector funds, or funds that seek to invest in specific aspects of the economy.

Individual Retirement Accounts help people save for retirement by allowing them to put away money without paying taxes until they withdraw funds. In this way, it is easier to build up money faster and accrue more interest.

What has been the **trend** in our **expectations** about the **age** at which we will **retire**?

In 1991, 50% of all workers in the United States thought they would retire before age 65. In 2010, that number dwindled to 28%.

What are the **main reasons** people are **delaying retirement**?

Twenty-nine percent cite the weak economy as the underlying reason. Other reasons include change in employment situation (22%), can't afford to retire (16%), need to make up for losses in the stock markets (12%), lack of faith in social security (7%), need to pay current expenses first (6%), increase assets to retire well (6%), unsure about stock market (5%), health care costs (4%), and changes in minimum age requirements (4%).

INDIVIDUAL RETIREMENT ACCOUNTS

What is an **IRA**?

IRAs, or Individual Retirement Accounts, were created in 1974, under an act of Congress called the Employee Retirement Income Security Act (ERISA), which gives indi-

73

viduals who do not have access to an employer-sponsored retirement plan the means to having one. It gives individuals the ability to preserve their tax advantages and growth opportunities of having a retirement plan when they leave their jobs.

How many **different types of IRAs** are there?

There are five different IRAs: Traditional; Roth; Simplified Employee Pension plan (SEP); Reduction Simplified Employee pension plan (SAR-SEP); and Simple.

What is a **traditional IRA**?

A traditional type IRA is an individual retirement account that allows employees to make tax deductible contributions up to a certain limit each year for the duration of their working lives, until they retire. The earnings and balance of the account, together with the employer's match, are then taxed at whatever tax rate you are at when you begin to withdraw this money at retirement.

What is a **Roth IRA**?

A Roth IRA is an individual retirement account, where contributions are made with after-tax dollars, meaning the income on your paycheck that you make after your employer has deducted taxes. You may make these non-tax deductible contributions to a Roth IRA up to a certain limit each year. Under certain circumstances, you may withdraw money from this account, tax free, before retirement or you can withdraw all of it, if you like, tax free, after the age of retirement (59 1/2). You may continue to add to this account up to the annual limit for as long as you like. You currently do not have to pay taxes on any distributions inside this account, so that your money may grow tax free.

What is a **SAR-SEP IRA**?

This is a Salary Reduction Simplified Employee pension, which is used in companies with fewer than 25 employees. In order to set up such an account, the employer must have 50% of the eligible employees contribute to this plan. Employees may make contributions in pre-tax dollars and deduct this amount from their current income, through salary reduction, thus reducing their current tax burden while saving for their retirement. After 1996, these plans were replaced by Simple IRAs, although plans set up before 1996 are still used by some employers.

What is a **SEP IRA**?

It is a Simplified Employee Pension plan that allows employees and small business owners the ability to save for their retirement. It allows employers to contribute into each employee's SEP IRA account up to 25% of the employee's annual earnings. The employee may also contribute to this account, and all contributions are tax deductible. Sole proprietors, partnerships, and corporations, including S corporations, can set up SEPs for their employees. You cannot take loans out against your balance. If you withdraw money from the account prior to retirement as income, you will pay a penalty of 10% additional tax on this money. When you retire, you may make withdrawals from the account, and pay tax on this amount as ordinary income at that time. You may move a SEP into another IRA anytime you like.

What is a **Simple IRA**?

A Simple IRA allows employers with fewer than 100 employees who earned $5,000 and above, to save for their retirement.

How much can an **employee contribute** to a **Simple IRA**?

Although this amount may change in the future, in 2010, employees could contribute (or defer) up to $11,500 of their salary per year, and set this money aside for retirement. Employers may match up to 3% of the employee's income into this account as well.

How much of our IRAs are tied up in **mutual funds**?

Forty-six percent of all IRAs are managed by mutual funds.

How much **money** is invested **in IRAs**?

About $4.2 trillion in assets, of which $1.9 trillion is in mutual funds, are invested in IRAs.

How many **households own IRAs**?

Forty-six million American households hold some form of an IRA.

What **percentage** of people are likely to **withdraw funds** from an IRA **before age 70.5**?

Thirty-seven percent are not at all likely, 27% not very likely, 20% are somewhat likely, and 16% are very likely to withdraw.

What do people do with their **IRAs** after they retire and begin **accessing their holdings**?

Forty-four percent use the money to pay for living expenses, 31% saved it in another account or reinvested it, 19% spent it on a health care expense, 15% used it for a home purchase, remodeling or repair, 14% used it for an emergency, 6% purchased a big-ticket item, 3% used it for education, and 12% used it for miscellaneous purchases.

What is **vesting**?

Vesting in a retirement plan means that after working for a defined period of time, the employee is able to own and keep whatever account balances and employer matching funds that have been deposited into one's "vested" account. A company may decide that an employee must be with the company for, say, five years in order to have 100% ownership in the employer's retirement plan or pension.

Why do companies have a **vesting period**?

This vesting period allows the company to reward long-term employees, and penalize employees who may not remain long with the company. Some vesting is immediate, while others follow a graduated period, increasing your ownership in the plan by 20% each year for five years. This is all determined in the fine print of your employer's retirement plan document

INVESTING IN GOLD

Why **invest** in **gold**?

Gold is used as another investment vehicle that is said to be a hedge against inflation, and perceived by investors as a safe haven from the fluctuations in values of currency, like the U.S. dollar. So investors believe that at certain times it may be better to keep a portion of an investment portfolio in gold, as it may appreciate better than holding the same amount in either cash or currencies, bonds, or other investments.

What affects the **price of gold**?

As in all aspects of the economy, supply and demand affects gold prices. As supplies of gold become scarce, prices tend to increase. As demand for gold decreases, in favor of other investments like stocks, the price of gold tends to decrease.

What is the biggest component of **demand for gold**?

Jewelry comprises roughly 68% of the demand for gold. This leaves 32% of the demand for gold emanating from technology and manufacturing demand, as well as investors purchasing physical bullion and holding it in hopes that it will appreciate in value.

Gold Prices 1850–2011

Year	Avg. Price	Year	Avg. Price	Year	Avg. Price
1850	18.93	1904	18.96	1958	35.10
1851	18.93	1905	18.92	1959	35.10
1852	18.93	1906	18.90	1960	35.27
1853	18.93	1907	18.94	1961	35.25
1854	18.93	1908	18.95	1962	35.23
1855	18.93	1909	18.96	1963	35.09
1856	18.93	1910	18.92	1964	35.10
1857	18.93	1911	18.92	1965	35.12
1858	18.93	1912	18.93	1966	35.13
1859	18.93	1913	18.92	1967	34.95
1860	18.93	1914	18.99	1968	39.31
1861	18.93	1915	18.99	1969	41.28
1862	18.93	1916	18.99	1970	36.02
1863	18.93	1917	18.99	1971	40.62
1864	18.93	1918	18.99	1972	58.42
1865	18.93	1919	19.95	1973	97.39
1866	18.93	1920	20.68	1974	154.00
1867	18.93	1921	20.58	1975	160.86
1868	18.93	1922	20.66	1976	124.74
1869	18.93	1923	21.32	1977	147.84
1870	18.93	1924	20.69	1978	193.40
1871	18.93	1925	20.64	1979	306.00
1872	18.94	1926	20.63	1980	615.00
1873	18.94	1927	20.64	1981	460.00
1874	18.94	1928	20.66	1982	376.00
1875	18.94	1929	20.63	1983	424.00
1876	18.94	1930	20.65	1984	361.00
1877	18.94	1931	17.06	1985	317.00
1878	18.94	1932	20.69	1986	368.00
1879	18.94	1933	26.33	1987	447.00
1880	18.94	1934	34.69	1988	437.00
1881	18.94	1935	34.84	1989	381.00
1882	18.94	1936	34.87	1990	383.51
1883	18.94	1937	34.79	1991	362.11
1884	18.94	1938	34.85	1992	343.82
1885	18.94	1939	34.42	1993	359.77
1886	18.94	1940	33.85	1994	384.00
1887	18.94	1941	33.85	1995	383.79
1888	18.94	1942	33.85	1996	387.81

Year	Avg. Price	Year	Avg. Price	Year	Avg. Price
1889	18.93	1943	33.85	1997	331.02
1890	18.94	1944	33.85	1998	294.24
1891	18.96	1945	34.71	1999	278.98
1892	18.96	1946	34.71	2000	279.11
1893	18.96	1947	34.71	2001	271.04
1894	18.94	1948	34.71	2002	309.73
1895	18.93	1949	31.69	2003	363.38
1896	18.98	1950	34.72	2004	409.72
1897	18.98	1951	34.72	2005	444.74
1898	18.98	1952	34.60	2006	603.46
1899	18.94	1953	34.84	2007	695.39
1900	18.96	1954	35.04	2008	871.96
1901	18.98	1955	35.03	2009	972.35
1902	18.97	1956	34.99	2010	1,224.53
1903	18.95	1957	34.95	2011	1,360*

*Predicted 2011 average gold price estimated by Natixis Commodity Markets.

Who is one of the **largest buyers of gold**?

From 2004–2008, the United States accounted for 11% of all gold purchases.

What **other places** in the world is the **demand for gold high**?

50% of the worldwide demand for gold in the form of jewelry comes from India, China, Turkey, and the Middle East.

What **percentage of world gold sales** comes by way of **investments**?

20% of world gold demand comes in the form of investments, with India, Europe, and the United States leading the world.

What else can **affect the price of gold**?

Central banks of countries are also big consumers of gold, and may buy or sell large amounts at any given time, and affect the global price of gold.

What are the **different ways of investing in gold**?

The most popular way of investing in gold is through the purchase of gold jewelry. Other ways include purchasing gold coins, bullion or bars, buying stocks in companies that extract gold, companies that sell gold jewelry, or by buying mutual funds that invest in precious metals, including gold. Investors may also buy exchange-traded gold funds, which may represent a certain holding or portfolio of gold purchases, as well as gold certificates that are issued by some banks, which represent a certain quantity of gold held by the bank.

The price of gold has skyrocketed in recent years, much faster than historically, with prices increasing about 500 percent over the last decade.

INVESTING IN REAL ESTATE

Why **buy** a **house**?

When you buy a house you own an asset that can appreciate over time. There is a sense of pride in owning one's own home. You no longer have to pay rent, or live with roommates or family. It is one of the first steps to financial security. It allows you to begin to create a credit history. It is a form of forced savings, since you must make monthly payments if you purchase your home with a loan or mortgage, and this money is going to both you (in the form of equity in the house) and the bank or mortgage company (in the form of a loan payment). It is also a good way to diversify your portfolio through real estate ownership. You can get tax deductions for a home office and deduct the interest on your mortgage. You may also qualify for special loan programs at lower interest rates to purchase a home. Additionally, you may sell the home at a profit, without paying capital gains tax, and use the proceeds to downsize and pay cash for your next home, thus saving the money that you would have used for mortgage and interest payments.

Why **else** should we **buy** a **house**?

Home ownership also represents one major aspect of the American Dream, to be independent financially, and to increase our wealth. This has been aided in part by many federal programs that make credit available, incentivize buyers through tax deductions, and provide mortgages and other credits for home purchase.

What are some **factors that affect** the general **prices of houses**?

On a macro level, the prices of houses follow the basic economic principle of supply and demand. The more houses there are for sale, the lower the price. The more buyers there are for houses, the higher the price.

Since the housing collapse, it has been a buyer's market and a seller's nightmare. Many home owners are upside down on their mortgages, meaning they owe more than the value of their homes. If you are lucky enough to be entering the housing market for the first time, now is the time to buy!

If I am thinking of **buying a house** in a certain city, how can I find **information about my target city** on the Internet?

There are many Websites, including www.city-data.com, www.neighborhoodscout .com, and www.realestate.yahoo.com, that provide valuable information on your future city, including house prices, unemployment rates, education quality, and crime statistics. It is essential to investigate these sites before buying or selling a house.

What is a **mortgage**?

It is the amount of money lent from a bank, which is the price of the house that is purchased, and financed by the bank in the form of a loan to the buyer, less any down payment and closing costs at the closing of the transaction.

What about **interest rates** and their **effect on housing prices**?

The higher the interest rate is for mortgage, the more the demand for mortgages is suppressed, since buying a house becomes more unaffordable. As interest rates or the price of our money ticks down, the more demand there is from buyers, and this would then make prices more buoyant over time.

PREPARING TO GET A MORTGAGE

Bring the following documents with you to your meeting with a mortgage lender.

- ❑ W2 forms from the last two years
- ❑ Pay stubs from the last month
- ❑ If you recently obtained a new job, bring a copy of the signed offer letter, which must include your new salary
- ❑ Bank checking and savings statements from the last two months
- ❑ Statements of mutual funds and brokerage accounts
- ❑ Special information pertaining to your particular situation, which may include divorce decrees, visas, resident alien cards, or other documents your mortgage lender may request

---

How low are **today's mortgage interest rates**?

Interest rates on loans for houses are lower than any time in the past 50 years. They may go even lower before we see a bottom in the interest rates for mortgage loans.

Why are there **fewer buyers** for **houses today**?

There are fewer buyers because many fear employment loss, inability to obtain a loan, inability to manage current expenses, and expectations from buyers that prices will further decline. They would rather wait out the decline in price than jump in at this point in time. Sellers are holding out for the best price because they need to pay off their mortgages in order to buy another house.

What does the term "**underwater on a mortgage**" mean?

It's when sellers can't leave their current home because they owe more on the balance of the home mortgage than they can make when they sell the house today.

How does **increasing our down payment** help to **protect us** from going "underwater"?

It protects us because if we put more money down to purchase the house, we owe less money on the mortgage in the future, and when it's time to sell, we will be able to sell at the market price, with less risk of owing more than the house is worth.

What about all of the **foreclosed houses** that are flooding the market?

The number of distressed mortgages or foreclosures in the area in which you are thinking of buying will have a depressing effect on all house prices. It not only increases the supply of available houses, but increases the supply of very cheap available houses, since the banks or lenders that own them want to get whatever cash they can, and are not looking to hold out for a better offer.

How much **cheaper** are **foreclosed houses** than currently **occupied houses** that may be on the market?

According to Moody's, an investment services provider, foreclosed houses sell for upwards of 40% less than occupied houses today.

What is "**shadow inventory**"?

It is the inventory of houses that most likely will move into foreclosure, thus increasing the supply of houses and depressing house prices.

How many homes are in **foreclosure**?

In 2010, the number of homes in some stage of foreclosure was about 1.1 million, which is up from 900,000 in 2009, an unprecedented number.

How many people are at **risk of foreclosure**?

In 2010, 1.7 million home owners were notified that they are at risk of defaulting on their loan because of missed payments. This means one in every 78 homeowners is at risk.

How many homes received **foreclosure filings** in 2010?

According to Realtytrac, more than 3.8 million foreclosure filings, which includes default notices, scheduled auctions, and bank repossessions, were reported on a record 2.87 million U.S. properties in 2010.

How long does it take for a home **to be foreclosed**?

Within 15 months after you stop paying the mortgage the home reverts to the lender and is then sold.

What **states** have the **highest rate of foreclosure**?

Nevada, Arizona, Florida, California, Utah, Georgia, Michigan, Idaho, Illinois, and Colorado.

The foreclosure problem affects more than just those losing their homes. Foreclosed homes lower property values in neighborhoods, and banks lose millions of dollars when they have to repossess houses that have been foreclosed on or even abandoned by buyers.

What does the **foreclosure rate** mean for American **home ownership**?

It means that home ownership most likely will fall to the lowest level since 1960, when 61.9% of American families owned their own home, and perhaps even lower in the next few years.

What was the **highest percentage** of households that **owned their own homes**?

According to U.S. census data, 69.4% of all households owned their own home in 2004.

What **tax advantages** are there to **home ownership**?

One of the great benefits of home ownership is the tax shielding aspect of having a mortgage. Essentially, the government allows you to deduct or not count the amount of mortgage interest you pay in one year against your income for that year. Another sizable advantage, and one of the principle benefits of home ownership, is that up to a certain value ($500,000 for a married couple), you do not have to pay taxes on the gain in value of your house. You may also deduct your property taxes when you file your income taxes, if you itemize deductions.

83

AVOIDING A FORECLOSURE

Be prepared before seeing a financial counselor or mortgage company before making an argument for keeping your home and avoiding foreclosure proceedings. The following checklist can help.

Monthly Expenses (put $0 if not applicable)

Mortgage: $ _____

Other Mortgage (second mortgage, home equity loans, etc.): $ _____

Property Taxes: $ _____

Insurance: $ _____

Homeowner Association Fees: $ _____

Utilities: $ _____

Other Real Estate or Property: $ _____

Car: $ _____

Other Vehicle (boat, motorcycle, RV, etc.): $ _____

Student Loans: $ _____

Child Care: $ _____

Credit Cards: $ _____

Other Expenses: $ _____

Monthly Income (put $0 if not applicable)

Gross Monthly Income: $ _____

Other Income (e.g., alimony, child support, commissions): $ _____

Other Financial Assets

Investments (stocks, bonds, mutual funds): $ _____

Retirement funds (401K, IRA): $ _____

Other Assets: $ _____

Hardship Information

Write down the reasons why it has become difficult to make mortgage or other payments.

_____
_____
_____
_____

Household income has gone down

_____
_____
_____

Increase in monthly debt payments

_____
_____
_____

Increase in expenses

_____
_____
_____

Other

_____
_____
_____
_____

85

What are the most **important rules** to follow when **buying a house**?

You have probably heard the answer before: Location, location, location. This means that the place where you purchase your house is probably one of the most important factors to help you maximize your return on your investment in this house.

Why is **location** so important?

Your house needs to be in an area where there are excellent schools, a place where taxes are used to support great city services, where upkeep and maintenance of neighboring homes is excellent, and near where your place of work is. It is great to live in a walkable community, a place where there is a sense of belonging, security, and friendliness. It is important that there be very little crime, if at all, as this will greatly increase the value of your home, and make it easier to sell your home in the long-term.

What if your **potential home** is in an **area** that has only **one major industry** or employer?

It means that if something were to happen to that industry or employer, it could become very difficult to sell your house, or even have any appreciation over time. So you must be very careful about location.

What about **buying houses** in "up and coming" locations?

This really depends on your preference for risk. Some buyers prefer to find a great house in a changing location, where they feel that the area is growing and desirable and that they may realize a high return on the investment, even though it has more risk. Other buyers may not move into these neighborhoods, depressing the values of the newly renovated houses down the block.

What about **great deals** on newly created **subdivisions**?

If you buy a house in a newly built subdivision, there is a risk that the builder may run out of money and not complete the project, leaving the initial buyers with houses in an area that is incomplete, making it very difficult to sell in the future.

What's **another general rule** about **location**?

Some people believe that one should consider buying the worst house on the best block, since the street already demonstrates that it is a very valuable area. And with some hard work, perhaps cash invested to fix it up, the house will be far more valuable over time than buying "the best" house on the block, one that requires no work or additional changes whatsoever but already commands a premium price.

If you buy a house in a newly built subdivision, there is a risk that the builder may run out of money and not complete the project.

How important are **property taxes** in **deciding to purchase** a home?

Property taxes could be a determining factor in choosing one area over another. Make sure you check what percentage of the home's sale price will be paid in taxes before deciding to buy a house. A city with very high taxes will charge you a larger percentage of the homes selling price than a more affordable city.

What is **another rule** of **buying a home**?

Buy as much house as you can afford. This means taking a hard look at your current expenses, deciding what you can live without, what you absolutely must have, and figuring out how much house you can afford. A larger house may require much more cash for utilities, such as electricity, heating and cooling, and maintenance.

How can I find out **how much house** I can **afford**?

There are many financial calculators available on the Internet that allow you to enter information about your income and expenses, and will roughly compute how much you can afford. Only a bank or mortgage adviser will really be able to tell you the amount that you can afford to mortgage.

What is the **general rule** for **obtaining a loan** for a house?

The general rule is that a good borrower can afford monthly payments, which would include principal, interest, insurance, and taxes, equal to 25% of his/her gross income.

87

What **factors** should I consider when **thinking about affordability**?

You have to look at such factors as your current income, your debts, and your existing monthly payments, and whatever money remains may go to your mortgage payment. The second big piece that will affect your mortgage payment is your down payment.

What is a **down payment**?

The down payment is the amount that you can comfortably pay in cash for the purchase of the house. This down payment, plus the mortgage amount, is the price that you pay for your house (plus some additional fees and expenses). The more cash that you put down, which is a percentage of the home price, the less your mortgage amount, and therefore your monthly payment, will be.

How do I know **how much to put down** for a house?

This is a tough question because it touches on the sentiment of the purchaser. You should have already saved at least four to six months of living expenses, in a cash account for your emergency fund, in case something should happen or change in your employment. This money should not be touched, not even for the purchase of a house. The money that you have managed to save in addition to that, money that you may have invested in other ways, should be used for your initial down payment.

What are the **general guidelines** for **down payments**?

Most lenders would prefer to have you put down 10%–30% of the price of the house in the form of a down payment. This enables you to possibly get better interest rates, lower fees or points, and reduce your monthly payments and interest over the lifetime of the loan. There are many programs offered by banks, including federal incentives, for the purchases of homes, especially for first time home buyers. Check with your bank or mortgage adviser.

What is an **appraisal**?

An appraisal is when your bank or mortgage company inspects the house to see if the amount of money that they wish to loan equals what they see is the value of the house.

What does the term **"appraise out"** mean?

If the house "appraises out," this means that the bank or mortgage company thinks that the value of the house is at least equal to the sales price; it is safe then to make a loan to the purchaser.

Home inspections are a vital part of home purchases. Buyers need to be fully informed of any defects or needed repairs in the spirit of full disclosure, and may not decide to buy a home if previously undiscovered problems arise.

What if the house **doesn't appraise out**?

You have two options: you can put more money down, if you really love the house, or you can try to negotiate the price of the house down, and get it nearer to what the bank thinks is the "real" price of the house.

What is an **inspection**?

An inspection is paid for and arranged by the buyer before the buyer purchases the house. A home inspector will check every physical aspect of the house, advising the buyer of all of the faults of the house, as well as an exhaustive list of all things that need to be repaired in the house.

What if I **find something** out about the house that **makes it unacceptable**?

You may write in your purchase agreement "offer contingent upon satisfactory inspection," and allow yourself the protection that if the house doesn't pass inspection, you don't need to go through with the purchase.

How can buyers **use this information when purchasing** a home?

It can be used to help you decide on your offer price, or in order to reduce the price of the house after you have made an offer. The inspection can also be used by the buyer to tell the seller what items need to be repaired before the buyer will choose to buy the house. In other words the buyer and seller negotiate either to make the necessary repairs, or knock down the price to accommodate the buyer, who will have to do the repairs later.

If I **pull out** of the deal **before the close**, won't I be **penalized**?

Most likely, yes. Another offer may come in that has no such terms, perhaps at an equal amount to your bid. The seller will of course choose the best deal of the two. You could also lose a portion of your deposit, which you must give to initiate the whole transaction. Check with your bank or mortgage adviser to find out exactly what their practice is, and at what point you can pull out of the deal without losing money.

How do **real estate agents** work?

Real estate agents are hired by the sellers and are paid a commission for the sale of the home. Real estate agents that work on behalf of buyers are knowledgeable of both your needs and the available listings in the areas that you choose. Their expertise is essential in guiding you to the right house.

What is the **MLS** or **multi-list service**?

This is an electronic database of every property for sale, nationwide. Realtors access this information to help search for all properties that are listed by other realtors in order to identify specific choices for their clients.

What are **comparables**?

Comparables, or "comps" as they are known, are houses that are physically similar to your house, which are in a specific radius of distance from your target house, and have sold in the recent past. You can gain intelligence as to the "market price" of the house by looking at the price that the comparable house actually sold for.

How can we use this knowledge to **negotiate a better price**?

You can find out what is deficient about your target house, compared with the "comps," and tell the seller and your realtor when you make your offer. You might say, "We are offering $5,000 less because all of the comps had central air conditioning and this one doesn't." If the sellers are motivated to sell, they may take your offer, and knock the price down. Comps are usually provided by each client's realtor.

What else can we **learn from "comps"**?

We may also see from the "comps" that we actually are getting a really great deal. Perhaps all of the recent comparable houses sold for $30,000 more than the offer price of your target house. Knowing what others have sold for may indicate that you are getting a very good deal. It could also indicate that the prices of real estate in this area have fallen precipitously, and perhaps the price may go even lower. Some people may reconsider buying or investing in the area, since prices of homes are not appreciating.

What is **mortgage fraud**?

Mortgage fraud involves a crime committed in order to secure or grant a mortgage, usually falling into two categories: misrepresenting information on a mortgage application (59% of all cases) and appraisal related misrepresentation (33% of all cases).

Which **states** lead the nation in **mortgage related fraud**?

According to a report issued by the Mortgage Asset Research Institute, Florida, New York, California, Arizona, and Michigan lead the nation in mortgage fraud.

How much did real **estate prices decline** from 2006 to 2009?

The average home lost 33% of its value during this period of economic decline.

What **percentage** of Americans saw their **house equity decrease** during this period of decline?

Twenty-seven percent of all Americans saw their home value cut by at least half.

How much money in real estate wealth was wiped out during the decline of 2006 to 2010?

Six trillion dollars in home values was wiped out.

What **percentage** of **online economic users** use the **Internet** to find **information** on the **value of their house**?

Eighteen percent of users use the Internet to find current home prices, trends, and data pertaining to the value of their own home.

What is **home equity**?

Home equity is the current market value of your home, minus any mortgages or liens on the home.

How do we determine the **market price of the house**?

The market price is derived from the recent sale price of comparable houses, the quality of the house, neighborhood, and market demand for the house at that price.

Can we **use the equity** in our home even if we do not sell it?

Yes, this equity can then be lent back to the home owner, and repaid over time. This is not advisable when house prices are falling.

How do people use **home equity loans**?

Most people use home equity loans to reinvest in their home, by making value-increasing improvements like new kitchens and bathrooms, or fixing up exteriors, etc. Some people use home equity loans to consolidate and pay off credit card debt, invest in a business venture, or even use the equity in their home to fund living or medical expenses in retirement.

SELLING YOUR HOUSE

What is **curb appeal**?

Curb appeal is the impression that your house makes to buyers when driving by, or as they first approach your house on the way in. Many buyers make instant decisions on whether or not to buy your house based upon these initial seconds or minutes.

What is **staging**?

Staging is the act of changing the furnishings, either by buying, renting, or rearranging the layout of each room, in order to present your house for sale in the best possible manner.

What are some of the most **important things** that you can do to **prepare your home for sale**?

Make the most important repairs that may increase both the curb appeal of your house, as well as necessary improvements on the inside that may sway a buyer to

Just a few minor fixes, such as a new coat of paint or planting flowers, can add tremendous appeal to a home and make a sale more likely.

decide to buy your house. Sellers will invest in exterior landscaping, kitchens, and bathrooms in order to improve their chances of attracting a buyer.

Why are **neutral colors** so important when **selling a house**?

You want to give buyers the least number of reasons to dislike your house. So if you really loved your red-walled kitchen, it's time to paint it white or beige, so that people do not use the color of the room as a reason to not buy the house. Also, neutral colors allow buyers the ability to see how big the house is, how spacious the space is, and allows them to imagine living in the house.

Should **I move out of my house** when I am trying to sell it?

Absolutely not. Unless your work forces you to move before selling the house, it is very important that your house look like it is currently lived in. Nothing detracts more from the sale price of a house than walking through a series of empty box-like rooms, with no signs of life. Your house is much more valuable when you are still living in it.

What about all of **my clutter**?

One of the best things that you can do when trying to sell the house is to go through each and every room of the house and de-clutter. This means taking a very minimalist

93

approach and removing all but the most essential things. This means no stacks of anything in each room, and no toys.

What about **photographs and personal art**?

Again, if you want to make your house appeal to the largest number of buyers, get rid of all personal artwork and photographs, unless they are completely neutral. The house should be perfectly clean and orderly.

How fast do people form **first impressions**?

The speed that we are able to decide whether something is good or bad is measured in tenths of seconds. With our ability to use the Internet to see pictures of houses, we are deciding whether we like a house or not in seconds. So unfortunately, it means as sellers, extra care needs to be taken to make your house as demanded as possible.

What does the expression "**price to sell**" mean?

It means that you are in competition with many other houses that are for sale, and you want to price the house low enough so that it will be among the first houses that people consider buying, instead of the last. That means to price it lower than its rivals at the outset.

How often are **sellers cutting their prices**?

According to Trulia, a real estate research firm, during the month of July 2010, 25% of all sellers in the United States cut their prices in order to sell their houses.

Why is the **speed of selling the house** so important?

Because the longer the house is on the market, buyers will perceive that there is something wrong either with the house itself, or the price, and will be more reluctant to even look at the house.

Why is **picking the right agent** to sell your house important?

Because it is the agent who will deliver the potential buyers to you. They are knowledgeable in the area that you are selling, they know the community and characteristics well. They have a lot of contacts, and are experts at showing the home in the best possible manner. Since they are compensated with a commission on the sale price, they are of course motivated to try to get the highest reasonable price for their client.

What **percentage** of buyers ultimately **pays cash to purchase** an existing house?

In 2010, more than 25% of all existing houses sold were purchased by cash buyers who didn't need to obtain a mortgage.

What is a depressed or **down real estate market**?

A down market or a downturn in the real estate market is when average prices are falling relative to some baseline measure.

Should we consider **selling** our home during a **down market** in real estate?

People may consider selling their homes during a down market because of some life change, perhaps employment or marital change. If you have been in the house for a long time, and do not wish to see your equity in the home further eroded, it may be the time to sell. But, thinking of your home as a long-term investment, some would argue that it is best to wait out market cycles, and sell when the prices are high or higher than they currently are. Each individual seller must evaluate his or her tolerance for losses, and appetite for risk, and decide the best time to sell.

What about **buying in a down market**?

If you are selling your current home in a down market, in order to purchase another home, you will benefit from the low prices of your potential new home.

If we stay in our home, what should we do **during a down market**?

You may think about refinancing your loan in hopes of getting a better mortgage and thus lowering your monthly payments. You may also think about reducing as many discretionary expenses as possible, and delaying the purchase of big-ticket items, in order to continue to grow your cash savings, during these uncertain times.

What else should we do if we stay in our home during a down market?

One should also focus on reducing or eliminating all credit card debt, and delaying or eliminating all non-essential purchases.

FINANCIAL PLANNERS AND INVESTMENT ADVISORS

How many financial planners are there in the United States?

There are approximately 300,000 people who call themselves financial planners.

How many of the financial planners are actually certified?

Of the 300,000 financial planners in the United States, only 60,000 have passed the rigorous examinations that allow them to be called a "certified financial planner," or CFP.

What is the difference between a financial planner and an investment adviser?

An investment adviser is able to offer advice on the many investment choices that are available to you, both from the company that he or she works for, as well as other choices outside the firm. A financial planner is a generalist that is experienced at looking at the big picture of your financial health, your entire portfolio, both assets and liabilities, and guide you on the proper choices that will allow you to reach your short-term and long-term financial goals.

So what does a financial planner do?

A financial planner can advise clients on how best to increase their assets and reduce their debt, help establish an expense budget and savings/investing budget, and help develop a detailed strategy or financial plan to realize short and long-term financial goals.

How are financial planners different from stock brokers, accountants, or insurance brokers?

Stockbrokers are versed in helping clients specifically invest and grow their wealth through the purchase of equities and other specific investment instruments that they represent. Accountants are able to give advice on taxes and tax strategies that can impact how much you must pay in taxes, what types of tax credits are available to you, and what you can do to limit your tax exposure in a given year. Insurance brokers are interested in selling policies to you, as a part of a larger investment strategy. Both stockbrokers and insurance brokers may earn commissions on what they recommend.

Why should we use a financial planner?

For people who are too busy to invest the time and energy involved in researching the myriad of financial options available to them, a planner may represent the one-stop

Be selective when choosing a financial planner. Not all people who describe themselves as such are fully qualified, and some may charge excessive fees for their services.

source of information that busy individuals need. Also, using an outside adviser may help enforce the sort of discipline that is needed to reach one's financial goals and may help steer you in the right direction.

How important is **experience** in identifying a **financial planner**?

Experience is very important since a financial planner has to have demonstrated many years of experience across a wide variety of clients in order to learn and be able to give the client proper advice.

Is it **important** for the **financial adviser** to have **similar clients** to me?

Yes, the best financial planners understand and advise people who share similar characteristics. You wouldn't want to go to a financial planner who specializes in the elderly if you are in your twenties and are relatively new to the work force.

How important are **certifications** when it comes to **choosing a financial planner**?

Certifications are very important and demonstrate that the planner has gone through the courses, examinations, and continuing education, as well as the ethical training

97

involved in the certification process. One should never use a financial planner who does not have such credentials.

Are investment advisers or financial planners **required to have credentials or certifications**?

No state or federal authority requires these credentials in order to give advice. Many states, however, do require that people advising clients on financial matters pass some proficiency tests.

How many **different financial planning certifications** are there?

There are many different designations of financial planners. The most important are: CFP (Certified Financial Planner), CFA (Chartered Financial Analyst), Certified Fund Specialist (CFS), Chartered Financial Consultant (ChFC), and Chartered Investment Counselor (CIC).

What is a **Certified Financial Planner** (CFP)?

Holders of the CFP are tested on their knowledge of over 100 areas of financial planning, including stocks, bonds, taxes, insurance, retirement planning, and estate planning. Candidates for this certification must also complete qualifying work experience, and adhere to the CFP code of ethics. The certification is granted by the Certified Financial Planner Board of Standards, Inc.

What is a **Chartered Financial Analyst** (CFA)?

People who hold this certification have to pass rigorous examinations, have a minimum of three years of work experience, and must show integrity, extensive knowledge in such financial areas as ethics, portfolio management, security analysis, and accounting. The certification is offered by the CFA Institute.

What is a **Certified Fund Specialist** (CFS)?

A certified fund specialist accreditation means that the adviser is an expert in mutual funds and the mutual fund industry. They have studied, and are tested for their knowledge in, portfolio management, dollar cost averaging and annuities. If they have a license to buy and sell funds, they will also be able to purchase funds on behalf of clients. The Institute of Business and Finance oversees the accreditation of the CFS.

What is a **Chartered Financial Consultant** (ChFC)?

These are advisers who hold an accreditation from the American College and have successfully completed an examination covering all areas of financial planning, including income tax, insurance, investment, and estate planning, and must have a minimum of three years of experience in the financial industry.

What is a **Chartered Investment Counselor** (CIC)?

In order to be a CIC, one must first be accredited as a Certified Financial Analyst. Candidates must study more advanced concepts in portfolio management, adhere to a strict code of ethics, and provide character references.

What is the **National Association of Personal Financial Planners**, and why is it an important resource when choosing a planner?

The NAPFA is the nation's leading organization dedicated to the advancement of fee based financial planning. This means that financial planners who have earned a registration with NAPFA cannot charge clients a commission and must go through rigorous examinations and continuing education.

Why else are the **NAPFA standards** so **good**?

NAPFA also believes that they are on the leading edge of standards of education, training, and method of practice, and with these standards, can help move people away from the debt, undisciplined financial practices, and lack of retirement planning that beset millions of Americans.

What is a **conflict of interest** in financial planning?

A conflict of interest is when the planner may benefit financially from the investment choices that they offer you. Those choices may be subjective and biased because the commissioned financial planners may limit the choices offered to you, and only steer you in the direction of the financial investments that help them earn commissions.

So should we steer away from considering **commission-based financial planners**?

Yes, it is best to find the most unbiased and objective fee only planners who do not directly benefit from the ideas and strategies that they present to you.

Can I **ask the potential planner** if they or their firm has **ever been involved in any litigation or disciplinary action**?

Yes, it is a very good idea to ask this question, and to obtain a letter from them that states that they have not. You should disqualify any individual or firm that has had any disciplinary action.

How can we **check the disciplinary history** of a potential financial adviser?

You may check if there has been any disciplinary action taken against either the person or the firm by going to the Websites of the following organizations: Certified Financial Planner Board of Standards, North American Securities Administrators Association, National Association of Insurance Commissioners, Financial Industry Regulatory Authority, or the Securities and Exchange Commission. You may enter their name and state and find out if there have been any actions taken against them.

Should we **ask potential financial planners what services** they offer?

Yes, it's important to know the range of services that they offer, as well as whether or not they earn commission on what they recommend, or do they only work based upon a one-time fee. A financial planner should not be able to offer advice without the proper licenses and registrations from the state or federal authorities.

What about the **financial planner's approach**? Should I pick an aggressive or a conservative planner?

Depending on your life situation and your short and long-term goals, the key is to match your situation and style with that of your planner. So it is important for you to find out what the approach is and if it matches what you wish to accomplish. It's also important for your adviser to have clients in similar life situations and a track record of success working with them.

Will the financial planner be **working with me alone**, or with a **team of other people**?

This is an important question, as we need to check the backgrounds of anyone else that the adviser partners with, including the insurance representative, mutual fund company broker, etc., that he or she may bring on to work with you.

How do **financial planners** get **compensated**?

Financial planners are compensated in many ways. Some planners charge an hourly fee, others a monthly fee, no matter what advice they give. Some planners charge a flat fee to draw up an annual financial plan, and others may charge a percentage of what you actually invest based upon the size of your portfolio. And still others earn a commission or percentage of whatever it is that they end up selling you. So you must be careful to consider how much you must pay out in fees before choosing an adviser.

HAVE THE FOLLOWING DOCUMENTS WITH YOU WHEN YOU MEET YOUR MORTGAGE COMPANY OR FINANCIAL ADVISOR

- ❏ Mortgage Information
- ❏ Current mortgage statement and any recent notices/letters received
- ❏ Current statement for any other loans/lines on the home
- ❏ If employed—need your last two pay stubs
- ❏ If self-employed—need your current Quarterly or Year-to-Date Profit/Loss statement
- ❏ If receiving benefits (Social Security, pension, unemployment, death, etc.)—benefit statement or letter showing the amount, frequency and duration
- ❏ If receiving alimony or child support—divorce decree (or other document) showing amount, frequency and duration
- ❏ Last two month's banking statements for checking/savings
- ❏ Last two years' tax returns

If my planner earns a **commission**, why could that be **harmful** to me?

If your potential planner earns a commission, he or she may likely steer you in the direction of purchasing investments that benefit him, not you. So you need to be careful in choosing commissioned based planners, and understand very well how they earn their income.

Should we find out if the **planner is benefiting** in other ways from **directing me** into a **certain investment**?

Yes, you should ask how else he or she may be compensated, if they earn a referral fee for selling you X mutual fund or insurance policy, and if his or her company earns something because of the referral.

What if my potential planner can't work with me because **my portfolio is too small**?

This is actually beneficial to you, since the adviser is saying that he specializes in higher net worth individuals. It's very good to work with an adviser who specializes in clients of similar size and issues.

101

How can I **check** if my **planner** has a **criminal history**?

Most states have a free, online criminal history or offender online database. Check first with the main Website for your state, and run a check to see if your planner has a hidden criminal past.

What if I find a **planner** who says his **clients make huge returns** of their investments, like 50%?

Any planner that boasts about the high rates of returns of his clients is probably not telling the truth, and is most likely not suitable for you.

Should I ask my **friends for referrals** when identifying a potential planner?

Most likely not, since this is the principal way in which fraudulent planners rope in new unsuspecting victims. Many people think that by asking friends for advice, they will somehow escape the hard research that we all must do to identify

Even people who pride themselves on being smart investors can be fooled. In one of the biggest scandals in recent years, investment advisor and stock broker Bernie Madoff was caught in a Ponzi scheme, paying his clients off with money from other clients instead of actual profits from investments. Madoff was one of the most trusted and well-connected figures in the financial world, but he fooled rich and famous alike out of millions of dollars.

the best financial planner. It's best to do the research yourself, do not skip any steps, and be diligent in your interviews.

What **other types of questions** can you ask a potential financial planner?

You might ask such questions as: Where did you go to school? What licenses do you hold? Are you registered with the SEC, a state, or financial industry regulatory authority? Can you recommend only a limited number of products or services, and why? If you are a registered investment adviser, can you give me a copy of your Form ADV?

Why is a **Form ADV** important?

The Securities and Exchange Commission's Form ADV is required by all licensed investment advisers who manage more than $25 million. Anyone who manages less than that must register with the state securities regulator. Part one of the form lists the adviser's education, business, and disciplinary history for the past ten years. Part two lists information pertaining to the adviser's fees and investment strategies.

My financial adviser mentioned that he is a **fiduciary**; what does this mean?

It means in all circumstances your adviser will put you, the client's interest comes first—above his own, or the firm or the investment companies that he may represent. Ask if your adviser is a fiduciary.

Why is **fiduciary responsibility important**?

Because under the current guidelines established by the SEC, an adviser merely needs to meet the "suitability standard," which means that advice "needs to be appropriate for the client," rather than "in the client's best interest."

What **percentage** of people actually **believe that their stock broker** is acting as a **fiduciary**, exclusively with their best interests in mind, when directing clients to a particular investment or trade?

In a recent study, 66% of all investors thought that their stock brokers were in fact acting as fiduciaries. They were not.

What **percentage of people think** that the **"financial advisers"** employed at a brokerage firm to sell **are held to a fiduciary standard**?

Seventy-five percent of those surveyed also thought these sales reps were acting with their clients' best interests in mind, when in fact they were not.

Do I really **need** a **financial adviser**?

It really depends on your own situation, your time, and the educational resources that are available to you. Some employers use very large companies to manage their retirement plans or mutual fund families, which offer free advice on financial planning. And to some, this information is sufficient to help guide them through the many choices that are offered in their retirement plans. Other people need more direct control over their portfolios, and wish to work side by side with an adviser as they move toward their financial goals. So the decision to use a financial adviser really depends on your own personal needs.

What is discussed in a **financial planning meeting**?

A financial plan discussion might include such items as: your financial goals both short and long-term, your net worth (all of your assets/savings/investments minus all of your liabilities/debts), your monthly budget (both income from your work and expenses), a discussion on how comfortable you are with risk (how much could you afford to lose), and finally an action plan.

INSURANCE

What is a **deductible**?

A deductible is the amount of money that the homeowner must pay toward a loss in order to collect on a claim.

What are **premiums**?

The premiums are the amount that you pay each month for your insurance coverage. Insurance companies take your premiums, invest them, use them to pay out claims from other insured members, and use the proceeds to help generate profits for the insurance company and provide a return on the investments for the shareholders of the insurance company.

HOME INSURANCE

Why do I need **home owner's insurance**?

Mortgage companies and banks that finance your loan for the purchase of a house require you to have a home owner's insurance policy. The policy protects your investment (your house) in case of damage or loss, due to a catastrophic natural event, like a hurricane or an earthquake, as well as damage because of snow, ice, or fallen trees.

Why do mortgage companies, banks and finance companies **require home owner's insurance**?

Because they technically own your home and want to be sure that they get paid for the mortgage loan plus interest, even in the event that the house burns down. The insur-

Insurance is designed to help you recover from tragic events such as fires and floods. It is best to file insurance claims only in cases when you cannot easily afford to repair or replace what you have lost.

ance will cover the costs to replace the house, and ultimately the home owner will be able to continue to pay the mortgage or sell the house.

How does **home owner's insurance work**?

The homeowner may get a policy covering the replacement cost of the home at current market rates. This premium is paid monthly and is in force for as long as the homeowner continues to pay the premium and retains ownership of the house.

Why are the **dwelling coverage limits** tricky?

The dwelling coverage limits, or computing the replacement value, may be a problem if your house either goes up in value, or declines in value, from the time that you agreed on your policy. If your home has gone up in value, or appreciated, you may not have enough coverage to replace your house. If your home declines in value, or depreciated, you may be paying for too much coverage.

Should I **change my dwelling coverage limits**?

It is good to reassess these amounts every year, and adjust your policy according to today's real estate market conditions.

With floods occurring frequently in recent years, flood insurance has been in the news. Flood insurance eligibility is affected by such considerations as whether or not you live in or near a flood plain and whether you are located in an area that is known to experience flooding on a regular basis.

What does the **policy cover**?

In general, your policy covers the costs to repair or rebuild your house and any other structures on your property, like garages or work sheds, from such events as a fire, water damage from a broken pipe or heating system, fallen trees, and damage due to wind or snow.

What **doesn't** my **policy cover**?

If you live in a flood plain, hurricane or earthquake prone area, your initial policy may not cover these occurrences. Your insurance company will tell you what additional coverage you may need in order to be properly insured.

What happens if there is **damage** to my house due to a **natural event**, like high winds pushing a tree onto my roof?

The insurance company will send out an insurance adjuster or claims adjuster to your house within a few days, and he or she will investigate the claim, and with a contractor, provide you with an estimate of what the cost of repair is. The policy then allows you to pay a small deductible and either use the insurance company's contractor to do the repairs necessary to bring the house back to its original condition, or to use your own contractor to complete the repairs.

107

HOME INSURANCE CHECKLIST

Review this checklist to make sure you ask the right questions of your home insurer and save as much money as possible.

- ❏ Do you have *enough* insurance? You need to have enough to replace the entire house if it is lost to floods, fires, earthquakes, or other disasters. Flood and earthquake insurance are not typically included unless you ask for such coverage; circumstances for such coverage depend on the location of the house, such as whether it is in a flood plain or near a geological fault line.

- ❏ Cover the items in your house completely. Take an inventory and take photographs of more expensive items; provide this information to your insurer. You might need additional riders for expensive jewelry, collectibles, antiques, and expensive electronics such as computers.

- ❏ Include liability insurance in case someone is injured on your property and files a lawsuit.

- ❏ Get umbrella insurance to cover the risks of having a swimming pool or other risky items on your property.

- ❏ Ask about the availability of additional coverage, such as for drain/sewer back-ups, inflation-guard to cover rising costs.

- ❏ Ask about discounts for safety features, including fire extinguishers, smoke detectors, burglar alarms, fire alarms, deadbolts, earthquake retrofitting, wind-resistant shutters, and so on.

- ❏ Ask about multi-policy discounts.

- ❏ If you are over 55, you may get a discount.

- ❏ Upgrades in plumbing, electrical, and AC systems may make you eligible for discounts.

- ❏ Take the highest deductible that you can reasonably afford, and don't file claims for minor damage to your property that you can afford to fix yourself easily.

What else does my home owner's policy cover?

Most home owner's policies cover personal property and effects in your house from damage or loss, such as artwork, clothing, jewelry, electronics, appliances, etc.

Should I document the purchase of certain things that I would like to have on my home owner's insurance policy?

Yes, it is not a bad idea to keep copies of receipts of these big ticket items, and to record a video of these items, room by room, so that you have some record of what you do own. Make sure that you store this information in a fire/waterproof safe place. Your insurance company can provide you with specifics on documenting the purchase and ownership of such items.

Does my home owner's policy cover **personal injury**?

Your policy may also cover personal injury and liability if someone falls or injures himself on your property. You may pay for certain amounts of coverage, depending on how much protection you need.

How do I know **how much personal injury insurance coverage** I need?

It is a good rule to have coverage that is equal to or exceeds your net worth, so that you will not lose any of your assets if you are ever sued.

How can I find out if I am dealing with a **legitimate insurance company**?

The National Association of Insurance Commissioners (www.naic.org) keeps track of all complaints lodged against insurance companies in each state. You may do a search and investigate your insurance company by going to its site and entering the name of the company to see if it exists, if it has any complaints, and if it is a legitimate company with which to do business.

Do I need to **pay for investigative information** on insurance companies?

No, you should never pay any company or Website to view its reports, as this information is available for free on many Websites, including that of your own state. Just do some digging and you will find the information that you seek without having to pay.

What are the **biggest complaints against insurance companies** that offer home owner's insurance?

According to the NAIC, in 2010, 25.1% of all complaints were due to delays in handling claims, 14.5% were because of denials of claims, and 14.3% were because the settlement or offer was unsatisfactory.

How can I **save money** on my home owner's insurance?

The easiest way to save money on your insurance is to increase your deductible, from say $500 to $1,000 or higher. This will lower your monthly premiums by as much as 25% for your coverage. You may also consider shopping around and obtain several quotes before deciding on one insurance company.

What should I look for in **deciding what** home owner's **insurance company to use**?

You should look for a company that provides excellent service, pays claims without hassle, is financially solvent and in good standing, has a long history of serving clients and, of course, competitive prices.

Can I be **overinsured** on my home owner's policy?

Yes, if you insured the replacement cost of your house to match what you paid for the house, you are most likely overinsured, since the price of your house included the price of the physical land beneath your house. Since your land does not incur any damage, you need to insure your house for the cost to rebuild the same size and type of house that you originally purchased, minus the land. The property appraiser that you used to buy the house will be able to give you an exact figure for the land, given today's real estate market rates in your area.

Can I **save money** if I buy my **home owner's insurance policy** from the **same company** that provides my auto or life insurance policy?

Yes, you may save additionally if you group several different policies together with the same company. Check with your insurance agent to see what kinds of discounts are available if you move your policies to one company.

What are some **other things** that I can do to **lower my home owner's insurance costs**?

Many insurance companies offer additional discounts for installing burglar alarm systems, fire alarms, and smoke detectors, retrofitting your house with storm windows, or fire retardant barriers to minimize the damage due to a fire. Check with your agent if these additional discounts are available.

INSURANCE FOR RENTERS

What is renter's or **tenant's insurance**?

The owners of your apartment carry some form of insurance that covers the physical buildings from loss. But their policy does not cover the loss incurred by the tenants in the building for their possessions.

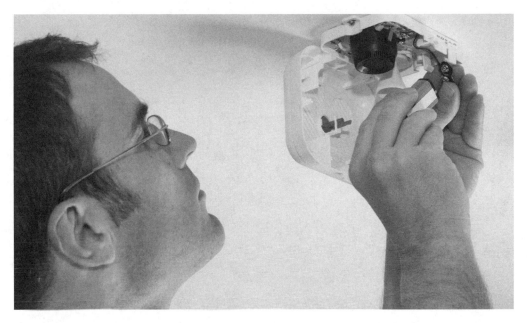

Taking sensible precautions, such as installing smoke or radon detectors in your house, or burglar alarms, can help you save on insurance costs.

How does **tenant's insurance work**?

A renter can make a list, or electronic record of the possessions inside the apartment, and their values, and have a file of receipts for these items. Then, the renter contacts an insurance company, and gets a policy covering their possessions, and can choose a deductible, and pay premiums each month. If there is a fire in your building, you will be able to collect money for the replacement value of your possessions.

What **percentage of renters** are **uninsured**?

According to a study released by apartments.com and reported by Allstate Insurance Company, 67% of the 81 million renters in the United States do not have renter's insurance. This means if there is a catastrophic loss, they would not receive any money toward replacing their lost possessions.

How expensive is renter's insurance?

A typical policy, depending on the value of ones possessions may be $100–$300 per year.

What if I own a condo, am I **covered under the condo association's policy**?

No, the condo association's policy covers the physical property itself, and not the possessions within. Check with your condo association to see exactly what is covered   111

To have complete car insurance coverage, you need collision, comprehensive, and liability insurance. Liability insurance protects you in cases when bodily or property damage to others has occurred; collision covers damage to the vehicle; and comprehensive insurance covers other contingencies, such as theft and vandalism.

under their policy, and what coverage they recommend, before purchasing a condominium. Most condominium owners believe that their possessions are covered, when they are not.

What does my **renter's or condo insurance cover**?

A policy covers damage due to fire or lightning, windstorm, or hail, explosion, riot or civil commotion, aircraft, vehicles, smoke, vandalism or malicious mischief, theft, damage by glass or safety-glazing material that is part of a building, volcanic eruption, falling objects, weight of ice, snow, or sleet, water-related damage from home utilities, and electrical surge damage. It does not cover flooding or earthquakes, as these disasters need to be covered under a separate policy.

What's the **difference** between "**actual cash value**" and "**replacement cost coverage**" in my renter's insurance policy quote?

Actual cash value means that the insurance company will pay you what your possessions were worth at the time of the claim, less your deductible. Replacement cost coverage is the value to replace the possessions, as new, at the time of claim. Make sure your policy covers the costs for replacement.

GETTING CAR INSURANCE CHECKLIST

Applying for car insurance will go smoothly if you remember to note the following:

- ❏ Your driver's license number
- ❏ Vehicle Identification Number (VIN)
- ❏ The year, make, and model of your vehicle
- ❏ Name and contact information of the company financing your car

---

AUTOMOBILE INSURANCE

Do all **states require** that we have **automobile insurance**?

No, every state and the District of Columbia requires that drivers have adequate insurance except for New Hampshire.

What types of **coverage** does one get when one buys an **auto insurance policy**?

There are three main types of automobile insurance coverage available to you: liability, collision, and comprehensive.

What is **liability coverage**?

Liability covers unintentional bodily injury and property damage to others when you are legally liable or substantially at fault in an accident.

What is **collision coverage**?

After payment of a deductible, collision coverage pays for any physical damage to your vehicle as a result of a collision.

What is **comprehensive coverage**?

After payment of a deductible, comprehensive coverage covers you for any non-collision losses including fire, theft, glass breakage, and vandalism.

113

Save money on your car insurance by installing a car alarm on your vehicle.

What if **my pet** is involved in an **accident in my car**?

Some insurers offer pet protection coverage for your pet dog or cat should they be injured or killed while in your vehicle as a result of an auto accident.

What **other types** of **supplemental coverage** is available?

Depending on which insurance company you choose, optional or required coverage is available, including personal injury protection, medical payments, uninsured/under-insured motorists coverage, loan/lease gap coverage, car rental coverage, and custom, electronic or extra equipment coverage.

Whom do I **call first** when I am **in an accident**?

The first place to call is the local police in the area where the accident occurred, in order to get a police report.

Can I **leave the scene of my accident**, and take care of things later?

You should never leave the scene of an accident, as police must arrive at the scene to see if anyone is substantially responsible, to interview the drivers, and to file a police report.

LOWER YOUR CAR INSURANCE

If your auto insurance is beginning to put a squeeze on your wallet or purse, there are many things you can do to lower payments.

❑ Ask your insurer about multi-car discounts.

❑ Keep your credit rating high. Insurance companies will charge drivers higher rates if their credit is bad.

❑ Purchase insurance a year at a time, rather than a six-moth policy, to lock in the rate.

❑ Avoid buying cars that are typically costly to insure, including sports cars, large SUVs, luxury cars, very small vehicles, and cars with a high track record of being stolen.

❑ Check if you are eligible for a group discount. Depending on the insurer, you might get a discount for belonging to various organizations, such as a credit union, or even for owning a certain credit card.

❑ Raise your comprehensive and collision deductibles. Check with your lender to see what it allows for a maximum deductible.

❑ Combine your policies into one. You can group your auto insurance with policies such as home or renter's policies to get a discount.

❑ Make payments electronically. Many insurers offer discounts for making EFT payments automatically, either directly through a bank account or through a credit card.

❑ Install anti-theft devices in your car.

❑ Check your mileage. Insurance costs can vary depending on how far you drive to work, so make sure the number is accurate and you aren't being charged for too much mileage.

❑ If you store your vehicle for long periods, check with your insurance company if you can just carry comprehensive coverage during those times.

❑ Check for discounts for safety devices, such as airbags, anti-lock brakes, and automatic seatbelts.

❑ Take a driving course. You can sometimes get a discount for taking a defensive driving course. Teenage drivers, in particular, can be eligible for discounts for getting good grades on driving classes beyond the usual driver's education courses.

❑ Before buying insurance on a rental car, check with your insurance company to see if you really need it. Many times, you will already be covered.

After the accident, what should I do to **begin the claims process**?

You need to contact your insurance claims adjuster, who will ask you to obtain and submit a copy of the police report and report number to him or her.

What information should I exchange with the other driver of the vehicle involved?

You need to exchange name, address, and telephone number, as well as driver's license number, and license plate number. It is advisable to take a picture of any damage, and the plate of the vehicle, just in case they decide to leave the scene. You should also exchange insurance information including the name of the insurance company and policy number.

What about **witnesses**? Do I need any **information from them**?

If the accident was critical, and the damage severe, it is not a bad idea to get the names of any witnesses that might have seen the accident.

How long does it take **to make a claim**?

Depending on the quality of service that your insurance company provides, it shouldn't take more than 15 minutes to process a claim, if you have all of the proper information available at the time of the call.

Will I have to **pay for anything after the accident**?

It depends very much on what type of coverage you obtained when you got your policy, and what your deductible is.

What should I look for in **identifying** a **good auto insurance company**?

Customer service is a very important consideration when choosing an auto insurer since you will need a company with very good service if you are ever in an accident and must make a claim. Price is also a consideration, and we always want to find the best service for the least price. Choose a financially sound company with a long history, and one that has served many people for many years. Great insurance companies also have established a network of repair facilities, and have established relationships directly with the people who can do the repairs necessary to get your car back on the road.

What are some **ideas** for **saving money** on **auto insurance**?

There are several ways to shave money off of your policy. One of the easiest ways is to shop around and compare prices for the same coverage. You may also try increasing your deductible, getting a group rate by belonging to a group that has coverage with the insurance company (like a credit union), insuring multiple vehicles with the same company, getting multiple insurance policies (like house and car) from the same company, installing anti-theft devices, and wearing seat belts. You may see savings of hundreds of dollars per year. See the checklist on page 115 for more ideas.

HEALTH INSURANCE

How much do Americans **spend on health care each year**?

Americans spend $2 trillion on health care each year.

How many Americans have **no health insurance**?

Forty-six million Americans have no health insurance coverage.

Who are the **people without health insurance**?

According to the U.S. Census Bureau, the uninsured are people who can't afford to pay for high insurance premiums, people who are poor but are eligible for Medicaid, young people who do not feel that they need insurance, and illegal immigrants.

How many Americans **lose their health insurance** coverage each day?

As many as 14,000 Americans lose their insurance every day.

What is **Medicare**?

Medicare is the U.S. government's medical insurance available to people of retirement age.

Can you get **Medicare** if you are **younger than age 65**?

Yes, people with certain disabilities may apply for Medicare before they reach the age of 65.

What is the **Affordable Care Act**?

The Affordable Care Act, passed by Congress and signed into law by President Barack Obama in March 2010, gives Americans better health security by putting in place comprehensive health insurance reforms that hold insurance companies accountable, lower health care costs, guarantee more choice, and enhance the quality of care for all Americans.

About 50 million Americans between the ages of 18 and 64 have no health insurance, according to the U.S. Centers for Disease Control and Prevention.

Will the **Affordable Care Act** have any effect on the **lifetime maximum expenses** that insurance companies impose on the insured?

Yes, in fact the Act removes all lifetime limits, so that if, for example, you are undergoing cancer treatment, and you have reached your old limit, you can continue to be treated.

What was it like **before the Affordable Care Act**?

Before, you could and would be cut off from all treatment by your insurance company, as soon as you reached the maximum, even if it meant that you would soon die without the treatment.

How many people will benefit from this provision?

Immediately, 20,400 people who previously would have exceeded their maximum insurance benefits each year will benefit, as well as 102 million Americans who will be treated for some chronic disease.

Does the Affordable Care Act **help our children**?

Yes, insurance companies must now keep your children covered under your policy, if you choose, until they reach the age of 26, instead of 18–21 years.

Does the Affordable Care Act **prevent insurance companies** from **dropping the very sick and ill** who need treatment the most?

Yes, before the Act, insurance companies could drop you from their plan, if you were diagnosed with a severe illness or you made a mistake on an application. The Act bans this practice, and allows people to keep their coverage, even as they are in the early stages of treatment, without fear of being dropped.

How many people can **benefit** from the provision that **increases the age limit to 26** for children covered under their parents' insurance?

About 1.8 million Americans may benefit.

Before the Affordable Care Act, could **insurance companies discriminate** against **children**?

Yes, before the Act, insurance companies would routinely deny benefits to children with pre-existing conditions. If a child had cancer, and the parents changed insurance companies, the insurance company could deny any coverage, because the child was already sick. Under the Act, this is forbidden, and all children under the age of 19 must be covered, regardless of their pre-existing conditions.

Will the **Affordable Care Act** deal with **annual limits** that insurance companies impose?

Yes, the Act will restrict how insurance companies establish these limits, and what the limits will be. Before the Act, if you reached your maximum benefits, you would either have to pay out of pocket for the expenses, or not receive any treatment, depending on the limits set by the insurance company.

Does the **Affordable Care Act** address **preventive services**?

Yes, services like mammograms, colonoscopies, immunizations, and pre-natal and new baby care will be covered, and insurance companies will be prohibited from charging deductibles, co-payments or co-insurance.

Will our **right to appeal** a decision by an insurance company be **protected** under the Affordable Care Act?

Yes, consumers will be guaranteed the right to appeal insurance company decisions (claims, denial of benefits) through an independent third party.

119

Does the **Affordable Care Act** deal with how we **choose** our **primary care doctors**, and out of network emergency coverage?

Yes, consumers will have their choice of providers within the plan's network of doctors, including OB-GYNs and pediatricians, without a referral, as well as out-of-network emergency care.

How do I **get health insurance**?

Most Americans obtain medical care coverage through their employers, who offer it as a benefit, in order to attract and keep employees.

Who **pays** for my **employer-sponsored medical insurance**?

The typical employee pays a monthly premium, which represents about 75%–80% of the actual cost. Your employer covers the rest.

What is a **medical deductible**?

A medical deductible is the amount of expenses that the medically insured must pay before the insurance company will pay for the covered services.

Medical insurance should ideally be designed to cover both emergencies and preventive care.

What is a **co-pay**?

It is a short form of the word co-payment, an expense that the insured must pay whenever medical services are rendered. Co-payments are not counted toward out of pocket maximums.

What are **out-of-pocket maximums**?

This is the amount of expenses that the insured would pay in any given year, up to a maximum amount as set forth in the medical insurance policy. The higher the maximum, the lower the annual premium.

What is **co-insurance**?

Co-insurance is similar to a co-payment, except that it may be counted toward your annual out of pocket maximum, and is a percentage payment after the deductible is paid, up to a limit.

Why do we have co-payments/co-insurance?

Insurance companies use this method as a way of limiting the misuse of the insurance, so that the insured only use doctors when necessary, by making the insureds pay a portion each time they use a doctor.

How does medical insurance work?

When you visit a doctor seeking treatment, the price/value for the service that is rendered is established by the insurance company, and the insurance company will pay for that service up to the amount that they have established. If the doctor charges higher than this amount, the insured must pay the difference. If it is less, the insured would get a discount, and may pay less for that service. Each insurance company establishes what types of visits are covered at 100%, 80%, 50%, etc., in your initial policy.

What is a Statement of Benefits?

The Statement of Benefits document is generated each time you have any treatment or consultation and describes exactly the service that was performed, what the cost was, what the insurance company thinks the cost should be, what your co-pay, if any, was for the service, and what you owe the service provider.

How do I check the accuracy of my medical bills?

If your medical insurance company offers an online version of your plan it is best to use this to help reconcile your bills. For extra protection, compare your statement of benefit report with the actual bill that you receive from the doctor. If you see any discrepancies, call up your insurance company and ask a representative to explain the discrepancies.

Why are there discrepancies in my medical bills?

Medical service providers use third parties to do their billing, and these companies may make mistakes when keying in information from your bill.

What types of discrepancies are there in medical bills?

Sometimes a doctor may charge you for a service that you were unaware of, charge you twice for the service, or charge you for a service that is already free according to your plan. So it is very important to understand your medical insurance plan, and per-

121

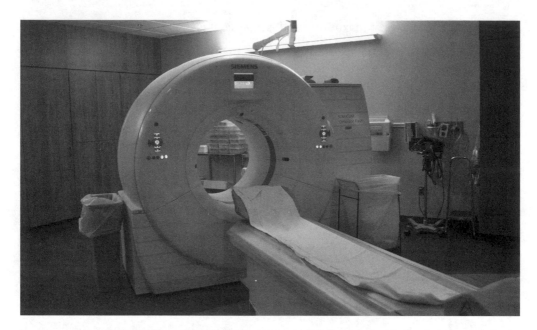

There are many items to check when reviewing health insurance plans, including reviewing what medical tests are covered. Tests, such as CT scans, can cost hundreds, even thousands of dollars for one hospital visit.

haps even call ahead to the doctor to find out how much out of pocket you will have to pay before your appointment so that you are not surprised.

Can a doctor give me a **quote before** I seek their help?

Yes, all you need to do is provide them with your insurance plan numbers, and some basic information, and they will be able to tell you pretty precisely what the charges for the visit or procedure will be, how much will be covered by your insurance and how much you will have to pay out of pocket.

What does **medical insurance cost**?

According to a 2009 America's Health Insurance Plans study, the average annual premium for an individual was $2,985 and for a family it was $6,328. Health insurance premiums rose about 119% from 1998 to 2009, and this rate of inflation shows no signs of slowing down soon.

How do **employers** react to **rate increases** by medical insurance companies?

According to annual survey by the firm Mercer, 40% of companies pass on the increases by having the employees pay a larger percentage of the premiums, while 39% will

HEALTH COVERAGE CHECKLIST

Before purchasing health care, you should compare coverage and costs of several providers. Use the following checklist to record the information in a handy place.

Health Insurer 1

Hospital care: _____

Office visits to your doctor: _____

Ease of getting an appointment: _____

Choice of doctors: _____

Location of doctors and hospitals: _____

Prescription drugs: _____

Immunizations: _____

Medical tests, X rays: _____

Mammograms: _____

Surgery (inpatient and outpatient): _____

Maternity care: _____

Well-baby care: _____

Mental health care: _____

Dental care, braces and cleaning: _____

Vision care, eyeglasses and exams: _____

Home health care: _____

Nursing home care: _____

Services you need that are excluded: _____

Minimal paperwork: _____

Waiting period for coverage: _____

Health Insurer 2

Hospital care: _____

Office visits to your doctor: _____

Health Insurer 2 (contd.)

Ease of getting an appointment: _____

Choice of doctors: _____

Location of doctors and hospitals: _____

Prescription drugs: _____

Immunizations: _____

Medical tests, X rays: _____

Mammograms: _____

Surgery (inpatient and outpatient): _____

Maternity care: _____

Well-baby care: _____

Mental health care: _____

Dental care, braces and cleaning: _____

Vision care, eyeglasses and exams: _____

Home health care: _____

Nursing home care: _____

Services you need that are excluded: _____

Minimal paperwork: _____

Waiting period for coverage: _____

Health Insurer 3

Hospital care: _____

Office visits to your doctor: _____

Ease of getting an appointment: _____

Choice of doctors: _____

Location of doctors and hospitals: _____

Prescription drugs: _____

Immunizations: _____

Health Insurer 3 (contd.)

Medical tests, X rays: _____

Mammograms: _____

Surgery (inpatient and outpatient): _____

Maternity care: _____

Well-baby care: _____

Mental health care: _____

Dental care, braces and cleaning: _____

Vision care, eyeglasses and exams: _____

Home health care: _____

Nursing home care: _____

Services you need that are excluded: _____

Minimal paperwork: _____

Waiting period for coverage: _____

increase the employee share of deductibles, co-pays/co-insurance, or out of pocket maximums.

What is a **health savings account**?

A health savings account (HSA) is a medical savings account that offers consumers a tax advantage, since they pay no federal income taxes at the time of deposit for the funds that are deposited. The money can be used to pay for health expenses or out of pocket expenses related to your medical care. The funds that are in the account can be rolled over from year to year.

What's a **flexible spending account**?

Similar to an HSA, the flexible spending account allows consumers to set aside money in an account to be used during the plan year, plus two and a half months free from payroll taxes, to be used for medical expenses. The money must be used during that time, and any unused funds can be used for future plan administrative costs, or given back to the employee as taxable income. The maximum allowed per year in contributions is $5,000 per plan year and will move to $2,500 in 2013.

125

LIFE INSURANCE

What is **life insurance**?

Life insurance represents a contract between the insured and the insurance company whereby, in exchange for premiums paid by the insured (at regular intervals, or one lump sum), the insurance company will pay out the value of the insurance policy, at the end of life of the insured, to his/her beneficiary. There are two main types of life insurance products: term and permanent.

How do I know **how much insurance** to buy?

It really depends on what your goal is, and how you and your beneficiaries will make use of the money. People often purchase life insurance to cover their outstanding mortgage balance, so that in the event of their death, their house can be fully paid, and their family can live comfortably, without having to worry about incurring a great debt. Other people buy insurance policies that allow them to take income or provide income to their family upon the insured person's death.

If I already have a well-funded IRA or 401k retirement plan that I am automatically investing in each month, **do I really need life insurance**?

If your retirement plan is well funded, your mortgage nearly paid off, and you are nearing retirement age, it's probably a good idea to save the money on expensive insurance premiums and insurance investments, which may have a return that is less than what you are getting on your retirement plan. The older you are, the more expensive the insurance premiums, if you choose to get an insurance policy later on in life. It may be more prudent to use the money that you would invest in an insurance policy, and redirect that money to your retirement fund.

Can you buy **too much insurance**?

Yes, the amount of insurance that one should get depends on the value of your assets and your debt situation. It also depends on the amount of income you wish to have in retirement years, and the amount of income you wish to leave your spouse in later years, should you die early in life. Many insurance companies have calculators available on their Websites that allow you to see how much insurance you would need to purchase in order to meet your goals.

What is **term life insurance**?

Term life insurance is a type of insurance that covers the insured for a certain period of time or term—10, 20, or 30 years—and pays a benefit to a beneficiary upon the

No one likes to think about death, especially one's own demise, but planning for the inevitable is the responsible course of action. Buying life insurance can help protect your family, and you can even borrow on the cash value, if needed.

death of the insured. The policy also expires when the term ends, so that if no death occurs during the term period, no payout is made.

Why is a **term life insurance** policy **favored** by people?

It is favored because it is relatively inexpensive. You can buy a policy for specific period of time, for example, until your children are financially independent. And you may not incur taxes as a beneficiary of the policy. Some also buy a term life policy to supplement other insurance policies that they might hold, and to cover the value of their home mortgage upon their death.

What if I **outlive** the term of my **term policy**?

Insurance companies will give you the option to continue your policy, for a much higher premium, convert it to a permanent policy, or just let it expire.

What is **permanent life insurance**?

It is an insurance policy that, in exchange for regular premiums paid throughout the lifetime of the insured, pays a death benefit upon the death of the insured. Part of the money that you pay in premiums is set aside in an account to grow in cash value, which you can later access by borrowing against it, and part of the premium is used to pay the death benefit.

127

Do I need to take a **medical exam** to get **life insurance**?

No, but it does depend on the company that you choose, and many insurance companies often require it. If you convert a term life insurance policy to a permanent policy, sometimes the insurance company will not require a second exam.

SMALL BUSINESS INSURANCE

Why would I need **business insurance**?

Since operating a home-based business may involve a significant financial investment, business owners need to protect themselves and limit the financial risks of events such as lawsuits that may arise from the operation of that business.

What types of **insurance** do I need if I operate a **home-based business**?

There are many types of insurance coverage available for small, home-based business, including contents insurance, general liability insurance, product liability insurance, professional liability insurance, errors and omissions insurance, and disability insurance.

What is **contents insurance**?

Contents insurance pays for loss or damage to possessions on the premises of your home-based business. Your home owner's insurance will not cover the loss or damage of equipment in your home-based office, and this needs to be covered under a separate policy.

What is **general liability insurance**?

General liability insurance covers the home business operator from general claims of liability or injury due to negligence. It also protects against payments as the result of bodily injury, property damage, medical expenses, libel, slander, the cost of defending lawsuits, and settlement bonds or judgments required during an appeal procedure. If a client is visiting your office, and injures himself, general liability insurance will cover the expenses related to this claim. Your home owner's policy will not.

What is **product liability insurance**?

Companies that manufacture, wholesale, distribute, and retail a product may be liable for its safety. If your home-based business represents these companies and sells physical products to people, product liability insurance will cover you for lawsuits that arise from injuries or damages caused by the product that you sell and its use.

What is **professional liability insurance**?

Also known as professional indemnity insurance, it protects professionals, like architects, accountants, and lawyers, from injuries or damages caused by the services that they provide, and may be available through the professional association/society to which the professional belongs. Depending on your profession, you may be required by your state government to have such a policy.

What is **errors and omissions insurance**?

It is an insurance policy used by people in the service and consulting businesses, which covers the insured from claims arising from a client who holds such company or an individual responsible for a service that was provided, or failed to be provided, which did not have the agreed upon results.

What is **disability insurance**?

It is an insurance policy that covers you for temporary or permanent loss of income, enabling you to continue to earn income for a period of time, as specified in the policy. Typical policies may have enough coverage so that income is being earned, for a period of time, until the insured can get back to work again.

Where can I **purchase insurance** for my **home-based business**?

It is important to shop around and obtain several quotes from reputable insurance companies or brokers, as prices for these and many other policies may vary greatly from company to company.

TAXES

FEDERAL TAXES

Who must file a federal income tax return?

If you are a U.S. citizen or resident alien, whether you must file a federal income tax return depends on your gross income, your filing status, your age, and whether you are a dependent.

How many people file individual tax returns by the deadline in mid-April?

About 140 million people file an individual tax return each year in the United States.

What percentage of households will owe no income tax in 2010?

According to a report by CNN, 45% of all households will owe no income tax. Many of these households make far less income in order to pay income taxes.

How many people file their taxes electronically using E-File?

Two out of every three taxpayers file their taxes electronically, using the IRS E-File service.

How quickly can I get my refund if I also opt for direct deposit?

If you opt for direct deposit, you may get your refund deposited directly into up to three accounts in as little as ten days.

Beginning in 2011, taxpayers may use their tax refunds to invest automatically in U.S. savings bonds.

Can I **automatically invest** in **U.S. savings bonds** using my **refund**?

Yes, beginning in 2011, taxpayers may purchase up to $5,000 of U.S. Treasury Series iSavings Bonds, low risk bonds that grow in value for up to 30 years.

What **types of forms** are there for filing a **federal tax return**?

There are three main forms—1040EZ, 1040, and 1040A

What **types of filing statuses** are there?

The five filing statuses are single, married filing jointly, married filing separately, head of household, and qualifying widow(er) with dependent child. If more than one filing status applies, you may choose the one that enables you to pay the lowest tax.

What is a **tax credit**?

A tax credit is an item that allows you to reduce the taxes that you must pay, and is more valuable to you than a tax deduction.

Why do we have **tax credits**?

We have tax credits to encourage some sort of behavior, giving a break to people who may need additional assistance. For example, we may get tax credits to encourage

---

COMMON TAX DEDUCTIONS

Whether or not you itemize your tax return, you are allowed certain tax deductions, including the following. Review this list to check off the deductions you should be taking.

Eligible Deductions Whether or Not You Itemize

❑ Business expenses

❑ Retirement contributions, including 401(k), IRAs, SEP accounts

❑ Interest on student loans up to $2,500 a year

❑ Capital losses

Eligible Deductions When You Itemize

❑ State and local taxes

❑ Medical expenses

❑ Contributions to charities

❑ Interest paid on home mortgage(s)

❑ Interest paid on home equity loan(s)

❑ Personal casualty and theft losses not covered by insurance

---

energy savings behavior by giving a credit for the purchase of energy saving appliances or improvements to your house.

Who creates the tax credits?

The U.S. Congress can enact different tax credits each year to help Americans for different purposes. Some remain for many years; others may be of short duration.

Are these tax credits available to everyone?

No, many of these credits phase out when certain income levels are reached, or if certain requirements are not met. See the IRS Website (www.irs.gov) for more details on any particular credit.

What is a tax deduction?

A tax deduction is an item that reduces your taxable income, which is then used to compute the amount of taxes you owe at the end of the year.

Just as gambling winnings are taxable, gambling losses can be deductible. However, they are deductible only if you itemize and do not take the standard deduction.

What are some **notable tax deductions**?

State sales tax (especially if you live in a state with no state income tax, you can choose between deducting your state's income tax or the sales tax); out of pocket charitable contributions (those cash expenses related to your work with a charity, like driving expenses, purchase of food, etc.); student loan interest paid by parents; employment-seeking expenses (as long as they do not exceed 2% of your adjusted gross income); moving expenses to take your first job; health insurance deduction for the self-employed (enabling you to deduct health insurance premiums for you and your family); state income taxes paid; property taxes paid; capital losses; and gambling losses.

What is better, a **tax credit** or a **tax deduction**?

A tax credit is more favorable, because the amount of the credit, dollar for dollar, is subtracted directly from the amount of tax owed. A deduction only reduces taxable income, which is then applied to a certain tax rate, depending on income, for computing the final tax owed.

Are **tax credits and tax deductions** the **same each year**?

No, tax credits and tax deductions may change each year. It is best to check the www.irs.gov Website to find out new changes to credits and deductions for each year that you file.

Do I need to have **income** to receive a **tax credit**?

No, as long as you are not filing your taxes under anyone else's tax return (e.g., a spouse), even if you reported no income, you still may be eligible for this year's tax credit.

What are some **notable tax credits**?

Some of the more notable tax credits include: the American Opportunity Credit (which covers educational tuition, books and fees related to post-secondary education); the Energy Credit (for purchase of certain energy efficient appliances); the Earned Income tax credit (for filers meeting certain income levels); and the First Time Home Buyers Credit (available for those who closed on the purchase of a first home before April 2010). In addition there are also: Schedule M, the Making Work Pay Credit (which offers $400 for individuals and $800 for families, off their taxes); The Foreign Tax Credit (if you earned income from work or investments in a foreign country); Childcare and Dependent Care tax credit (which allows you a credit of between 20% and 35%, depending on your income); general business credit; child tax credit; alternative minimum tax credit; and lifetime learning credit.

What is a **progressive tax rate**?

A progressive tax rate is a tax rate that changes depending on the amount of income earned in a year. As someone earns more income, the percentage of that income to be paid in taxes increases. The higher income you make, the more able you are to pay the tax. It is also known as marginal tax rate or marginal tax bracket.

Federal Tax Rates

Tax Rate 2010	Single	Married Filing Jointly
Standard Deduction	$5,700	$11,400
10%	$0–$8,375	$0–$16,750
15%	$8,375–$34,000	$16,750–$68,000
25%	$34,000–$82,400	$68,000–$137,300
28%	$82,400–$171,875	$137,300–$209,250
33%	171,850–$373,650	$209,250–$373,650
35%	>$373,650	>$373,650

Tax Rate 2011	Single	Filing Jointly
Standard Deduction	$5,800	$11,600
10%	$0–$8,500	$0–$17,000
15%	$8,500–$34,500	$17,000–$69,000
25%	$34,500–$83,600	$69,000–$139,500
28%	$83,600–$174,400	$139,500–$212,300
33%	174,400–$379,150	$212,300–$379,150
35%	>$379,150	>$379,150

COMMONLY MISSED TAX DEDUCTIONS

Review this list of tax deductions for which you might be eligible before filing.

❑ Health insurance premiums paid exceeding 7.5% of your Adjusted Gross Income.

❑ For self-employed individuals, health insurance premiums can be deducted 100%.

❑ In states without state income tax, deduct your state sales tax. Keep records of state sales tax paid on large items, such as automobiles, but you don't have to keep receipts on every small purchase unless you wish to. You have the option of using a tabled value provided by the IRS.

❑ You can deduct any state taxes that you may have owed when you filed the previous April.

❑ A retirement tax credit for people with an adjusted gross income of less than $25,000 ($50,000 for joint filers) provides a credit up to $1,000, or up to 50% of the first $2,000 put into a retirement account, such as an IRA or SEP.

❑ Estate tax on IRAs are deductible; in other words, if you inherit an IRA, you can deduct the amount of estate tax you paid on the inheritance.

❑ Expenses accrued for tax preparation and investments are deductible if they exceed 2% or your adjusted gross income. This includes brokers fees, phone expenses when calling a broker, and even safety deposit box fees.

❑ Higher education expenses up to $4,000 when your adjusted gross income is less than $65,000 ($130,000 for joint returns).

❑ The Lifetime Learning Credit is available for undergraduate and graduate students, as well as adults taking courses in order to get better jobs.

What are the **different marginal tax rates**?

Currently, the marginal tax rates or brackets are 10%, 15%, 25%, 28%, 33% and 35%.

How does the **marginal tax rate** work?

If a single person were to make $10,000 in income, they would be taxed 10% on the first $8,375 ($837), and then 15% on the amount of income from $8,376–$10,000 (which is $243) for a total of $1,080.

What is a **tax schedule**?

It is a rate sheet used by individual taxpayers to approximate their estimated taxes due. There are four main schedules used, based on the filing status of the individual and

- ❑ The American Opportunity Credit, which replaced the Hope credit beginning in 2011, is for undergraduate students going to school at least part time. It is a change from the Hope credit in that it applies even to low-income people who owe few or no taxes.

- ❑ Students who are not declared as dependents on their parents' tax returns can deduct up to $2,500 off any loan interest paid by their parents.

- ❑ "Above the line" credit up to $250 for educators who spend money out of their own pockets to purchase educational materials for their classes.

- ❑ Child care expenses are often tax deductible when such expenses are required to take care of your children while you work.

- ❑ Refinancing a mortgage allows you to deduct money paid on new or old points.

- ❑ Moving expenses, when necessary to relocate for a new job, are tax deductible when searching for your *first* job when you must move more than 50 miles from your current residence.

- ❑ National Guard or military reserve tax filers can deduct travel expenses when they need to travel more than 100 miles and must pay for a place to stay overnight. This deduction includes lodging, half of meal expenses, mileage, tolls, and parking.

- ❑ If your employer paid you a salary while you were on jury duty and then demanded you repay your company for the amount you received in jury pay, you can then deduct the jury pay on your next return.

- ❑ Non-cash charitable contributions are worth a tax credit. This applies to goods donated, such as clothing and used cars. Make sure you get a receipt from the nonprofit organization to which you are contributing. You can also deduct mileage when you have to drive as a result of volunteer work you are doing.

include: Schedule X (single), Schedule Y-1 (married filing jointly, qualifying widow[er]); Schedule Y-2 (married filing separately); Schedule Z (head of household).

What else does the term **tax schedule** refer to?

It is also a term used to describe the addendum worksheets that accompany the IRS Form 1040, and include Schedules A (itemized deductions), B (dividend & interest income), C (business profit or loss), D (capital gains), and E (supplemental income and loss)

What is a **capital asset**?

Nearly everything that you have purchased and own, or have used for personal purposes, is a capital asset. It could be an individual stock, the value of your rental house, etc.

137

What is a **cost basis**?

It is the amount of money that you used to purchase an item that you own.

What is a **capital gain or loss**?

It is the difference between your cost basis, or what you paid for it, and what you sold it for. If the difference is positive, meaning its value increased, it is called a capital gain. If the price decreases from the time of purchase, then it is called a capital loss. Both situations are given attention when you file your taxes each year.

What is the **maximum** that we can claim in a year for a **capital loss**?

After we total what all of the capital gains were for the year, $3,000 is the limit that can be applied each year for a loss, until the total loss is fully utilized. That means if you lost $9,000 on a stock investment, you can claim $3,000 in losses, each year, for three years.

Are the **tax rates the same** for **capital gains** as they are for **individuals**?

No, the tax rates that apply to capital gains are lower than the tax rates that apply to other income. The maximum rate for some capital gains is 15%. For lower-income individuals, the rate may be 0% on some or all of the capital gain. Special types of net capital gain can be taxed at 25% or 28%, depending on what they are, and whether there are any penalties involved.

Can I **deduct capital losses** on the **sale** of my **personal property**?

No, you may only deduct capital losses on investment property, not on property purchased for personal use.

How do we use the **tax tables** to determine what our **tax liability** is for the year?

After taking into consideration your filing status, what forms you file, and any adjustments to your taxable income (tax deductions), you look up what your adjusted gross income is in the table, and see how much tax you are required to pay. Then, you may subtract any credits or payments from this tax in order to compute your final tax bill.

What is the **difference** between a **short** and **long-term capital gain**?

If you hold the asset before selling for less than a year, it is a short-term gain. If you hold the asset longer than a year before selling it, it is a long-term capital gain.

DEDUCTIBLE MEDICAL COSTS

The following medical costs are deductible on your federal taxes. Make sure you claim all deductions for which you are eligible!

❑ Hospital services

❑ Medical treatments

❑ Prescriptions and other drugs administered

❑ Medical supplies and equipment

❑ Medical insurance premiums, such as Medicare Parts B and D

❑ Professional service fees (including those by unlicensed care-givers, such as those offering in-home care, including dressing, bathing, and giving medicines)

Is there a **difference** in how long and short-term **gains** are **treated on our taxes**?

Yes, if the gain is a long-term one, it is taxed at 15%. But a short-term gain is taxed as ordinary income.

What is the **standard deduction**?

The IRS gives all tax filers a standard deduction depending on their filing status. If you think your itemized deductions may be higher than the standard deduction, it may make sense to submit itemized deductions on Schedule A with your Form 1040.

How much is the **standard deduction worth**?

While it changes every year, and depends on your filing status, for a single filer it was $5,700 in 2010, and it is $5,800 in 2011.

Can I **deduct my home office**, if I am **self-employed**?

If you use part of your home exclusively and regularly, for the sole purpose of conducting your business, you may be able to deduct expenses related to the use of that room from your taxes. Depending on what percentage of your house is actually being used for business purposes, you may deduct that same percentage of your bills such as mortgage interest, insurance, utilities, repairs, and depreciation of the house.

What are some **typical deductions** that we may use?

Typical deductions may include contributions to an IRA or retirement plan, student loan interest, capital losses, home mortgage interest, home equity financing, state and

Women participate in a run for a breast cancer research fund raiser. This and many other nonprofit activities are tax deductible.

local taxes (including property taxes), medical expenses (if greater than 7.5% of your adjusted gross income), charitable contributions (cash and non-cash), unreimbursed business expenses (like license fees, travel expenses, meals, car expenses, education), job search expenses, and casualty and theft losses.

Do the allowable **deductions change** from year to year?

Yes, the list of allowable deductions changes from year to year, so it is important to check with your tax preparer or accountant, or the IRS Website (www.irs.gov) to see new changes in deductions for each tax year. Some deductions are allowed only up to a certain level of income.

If I were married recently, would the **IRS consider me** to be **married** for the **full year**?

As long as you were married at any time before the last day of the year, you are considered married for that tax year.

What if I got a **divorce** in the **last year**? Should I **file as married**?

No, if your divorce decree occurred on or before the last day of the year, you may not file as married.

How do I qualify for **head of household** filing status?

You may qualify for head of household filing status if you are unmarried during the filing year, you filed a separate return than your former spouse, pay more than half of the upkeep of the household during the year, your spouse did not live with you during the last six months of the year, your home was the main household for your dependent child or children (including step and foster children), and you can claim an exemption for the child.

When may I use **Form 1040EZ**?

You may use 1040EZ if you meet all of the following requirements: your filing status is single or married filing jointly; you claim no dependents; you, and your spouse if filing a joint return, were under age 65 on January 1, 2011, and not blind at the end of 2010; you have only wages, salaries, tips, taxable scholarship and fellowship grants, unemployment compensation, qualified state tuition program earnings, or Alaska Permanent Fund dividends, and your taxable interest was not over $1,500; your taxable income is less than $100,000; your earned tips, if any, are included in boxes 5 and 7 of your Form W-2; you did not receive any advance earned income credit payments; you do not owe any household employment taxes on wages you paid to a household employee; you are not a debtor in a Chapter 11 bankruptcy case filed after October 16, 2005; you are not claiming the additional standard deduction for real estate taxes, net disaster losses, or qualified motor vehicle taxes; you do not claim a student loan interest deduction, an educator expense deduction, or a tuition and fees deduction, and you do not claim an education credit, retirement savings contributions credit, or a health coverage tax credit.

When may I use **Form 1040A**?

You may use Form 1040A if you meet all of the following requirements: your income is only from wages, salaries, tips, taxable scholarships and fellowship grants, interest, or ordinary dividends, capital gain distributions, pensions, annuities, IRAs, unemployment compensation, taxable social security or railroad retirement benefits, and Alaska Permanent Fund dividends; your taxable income is less than $100,000; you do not itemize deductions; you did not have an alternative minimum tax adjustment on stock you acquired from the exercise of an incentive stock option; you received

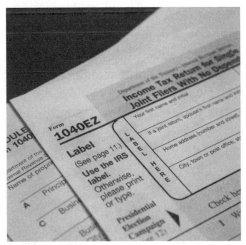

The 1040EZ form is the simplest tax return form you can file, but should only be used if you don't want to itemize your deductions and do not have complicated income considerations.

advance earned income credit payments, dependent care benefits, or if you owe tax from the recapture of an education credit or the alternative minimum tax, and your only adjustments to income are the IRA deduction, the student loan interest deduction, the educator expenses deduction, and the tuition and fees deduction.

When may I use **Form 1040**?

You may use Form 1040 if you meet the following requirements: your taxable income is $100,000 or more; you have certain types of income such as unreported tips, certain nontaxable distributions, self-employment earnings, or income received as a partner, a shareholder in an "S" Corporation, or a beneficiary of an estate or trust; you itemize deductions or claim certain tax credits or adjustments to income; or you owe household employment taxes.

What is a **Schedule A**?

Schedule A is used in conjunction with Form 1040, which enables you to report all of your itemized deductions for the tax year, including medical and dental expenses, taxes paid to state authorities, city taxes, interest paid on loans (like mortgage interest), and charitable gifts, etc.

Is there a **minimum amount** that I **must earn** in a year in order to be required to file my **federal income taxes**?

No, it is not that simple. There are a series of questions that the IRS has, which, if you answer yes to any, indicates that you need to file a return, including:

- Did you have federal taxes withheld from your pension and wages for this tax year and wish to get a refund back?
- Are you entitled to the Earned Income Tax Credit or did you receive Advance Earned Income Credit for this tax year?
- Were you self-employed with earnings of more than $400?
- Did you sell your home?
- Will you owe any special tax on a qualified retirement plan, including an individual retirement account (IRA) or medical savings account (MSA)? You may owe tax if you:
  —Received an early distribution from a qualified plan;
  —Made excess contributions to your IRA or MSA;
  —Were born before July 1, 1939, and you did not take the minimum required distribution from your qualified retirement plan;
  —Received a distribution in the excess of $160,000 from a qualified retirement plan; or

> ### What if I do not wish my employer to pay the taxes for me, and I wish to pay them all at once at the end of the year?
>
> You may increase your allowable number of exemptions with your employer, which will in turn increase the amount of money that you are seeing on your pay check. However, you must pay any taxes owed for that year when you file your income taxes in April of the following year.

> —Will owe social security and Medicare tax on tips you did not report to your employer.

- Will you owe uncollected social security and Medicare or railroad retirement (RRTA), or tax on tips you reported to your employer?
- Will you be subject to the Alternative Minimum Tax (AMT)? (The tax law gives special treatment to some kinds of income and allows special deductions and credit for some kinds of expenses.)
- Will you owe a recapture tax?
- Are you a church employee with income in wages of $108.28 or more from a church or qualified church-controlled organization that is exempt from employer social security or Medicare taxes?

How do I **pay** my **taxes?**

If you are employed, your employer will deduct a certain amount from each of your paychecks to cover the expected amount of taxes that you may owe by the end of the year.

What are the **benefits** of **increasing my exemptions** with my employer?

People tend to want to increase their exemptions with their employer if they are continuously paying too much each week in income taxes, and are receiving a large refund at the end of the year. These people may want to invest the money for that year, and earn more income on it, rather than overpay the U.S. government during the year, and earn no interest on that amount. If you earn more than $75,000 per year as a single filer, you must file and pay taxes quarterly.

What if I am **self-employed** and I am my own employer?

You are responsible for making a deposit with the IRS for any taxes that you owe on a quarterly basis. Quarterly taxes need to be filed on January 15, April 15, June 15, and September 15 each year.

Self-employed individuals need to pay taxes out of pocket, paying estimated federal taxes (and possibly state government, if applicable) four times a year.

What is a **tax refund**?

A tax refund is a check from the U.S. Treasury (after taking into consideration income tax, withholdings, tax deductions or credits, and other factors) that represents the amount of money you overpaid in taxes during that year.

What is **forced savings**?

Forced savings is a method of saving whereby an individual puts aside a certain amount of money each week that is not used on consumer purchases during the year. In a sense, receiving a refund from the IRS is actually a way of forced savings, since you cannot access this money until your refund arrives in the following year, after you have filed your income taxes.

Where do I go to find **changes to the tax code** to help me with my filings?

Go to www.irs.gov, click on "individual," and you will see links to new changes to the tax code that may impact your filing each year.

When should you **do your own taxes**?

If your financial situation is not very complex, you may consider doing your own taxes. With up-to-date tax software for both federal and state taxes readily available, it is relatively easy to file your own taxes, even if you have itemized deductions.

What are some of the **best software** titles available for **individuals** to manage and **file their taxes**?

Some of the best-selling programs include Turbo Tax, H&R Block, TaxAct, and Complete Tax.

ACCOUNTANTS AND TAX PAYERS

Why should people **use an accountant**?

People make the decision to begin using an accountant when their financial situation changes. They may have received a large raise, and have now moved into a more complex financial situation that warrants the advice of an accountant. They may have invested in real estate property or a small business, and need to set up a company of their own, and seek the guidance of an accountant to maximize their tax strategy, so that they are not paying too much or too little in taxes each year. They also may not have the time to manage the somewhat complex filings that may occur when their financial picture changes.

What is a **CPA**?

A CPA is a certified public accountant, which means that they have passed the CPA examination, administered by the American Institute of Certified Public Accountants, and have been certified by their state to practice accounting. CPAs also must have five years of education and coursework, real life work experience, and must complete continuing education coursework each year.

How do you **find** an **accountant**?

People seek the guidance of friends and trusted associates in order to find an account, so recommendations are important. Some use the American Institute of Certified Public Accountants Website (www.aicpa.org), which has a search link, allowing you to find the nearest CPA to where you live. After you have selected a few, it is good to then interview them to see if they meet your needs.

What **types of questions** might I **ask** if I am choosing an accountant?

It's best to find out if they have passed the CPA exam, which allows them to call themselves a CPA. You may want to find out how long they have been practicing as a certified public accountant, where they went to school, if they participate in continuing education courses, if they represent you in the event that you are audited, the type of software that they use to run their practice, what their rates/fees are, whether they

When looking for an accountant to hire, many people trust the recommendations of friends and family members. If you do not have the advantage of a trusted family accountant, you can search for nearby accountants on the Web and conduct interviews to select the one who is best for your needs.

handle clients in a similar financial situation, and do they have staff necessary to handle tax season.

What are some **reasons to switch accountants**?

It may be a good time to switch accountants if you have seen errors on your returns, if you are receiving letters from the IRS indicating that your filings were late, if you received what you feel is improper advice, or if your accountant chronically misses deadlines. If your tax situation has changed, and you do not feel that your accountant can handle these financial changes, it's not a bad idea to seek some advice elsewhere.

What is a **bad reason to change accountants**?

It's probably not a good idea to measure the abilities of your accountant based upon the size of your refund or taxes due, as most accounting professionals will do whatever is legally and ethically possible to ensure that you receive whatever you are due from the U.S. Treasury.

What is a **tax preparer**?

A tax preparer is someone who, for a fee, may prepare your tax filings. They have had some sort of formal training, may have their own practice or work at some of the

CHOOSING A TAX PREPARER

Use the following checklist to help you decide if a tax preparer is right for you. Check all that apply.

❑ Has professional degree or designation(s)

❑ Education includes Individual Income Tax Preparation

❑ Belongs to a professional organization, such as the National Association of Tax Professionals

❑ Has been in business for at least three years

❑ Will provide you with professional references if asked

❑ Will discuss with you his/her philosophy of tax preparation

❑ Offers computerized processing, including electronic tax returns

❑ Provides extra assistance guarantee, including covering for penalties due to errors by the tax preparer

❑ Provides audit assistance, if needed

❑ Has reasonable, competitive fees

❑ Has convenient location and office hours

❑ Provides convenient service even when it is not tax season

nationwide chains like H&R Block and Jackson Hewitt. They may have had formal training, some at a college or university, as well as experience working with tax matters, and may offer professional advice to you, and are fully capable of filing both federal and state and local taxes.

Are **tax preparers regulated** in anyway?

Until 2011, tax preparers were not regulated in any way. The IRS recently mandated that all tax preparers be registered, pay a registration fee, take competency exams, and have at least 15 hours of continuing education each year in order to remain in good standing.

How many **states regulate tax preparers**?

Only two states, California and Oregon, regulate tax preparers.

147

When choosing a **tax preparer**, should I ask if they are **registered** with the **IRS**?

Yes, you should ask if they have recently registered, and if so, what their Preparer Tax Identification Number (PTIN) is. This will ensure that your preparer is competent in the field of tax preparation.

Can a **tax preparer appear in my place** at audits, collection actions, or appeals?

No, only CPAs, enrolled agents, and attorneys specializing in tax matters may appear in place of you at audits, collection actions, or appeals activities involving your taxes. A tax preparer may not.

Will I be penalized if I use a tax preparer who is **not registered**?

Although you are responsible for what errors may appear on your tax returns, you will not be penalized if your preparer is not using a PTIN. The IRS will, however, identify that preparer and work with them to comply with the new regulations.

What **percentage of taxpayers use tax preparers** to assist in the filing of their taxes each year?

Sixty percent of all Americans use a tax planner.

What **percentage of taxpayers use tax software** to file their income taxes?

Thirty percent of taxpayers use home software to manage and file their taxes each year.

IRS AUDITS

What **percentage** of all **individual tax returns** are **audited** each year?

One percentof individual returns are audited in some way by the IRS, or about 1.426 million returns.

If I make **more money**, do my **chances** of being **audited increase**?

Yes, in fact for people earning between $200,000 and $1 million per year, the percentage of completed audits is 2.3%. For those earning incomes greater than $1 million per year, the audit percentage increases to 6.4%.

The Internal Revenue Service headquarters is located in Washington, D.C.

What are some **audit red flags**?

Some actions that may trigger an audit include: making math errors on your tax forms, not including all of your income earned during a year, reporting a small business loss for the year, large charitable gifts outside of the average without supporting IRS form and receipts, home office deductions, excessive deductions as a percentage of your income, excessive medical expenses, and undocumented business use of your car.

What is a **DIF score**?

It is an acronym for Discriminate Information Function system average, an analytical formula that allows the IRS to see which returns are falling outside the norm in terms of income, deductions, credits, etc. The IRS then targets those returns for audits to see if they can get taxes due.

If I am ever audited, **should I represent myself**?

It is always better to have a tax professional represent you during an audit or inquiry. Seek the help from either your tax preparer (a CPA) or a tax attorney for a better outcome.

STATE TAXES

What **states** have **no income tax**?

The nine states with no state income tax are Washington, Nevada, Alaska, Wyoming, South Dakota, Texas, Tennessee, Florida, and New Hampshire.

What **states** have the **highest income tax rate** (based on the highest tax bracket)?

New York, Connecticut, New Jersey, Maryland, and Hawaii.

What **states** have a **flat rate income tax**?

The seven states that have a flat rate income tax are Colorado, Illinois, Indiana, Massachusetts, Michigan, Pennsylvania, and Utah. All other states either have no income tax, or use a marginal or bracket system, depending on income, similar to the federal marginal tax system.

How many **states increased their taxes** from 2009 to 2010?

According to the National Conference of State legislatures, 12 states increased their taxes by more than 1%, 37 made no significant changes to their states taxes, and one state actually decreased its taxes by 1%. The good news is that for the most part, states decreased the personal income tax, but increased many taxes on consumption items, like fuel and tobacco.

Do I need to **file my state income tax each year**?

Depending on what state you live in, and if your adjusted gross income is higher than what the personal exemption amount is on your state's form, if you have filed a federal tax return, you should also file your state's income tax return each year.

How do I find out if I have been **delinquent in paying** for my **state taxes** in previous years?

You may write to the customer inquiries department at your state's Treasury Department, or check with the Website for the state that you live in, to find out if you owe any past due amounts.

What is a **sales tax**?

A sales tax is a tax levied by states on the sale of goods and services.

The State Capitol Building in Sacramento, California. California imposes the highest state sales tax of any state in America.

Do **all states** have **sales taxes**?

No, in some states, there are no sales taxes. In others, the sales tax can be anywhere from 2.9% to 8.25%.

What **state** has the **highest sales tax**?

California has the highest state sales tax rate of 8.25%.

What **states** have **no sales tax**?

The five states with no sales tax are Oregon, Alaska, Montana, Delaware, and New Hampshire.

CITY AND LOCAL TAXES

What **states** have laws that **allow cities** to impose an **income tax**?

The 14 states that allow cities and municipalities to impose an income tax are Alabama, Arkansas, Colorado, District of Colombia, Delaware, Iowa, Indiana, Kentucky, Maryland, Michigan, Missouri, New York, Ohio, Oregon, and Pennsylvania.

What is **property tax**?

It is a general term meaning the taxes levied on the value of one's principle residence, with the proceeds going to financing of local services, education, operational costs for the city and county in which you live, and the financing of special projects like sewers, streets and parks, and, depending on the state in which you live, state services as well.

When do we **pay** our **property taxes**?

Property taxes are normally paid twice per year, in the winter and summer.

What is **equalized value**?

This is the value of your property after assessment, which is then adjusted so that all similar properties are equally and uniformly assessed. This ensures that a school district, city, or township in which property is under-assessed does not get more than its fair share of state aid or funds. In some states, the state equalized value represents 50% of the true cash value of the property, although this may or may not be the same as the market value (the value which the property would sell for).

What is a **millage**?

A millage or tax rate is the number of tax dollars that a property owner must pay per $1,000 dollars of taxable value of their property.

What **affects** the **assessed value** of the property?

If the house has recently sold, or if you have made any significant improvements to the property, this will affect the city's assessment on the value of your property.

Do I have the right to **appeal** my **city tax assessment**?

Yes, when your assessed value statement is sent to you (with your tax bill), you have a right to appeal their assessment, and have a local hearing where you can state why the value should be changed. If you are still unsatisfied, most states have provisions to allow for the appeal at the state level in a hearing at the state's tax tribunal.

LOANS

PAYING FOR HOUSES

What is a **mortgage**?

A mortgage is a loan to purchase a property.

What **percentage** of homeowners and renters **thinks** that **home ownership** is a **smart decision** over the long-term?

According to the National Association of Realtors "American Attitudes about Home-ownership" survey, 95% of owners and 72% of renters believe that over a period of several years it is more sensible to own a home.

What **types** of **mortgages** are there for the purchase of a home?

There are many types of mortgages available, depending on your financial situation, including fixed rate, FHA loans, interest only, and adjustable rate mortgages.

What is a **fixed-rate mortgage**?

A fixed-rate mortgage is a mortgage that has a fixed interest rate for the period of the loan, and allows the purchaser to pay off the loan over a period of time: 10 years, 15 years, 20 years, 30 years, and even 40 to 50 years.

What is the **difference** between the different **loan periods**?

The shorter the period of the loan, the higher the monthly payment and the less interest that you have to pay over time, since you are borrowing the money over a shorter period of time.

153

What is an **FHA mortgage**?

The Federal Housing Administration (FHA), which provides mortgage insurance through FHA approved lenders, is the largest insurer of residential mortgages in the world. Depending on the state that you live in, the amount that you can borrow may be different.

Who uses **FHA mortgages**?

FHA mortgages are used by first time homeowners, because they require less of a down payment than conventional mortgages.

How long must I **pay** for **mortgage insurance** with an **FHA loan**?

FHA loans require the borrower to pay for the insurance for five years, or when the loan-to-value ratio is at 78%, whichever is longer.

What is a **loan-to-value ratio**?

A loan-to-value ratio is the loan amount divided by the selling price of the house.

What is **mortgage insurance**?

Mortgage insurance is a type of insurance that protects lenders from losses if a mortgage is not paid off in full. Depending on the amount of your down payment to purchase a home, you may be required to obtain mortgage insurance until you have paid off enough of the loan, so that the risk of defaulting on the loan is minimized.

What is a **front-end ratio**?

It is your total monthly housing cost divided by your gross monthly income.

What is a **back-end ratio**?

It is your total monthly housing cost plus all other debts divided by your monthly gross income.

Why use a **debt-to-income ratio**?

In order to prevent people from buying a house that they may not be able to afford, lenders will establish how much debt you can handle, and use this as one factor in determining your loan amount.

You bought the house! Good for you! But now you have a mortgage. Don't forget mortgage insurance, which you can either pay yourself or put in escrow.

Why are front and back ratios important?

Because they indicate to lenders and creditors how much debt can you afford.

What are the general guidelines on debt ratios in order to qualify for a mortgage?

You should have a debt income ratio of about 28% for your mortgage, insurance and taxes. You should also have a total debt income ratio (of all of your debts plus the mortgage payment) of less than 36% if you wish to qualify for a mortgage.

What is an interest-only loan?

It is a loan that allows a person to pay, for a period of time, only the interest on a loan. At the end of this period, the borrower must make a balloon payment of the value of the entire loan, or refinance the loan into a conventional loan.

What is an adjustable rate mortgage?

It is a loan that offers a fixed rate of interest for a short period of time: three, five, or seven years. At that point, the interest rate may change up or down, depending on what index the interest rate is tied to. These loans also have limits as to how high the

155

rate can change in a year and in the life of the loan. The borrower may continue to pay the loan at this variable or adjustable rate, or may also refinance the loan to a fixed rate conventional mortgage.

What are the **steps involved** in **getting a mortgage**?

The first step is to order your credit report, so that you may find if there are any errors and inaccuracies in it. The bank will also order the credit report to initiate your loan. The credit report will be used by the loan officers in determining whether or not you are a good candidate for a loan, as well as how much of a loan you can obtain. Next, it is important to have a clear picture of all of your debts, what the balances are, and what the monthly payments are. You should also have a most recent pay stub, showing what your current income is, and the last two to three years of IRS W2 forms, showing your income, as this will be used in determining your eligibility. You should also have the most recent bank and investment account statements showing your most recent balances. At this point, you should also know how much money you will use toward a down payment on the loan.

Does it **matter** to lenders **how much** my **down payment** will be?

Keep in mind that the more that you put down for the house, the more favorable your application will be for a mortgage, and the better terms you will have. You will also benefit from paying less interest over the life of the loan.

Should I **pay down** any **debts** before **applying** for a **mortgage**?

If at all possible, in order to reduce your monthly expenses, it is a good idea to try to reduce your debt load, as it will help in securing a mortgage. You also benefit by eliminating high interest rate debts before taking on a relatively lower interest rate mortgage.

What are **points** or **loan origination fees**?

These are fees that lenders charge for a fixed fee mortgage, with 1 point being 1% of the loan amount. Not all lenders charge points for loans, so shop around to find the lowest fees.

How should I **choose** a **lender**?

You should choose a lender by comparing the interest rates, amount of money required for a down payment, and any fees or points associated with the loan. You may also want to inquire how fast it will take to process your loan. Always speak with several different lenders, and beware of lenders offering comparatively low interest rates, as

COMPARING LENDERS WORKSHEET

Use the following worksheet to write down essential data from three potential lenders. This will make it easier to compare what each lender has to offer.

Lender 1

Company Name _____

Contact Phone _____

Contact email _____

Contact Website _____

Contact Address _____

Loan

Loan Amount _____

Length of Loan _____

Minimum Down Payment _____

Interest Rate _____

Estimated Escrow _____

Estimated Principle and Interest (P&I) _____

Private Mortgage Insurance (PMI) _____

Loan Fees

Application _____

Origination _____

Credit Report _____

Legal _____

Appraisal _____

Home Inspection _____

Flood plain determination _____

Title Search _____

Title Insurance _____

Title Binder _____

Closing Fee _____

Document Preparation _____

Document Recording _____

Surveys _____

Other fees _____

TOTAL FEES _____

Lender 2

Company Name _____

Contact Phone _____

Contact email _____

Contact Website _____

Contact Address _____

Loan

Loan Amount _____

Length of Loan _____

Minimum Down Payment _____

Interest Rate _____

Estimated Escrow _____

Estimated Principle and Interest (P&I) _____

Private Mortgage Insurance (PMI) _____

Loan Fees

Application _____

Origination _____

Credit Report _____

Legal _____

Appraisal _____

Home Inspection _____

Flood plain determination _____

Title Search _____

Title Insurance _____

Title Binder _____

Closing Fee _____

Document Preparation _____

Document Recording _____

Surveys _____

Other fees _____

TOTAL FEES _____

Lender 3

Company Name _____

Contact Phone _____

Contact email _____

Contact Website _____

Contact Address _____

Loan

Loan Amount _____

Length of Loan _____

Minimum Down Payment _____

Interest Rate _____

Estimated Escrow _____

Estimated Principle and Interest (P&I) _____

Private Mortgage Insurance (PMI) _____

Loan Fees

Application _____

Origination _____

Credit Report _____

Legal _____

Appraisal _____

Home Inspection _____

Flood plain determination _____

Title Search _____

Title Insurance _____

Title Binder _____

Closing Fee _____

Document Preparation _____

Document Recording _____

Surveys _____

Other fees _____

TOTAL FEES _____

they may just be teaser rates designed to get you to come in and speak with them. It's best to meet with lenders after you have learned as much about the current rates and practices, as well as fees, so that you will know who is giving you the best deal.

Should I **sell my house** before **getting a loan** for the **next home** purchase?

Your chances of obtaining a mortgage will be far better if you sell your current house, as your income may not support the payment of two mortgages. Also, sellers look more favorably on offers without house sale contingencies.

What does it mean "to be **pre-approved**" for a loan?

When someone is pre-approved, their lender has already investigated their credit worthiness and has established that the client can borrow up to a certain amount from the lender. Buyers of homes often get pre-approved, before making offers on the house, in order to make their offer more attractive to sellers.

Why is it **important** to be **pre-approved** for a loan?

Again, sellers of houses, when comparing offers to buy their homes, would prefer to consider an offer from someone who has a letter from a lender stating that they are already approved to borrow the amount of the sale price of the house than someone who makes the purchase of the house contingent upon getting a mortgage.

What does it mean "to be **pre-qualified**" for a loan?

This means that the bank or mortgage company has looked at the borrower's income and debt to determine the approximate amount of the loan. It does not mean that they have been approved for a loan.

HOME EQUITY LOANS

What is **home equity**?

Home equity is the difference in what your house was worth when you purchased it, and what it is worth if you were to sell it today, minus any loans that you may have on the home. The difference is the profit or equity that you have in your home.

What is a **home equity loan**?

After you have been living in your house for some time, assuming that real estate prices have been increasing, you begin to build equity in your house. Banks allow you to bor-

Home equity loans can be used for many purposes, such as buying a car or going on vacation. A better use, though, would be home improvements such as a kitchen remodel, which could then increase the value of your home.

row from them this value or equity as a line of credit that can be paid off over time at the prevailing interest rate at the time that you secure the loan. Many people use this loan to do necessary improvements in their home, which may increase the home's value.

What is the **downside** of using a **home equity loan**?

Often home equity loans are given to people with terms that allow them to pay only the interest on the balance of their line of credit each month. This means that the borrower never pays off the principal of the loan, and could end up paying out a significant amount of money just to have the loan. This is often written in the fine print of the loan documents, and is concealed from borrowers to make the loans more attractive.

How do people **use** home equity **loans incorrectly**?

Some people use home equity loans to buy cars, clothes, fund vacations, or purchase second homes. This may lead to major financial problems in the future, if not correctly managed.

Is it **easy** to get a **home equity loan**?

Yes, if you have owned your home for many years, and have a good credit history, an equity line may be obtained as soon as the bank can schedule an appraisal of your home   161 to determine the home's present value. Assuming you do not have any other loans on the property, you can usually obtain a home equity loan in a matter of days or weeks.

What **other considerations** or requirements to **obtaining** a **home equity loan**?

You must have a good income-to-debt ratio and you are required to make the minimum monthly payments for the loan.

REVERSE MORTGAGES

What is a **Home Equity Conversion Mortgage**?

It is another name for a reverse mortgage.

What is a **reverse mortgage**?

A reverse mortgage is a way for people aged 62 and older who have significant home equity to be able to pull out this equity in the form of a mortgage, where the bank actually pays the home owner either a lump sum, or monthly checks, or a line of credit, for the amount of equity that the homeowner wishes. There are significant fees in order to do this—usually 10% of the value of the home. It allows retirees to pull out equity in their home without having to incur a home equity loan, which allows them to get additional income. The reverse mortgage is then paid off when the home is finally sold. The reverse mortgage also incurs interest fees, which are also paid back when the home is sold.

What are the **requirements** for **obtaining** a **reverse mortgage**?

The requirements for obtaining a reverse mortgage are that you must be at least 62 years of age, own your home (meaning you do not have any mortgage on your home or a very small balance due), and you must live in the home.

What is the **amount** that I may **pull out** in equity in a **reverse mortgage**?

This really depends on the age of the youngest borrower/owner of the home, the current interest rate, the current appraised value of the home, and any mortgage insurance you may be required to purchase.

Why are **reverse mortgages controversial**?

They are controversial because many lenders target an older, less informed market of potential clients, who may not be aware of the many risks of pulling out equity from their

Advertisements for reverse mortgages are on the increase. They may sound like a good deal for those who own their own home and are looking to have a more comfortable retirement, but be careful. Reverse mortgages often come with hefty fees, and you could find yourself in trouble if your house does not increase in value.

home. The fees themselves are very large, compared to other forms of loans, and there is a risk that home prices may not increase, and therefore make it very difficult for the loans to be paid off. There are no income requirements for obtaining this type of loan.

When must I pay off my reverse mortgage?

You must pay off the reverse mortgage when you die, sell your home, move out of your home for 12 consecutive months, or fail to pay the property taxes or property insurance on the home.

What is an alternative strategy to using reverse mortgages?

Many retirees choose to downsize their lives, and sell their principal residence, pull the home equity out when they sell their house, and pay cash for a smaller place to live. This strategy contributes more to sustaining our wealth than pulling equity from the house in the form of a home equity loan or reverse mortgage.

CAR LOANS,
LEASING AND BUYING

What is a **depreciating asset**?

A depreciating asset is something that loses value over time.

How much **value** does a brand **new car lose** over time?

Depending on the car, its perceived value in the market place, and inventory available at the time that you wish to sell, a car loses between 20% and 40% the minute you drive it home from the dealership. In the second year of ownership, it will on average lose another 15%, and 13% the third year, etc.

Is the **purchase** of a **new car** ever an **investment**?

The purchase of a new car is never an investment. If it were an investment, it would be an investment that has a very large negative return, starting from day one.

So if I paid $20,000 for my **new car** yesterday, what is it **worth** after **two years**?

The minute you take it home, it is conservatively worth $16,000. After year two, it will be worth $13,600. The car that you just purchased is losing $266 every month.

What **types** of **loans** are available for the **purchase** of a **car**?

Loans for the purchase of a car fall into two categories: loans for new cars and loans for used cars.

How do **loans** for **new cars** work?

Banks, credit unions, and other financial institutions will make loans available for people with good credit histories, with three pay-off terms: 36 months, 48 or 60 months, and 66 or 72 months. Some credit unions will even finance a new car up to 84 months.

How do I **figure** what the **monthly payment** will be for a **car loan**?

Depending on the interest rate, how much you pay for a down payment, as well as what term you choose, will determine what your monthly payment will be.

WHAT YOU NEED TO APPLY FOR A CAR LOAN

It's a good idea to have the following documents on hand when you apply for a car loan.

- ❏ Proof of income. Bring pay stubs from the last month or two, along with how much you made during the last calendar year. If you are self-employed, bring tax returns from the last two years.

- ❏ Mortgage/lease agreements. These statements from your lender establish what your major monthly financial obligation is. Also establishes proof of residence.

- ❏ Bank and credit history. Other loans and financial information will be of interest to the lender, as well.

- ❏ Vehicle information. For a used car, bring the title, vehicle identification number (VIN), dealer sheet (if not purchased from a private owner), car mileage information, year, make, and model of the car. If buying a new car, the dealer sheet or buyer's order, year, make and model are sufficient.

- ❏ Proof of insurance.

What is the **difference** in **terms** of the **new car loans**?

The shorter the payback period for the loan, the lower the interest rate, and therefore the less interest you will pay.

Is the **interest** that I must pay for the **car loan deductible** from my federal taxes?

No, interest for a car loan used for personal purposes is not deductible.

How do **loans** for **used cars** work?

They work in a similar fashion to purchasing a new car. Finance companies will require that the loan be of a certain minimum, say $20,000. They also will have similar terms for the payback period of the loan, but about 1% higher than a new car loan. They also limit how old the car can be for financing. The car should be not older than seven years old.

Are the **interest rates** the same for the purchase of a **three-year old car,** as for the purchase of a **seven-year old car**?

No, a seven-year old car may be 1/2% annual interest higher than the three-year old car.   165

DECIDING TO BUY A NEW OR USED CAR

Which is better for you? A pre-owned car or a new purchase? Check the items that are important to you, adding a point for each item that is a benefit and subtracting a point for each item that is an important drawback to you. Add them up to see which car—old or new—has the higher point value and that will be the best choice for you!

Add a Point   **New Car Benefits**

_____   You are the first owner, so there should be nothing wrong with the car mechanically

_____   New cars come with manufacturer warranties, covering many repairs for several years

_____   Includes updated safety features

_____   May be eligible for insurance discounts for safety features

_____ **TOTAL**

Subtract a Point   **New Car Drawbacks**

_____   Cost is higher than a used car

_____   New cars lose 25% to 40% of their value as soon as you drive them off the lot

_____   Auto insurance is often higher than on a used car

_____ **TOTAL**

Add a Point   **Pre-Owned Car Benefits**

_____   Costs less than a new car (making it possible to buy a luxury or upgraded vehicle)

_____   Auto insurance often lower than for a new car

_____   Rate of depreciation is less

_____ **TOTAL**

Subtract a Point   **Pre-Owned Car Benefits**

_____   No car warranty, though used-car warranties might be available

_____   Repair history might be more difficult to determine

_____   Higher maintenance costs as parts wear out

_____   May have fewer safety features

_____ **TOTAL**

What **percentage** of consumers **buys** cars, **rather than leases cars**?

About 84% of consumers will buy cars, while 16% will choose to lease cars.

How do **leases work**?

When you lease a car, the leasing company establishes the value of the car for the period of time that you use the car. Your payments represent the portion of the car's value that you actually use, plus any fees or charges associated with the lease.

Why do people **lease cars**?

People lease cars instead of purchasing them outright for many reasons. If you are self-employed, and wish to deduct your monthly payments as a business expense on your tax return, you may be able to when you lease a car. Some people would like to be able to drive a fancy, luxury car with lower payments and cash outlay. When you lease you may not have

Buying a used car can be a wise choice. You can save a lot of money on a vehicle that is still in good condition, though you might also have some unexpected repairs.

to put a large amount of money down for a down payment, and your monthly payments may be relatively lower than buying the car or financing the purchase of a new car. Some do not like the idea of being locked into a 60-month loan to buy a new car. Others like the convenience of being able to essentially rent such a car and turn it in after a few years of driving. And still others lease so that they can test drive the car for a few years, and if they like it they can get financing or pay cash to buy the car outright. And they do not have to pay for the upkeep of the car during that time, as it is a leased vehicle.

What is **residual value**?

The residual value is the amount of money that the finance company says the car is worth at the end of a lease period.

How do they **arrive** at the **residual values**?

They look at data of past values, and predictions as to what demand from consumers will be at the end of the period. It is their best guess as to what the value of the car will be at the time the lease ends. It may be different, depending on which finance company you choose.

Why do **manufacturers manipulate** the **residual price**?

Sometimes, in order to reduce the inventory of slow-selling cars, manufacturers may artificially inflate the actual residual value of the car in order to make your monthly payments less. Since you are using only a small portion of the car's inflated value during the lease period, your monthly payments would be lower. In the end, however, you may end up paying much more to buy the car after the lease period ends than purchasing a used car of the same model, year, and type at that same time.

What is the **risk** of **leasing** a car?

One of the greatest risks in leasing is that the car depreciates more during your lease period, and the value of the car at the end of the lease period may be less than what the dealer says you must pay to purchase the car. There may be many of the same types of cars coming off of the lease, and the real price of the car may have dropped more than what the finance company predicted some years before when you signed the lease.

What about **mileage** on the **leased vehicle**?

Leased cars have limits as to how many miles they may be driven each year. If you are over, you may have to pay a high-per-miles charge at the end of the lease period as a penalty for driving the car too much.

Probably the toughest restriction concerning leased vehicles is that your contract limits you to how many miles the car can be driven. Penalties are imposed if you drive the car too far.

So how do I **shop** around for a **lease**?

You want to speak with different dealerships and compare the purchase prices, the residual values that each come up with, as well as what the monthly payment would be, the fees and finance charges, and the cost per mile for overages.

So what is a **general rule** about **leasing** a car?

If you choose the right car, one that depreciates less than others, you will have to pay less for the use of the car during the lease period. In other words, the more that the value of the leased car depreciates, the more expensive that the car will be.

PAYING FOR EDUCATION

What **percentage** of **undergraduates** receives any type of **financial aid** to attend **university or colleges** in America?

According to the National Center for Education Statistics, 68% of all undergraduates are receiving some form of aid to attend university or college.

169

Paying for college is a huge expense, but there are many grant and loan programs available that can make a higher education more affordable, such as Pell Grants and Stafford Loans.

What is the **average** amount of **student aid** that students in undergraduate programs are receiving?

In the National Center for Education Statistics study, the average amount of aid was $9,100 per student.

What types of **programs** are **available** to help **fund** my children's **education**?

If you are eligible, the federal student aid office has a myriad of programs to help parents and students fund their college/university expenses, including grants, campus based aid, Stafford loans, PLUS loans for parents, PLUS loans for graduate/professional degrees and loan consolidation. More detailed information is available on each of these programs at http://studentaid.ed.gov.

What is the **first step** in obtaining **federal assistance** for education?

The first step is to fill out the FAFSA (Free Application for Federal Student Aid) application form and submit it, along with the required documentation, in order to demonstrate the need for assistance. Be sure to avoid any Website that charges anything to submit this application, as there is no charge.

What does the **FAFSA application** cover?

It covers all types of student aid, from grants, loans, and work study, to non-federal aid.

PAYING FOR COLLEGE CHECKLIST

Use this checklist to maximize the number of ways you can save for college. Check off each item for which you are eligible and have applied, then, when you get financial aid, write the amount next to the award or loan.

Savings/Investments

❏ 529 College Savings Plan: $_____

❏ 529 Prepaid Tuition Plan: $_____

❏ Coverdell Education Savings Account: $_____

❏ Savings Bonds: $_____

❏ Taxable investment account for college: $_____

❏ Automatic payroll deductions for college savings account: $_____

❏ Private gifts: $_____

TOTAL: $_____

Grants/Scholarships

❏ Pell Grant: $_____

❏ School grant: $_____

❏ Employer grant: $_____

❏ Community grant: $_____

❏ Work-study: $_____

TOTAL: $_____

Loans

❏ Stafford: $_____

❏ Perkins: $_____

❏ PLUS: $_____

❏ Home equity loans: $_____

❏ Private loans: $_____

TOTAL: $_____

171

Which **colleges and universities** use the **FAFSA application** to help you finance your college/university experience?

Nearly every college and university in the United States, both private and public, uses FAFSA to assist with the funding of a student's education.

Why are there **so many questions** on the **FAFSA application**?

The questions are designed to help families demonstrate that there is indeed a financial need for receiving financial aid. It ensures that people who have real financial need get the most assistance available to fund their college/university experience.

What is **expected family contribution**?

After filling out the form, which includes information on your personal financial picture and whether the student is a dependent or not, the authorities will determine how much the family should contribute to the educational expense, and how much will be in the form of financial aid to cover the gap. As each institution has different fees and expenses, the amount of financial aid may be different.

What if I have had some **unusual expenses**, which make my **ability to pay** for my children's education **more difficult**?

If you have had unusual medical expenses or large change in income, these circumstances should be noted on your application, and discussed with the financial aid office of the school that you are attending.

How does the **financial aid** actually **come to me**?

The financial aid in general will be paid directly to the institution to cover tuition and room and board if necessary. Any remaining amount may be dispersed to you to cover other living expenses.

If I am applying to **different schools**, do I have to submit a **separate FAFSA application** to each one?

No, your printed application can be used at up to four schools that you list on the application. If you intend to include more than that, you may add up to ten schools by going online and setting up an account and PIN.

What is an **educational grant**?

172   An educational grant differs from a loan in that it does not need to be repaid.

Work-study programs, such as tutoring jobs, can really help to pay for your education.

What **types of grants** are **available** for education?

There are many types of educational grants available for students, some based on financial need, and others based on the student's academic ability or subject interest, or whether or not they have served in the armed services. Some of the more popular grants include TEACH grants, Federal Pell Grants, FSEOG grants, ACG grants, National Smart grants, Institutional Grants, and Iraq/Afghanistan Service Grants.

What is a **Federal Pell Grant**?

A Pell grant, the most popular grant, is awarded to undergraduate students who have not yet earned a bachelor's or professional degree. The Pell grant can be used in conjunction with other forms of financial aid as well. The maximum amount of the grant changes from year to year, and most recently was $5,500. It is dependent upon your financial need, the costs associated with attending your school, whether you are a full- or part-time student, and whether or not you plan on attending the school for the full academic year. You may receive up to two Pell grants in a single academic year for up to 18 semesters.

What is **campus-based aid**?

Campus-based aid are programs designed to help students fund their education based upon financial need, how much other aid they currently receive, and what funds are

173

available from their institutions at the time that they apply. It is available on a first come, first served basis. There are several federally funded campus-based aid programs available to students, including the Federal Supplemental Educational Opportunity Grant (FSEOG), Federal Work Study (FWS), and Federal Perkins Loan Programs.

What happens if the **university runs out** of **campus-based aid** funds?

When the pool of funds is used up, no additional funds are available, so it is best to apply early for these programs. As each school determines the deadlines for applications for these funds, the cut-off period may be earlier than your FAFSA application, so be sure to check with your institution on when the deadline for campus-based aid is, and apply to schools accordingly.

What is a the **Federal Supplemental Educational Opportunity Grant** (FSEOG)?

These are grants for students with exceptional financial need, and fund between $100 and $4,000 per year, depending on when you apply, so apply early. The money will either be paid directly to you, the school, or a combination of the two, depending on the school.

What is a **Federal Work-Study grant**?

It is a program that provides part-time jobs to students in undergraduate and graduate programs, allowing them to defray the costs of education and gain valuable work experience at the same time. Your institution will pay you directly, and the minimum that you can make must be equal to, or higher than, the federal minimum wage. You are not allowed to earn commissions or fees in this work, and you are limited in the amount that you can earn by the size of your work-study grant amount.

Can I **work anywhere** in a **work-study program**?

Most of the on-campus jobs will be at the institution that you attend. You may also opt to work in some capacity off-campus, at private not-for-profit organizations in town, or with private companies that have special work-study programs sanctioned by the institution that you attend.

What is a **Federal Perkins Loan**?

A Federal Perkins Loan is a low interest (5%) loan made available through the institution's financial aid office to undergraduate and graduate students who have demonstrated exceptional financial need. The school is in fact the lender of the money, and therefore the loan is paid back to the institution directly, although the funds are from the government.

How much can I **borrow** under the **Federal Perkins Loan**?

You may borrow $5,500 per year for each year of undergraduate study, up to a maximum of $27,500. If you are pursuing graduate studies, the maximum amount is $8,000 per year, up to $60,000 (which includes the $27,500 for undergraduate study as well). The amount available to you depends on your financial need, when you applied, and how much funds are available at the school you attend.

When must I **pay** these loans **back**?

In general, you must pay the loans back nine months after you graduate, or drop below half time status. You may be given a grace period to repay these loans, so check with your school's financial aid office.

What is a **Direct Stafford Loan**?

The Direct Stafford Loan, from the William D. Ford Federal Direct Loan Program, is a low interest loans for eligible students to help defray the costs of undergraduate education at a four year college or university, community college, or trade/career/technical school. Eligible students borrow the money directly from the U.S. Department of Education at all participating schools.

How many **types** of **Stafford Loans** are there?

There are two types: direct subsidized loans and direct unsubsidized loans. Subsidized loans are based on financial need, and the amount is determined by your FAFSA application. No interest is charged on the loan as long as you are enrolled in school at least part time, and during grace periods and deferment periods. Unsubsidized loans do not require the student to show financial need. The amount of this loan is also determined by the institution that you attend, and interest will accrue from the time that you actually get the loan. While you are in school, you may opt to just pay the interest on this loan, or let the interest accumulate over time, and then have this amount added to your original loan

If all else fails, student loans are a sensible way to pay for college. These loans typically offer low interest rates, and you do not have to start paying them back until after you have graduated or are earning an income.

amount for repayment. If you choose this option, the original loan amount will be larger, since you will be adding to the value of the loan, the amount of interest that you must repay.

What are the **interest rates** for these **subsidized and unsubsidized loans**?

Both loan types give borrowers the option to have a fixed interest rate or a variable rate. As the interest rates change from year to year, it is best to check with your school's financial aid office for specific rates.

How much may I **borrow** in the **Stafford Loan** Program?

The amount that you may borrow varies, depending on what year you are in, what other loans or aid you have, and whether or not you are in graduate school.

What is a **Plus Loan for Parents**?

Plus Loan for Parents enables parents of dependent students to seek financial aid in the form of a low interest loan to help fund their dependent's education. Parents must meet certain eligibility requirements in order to receive the aid, and as with many of these loans, only the amount of the education expense, minus any other financial aid that you might already have, will be the maximum allowed for the loan.

What are some of the **requirements** for a **Direct Plus Loan**?

The parents must be the biological or adoptive parents for the dependent student. The student must be enrolled at least half time at a participating school. The parent borrower must not have an adverse credit history, and must be a good credit risk. The student and parents must be U.S. citizens or eligible non-citizens, and must not be in default on any other federal educational aid.

What if I am a parent with **poor credit history**, and I am **denied**?

If you have poor credit history, you may identify an endorser who will in effect cover the loan, if you do not pay it back.

What is the **interest rate** on a **Plus Loan for Parents**?

The interest rate is around 7.9% per year, and interest begins to accrue when the loan money is dispersed.

REDUCE THE COST OF COLLEGE

Here are some quick strategies for lowering the cost of college.

- ❏ Enroll in community college the first two years. Many two-year schools partner with four-year colleges to make transferring credits easier.
- ❏ Avoid going to out-of-state schools. Out-of-state tuition is typically higher than in-state tuition.
- ❏ Attend a nearby college or university and live at home.
- ❏ Join the military, which will help pay for your schooling.
- ❏ Take Advanced Placement classes in high school that will allow you to place out of college courses.
- ❏ Take long-distance learning classes.
- ❏ Participate in for-credit internship programs.

Are there any **other fees** associated with a **Plus Loan for Parents**?

Yes, parents have to pay 4% of the loan amount as a fee each time money is dispersed.

And when does a **Plus Loan for Parents** need to be **paid back**?

Payment begins 60 days after the last disbursement. Parents may defer payment of the loan until six months after the student ceases to be enrolled at least half time.

How long do parents have to **repay** the **Plus Loan for Parents**?

They may pay off the loan over a period of 10 or 25 years.

Can a **Plus Loan** be discharged or cancelled, and **never be repaid**?

Yes. Under the Loan Forgiveness for Public Service Employees Program, if the student becomes a full-time public service employee and makes 120 payments on the loan, the loan can be discharged without paying in full.

What are **Plus Loans** for **graduate/professional degree** students?

The terms are almost exactly the same as the Plus Loan for Parents, except graduate students must fill out the application themselves (FAFSA application), and cannot have an adverse credit history.

Plus Loans for graduate and professional degree students must be filled out by the students themselves, unlike FAFSA forms.

After I receive all of these **loans**, is there any way they can be **consolidated**, so I only have to make **one payment**, instead of many each month?

Yes. Direct Loan Consolidation will allow the borrower to consolidate all of the federal student loans into one convenient monthly payment.

What if I have several **different interest rates**?

When you consolidate, the new loan interest rate will be a weighted average of the existing interest rates, not to exceed 8.25%.

How long until I have to **repay a consolidated loan**?

You have between 10 and 30 years, depending on the amount of your loan, and what repayment plan you have selected.

LOANS FOR SMALL BUSINESS

What does the **U.S. Small Business Administration** do to **assist small business owners**?

The SBA provides many financial assistance programs to help small business owners to become successful. These programs include loans, grants, venture capital and bonds.

How does one **get** a **Small Business Administration loan**?

The SBA creates the guidelines used by banks that offer SBA loans. Because the SBA has worked with you in understanding the business and securing the loan, the SBA guarantees repayment for the loan, so banks are more secure in making these loans available.

Is the **SBA loan** a **commercial loan**?

Yes, it is a type of commercial loan, a loan made to business, but structured according to SBA requirements.

What if I have **other business loans** available to me, like a **line of credit**?

SBA guaranteed loans may not be made if the borrower has access to other forms of financing at reasonable terms.

What **types of loans** are available through the **SBA**?

There are many loan programs available depending on your business, your location, your ownership, whom you serve, etc. Some of the programs include the 7(a) Loan Program (loans for business with special requirements, like exports assistance, companies impacted by NAFTA, rural business loans, loans in under-served communities, etc.), the cdc/504 program (long-term financing that helps develop communities), and the Microloan Program (small, short-term loans for certain types of business).

What is the **SBA CAPlines** Program?

This is a short-term loan program that helps small businesses gain access to working capital when their businesses require it. The different types of CAPlines available include Seasonal Line (for businesses that need to adjust their capital because of the seasonality of their business), Contract Line (capital needed to fulfill a contract), and Builders Line (for general contractors and builders), Small Asset based lines of credit (based upon the assets of the company, up to $200,000).

Small businesses make up the meat of the U.S. economy, yet they have been struggling even more than big corporations. Lack of capital is a big reason. If you are a small business owner, working with local city governments or doing some research on the Web may turn up opportunities for grant and loan monies.

What are the **typical loan maturities** for the **lines of credit**?

The loans can mature anywhere from a few months to five years, depending on the small businesses' needs.

Who **guarantees** these **short-term loans**?

Anyone who has ownership of more than 20% in the business is required to guarantee the loan.

How do **small businesses finance** the **operations** of their business?

According to a survey by the National Small Business Association, 59% of small businesses finance their business through the use of credit cards; 23% of those surveyed used four or more credit cards during the past year.

What about other sources of **loans** for **small business**?

Contact your local bank loan officer for information on business loans and lines of credit. Check with your state, city, and county economic development authority to find out what funds are available from these entities. Many cities, especially those in distressed areas, have set up programs that mix both private and public funds to help small businesses succeed. You may also search the Internet for sites that provide more specific information on local or regional programs available to you.

How else do small business owners fund their companies?

In the same survey, 51% of respondents funded their business through the earnings of the company, 45% had access to a bank loan, 30% were extended credit by a vendor, 19% had a private loan through friends or family, 7% used leasing, and 5% used an SBA loan.

What percentage of debt of small business owners is credit card debt?

Approximately 34% of respondents have more than 25% of their debt tied up with credit cards, with 20% of those surveyed paying interest rates of 20% or more per year on this debt.

Are small business owners happy with the terms of their credit cards (interest rate, fees, credit limits)?

About 79% of all respondents said that over the past five years the credit card terms have gotten worse.

Are grants available for the start up of a business?

No, there are no such grants available from the federal government to start a small business.

LOANS FOR VACATIONS AND PAYING OFF LOANS

Is it ever okay to take out a loan to finance a vacation or a large purchase?

It is never a good idea to take out a loan to finance a vacation, or pay for a new toy. Save the money first and use the money that you saved for these types of expenses.

What is the order of priority of paying off loans or other debt?

You want to make a list of all debts that you currently have, what the interest rate is on each of these obligations, and what the monthly payment is. Give highest priority to the debt that is carrying the highest interest rate and highest monthly payment.

Everyone could use a good vacation now and then, but taking out a loan to pay for a trip is almost never a good idea.

Give higher priority to debts like credit cards with no tax advantages, than to debts like mortgages, as there are tax advantages to having the mortgage.

Amount paid per $1,000 of principal borrowed

Term of Loan

Rate	10	15	20	25	30	40
2%	$9.20	$6.44	$5.06	$4.24	$3.70	$3.03
2.125%	9.26	6.49	5.12	4.30	3.76	3.09
2.25%	9.31	6.55	5.18	4.36	3.82	3.16
2.375%	9.37	6.61	5.24	4.42	3.89	3.23
2.5%	9.43	6.76	5.30	4.49	3.95	3.30
2.625%	9.48	6.73	5.36	4.55	4.02	3.37
2.750%	9.54	6.79	5.42	4.61	4.08	3.44
2.875%	9.60	6.85	5.48	4.68	4.15	3.51
3%	9.66	6.91	5.55	4.74	4.22	3.58
3.125%	9.71	6.97	5.61	4.81	4.28	3.65
3.25%	9.77	7.03	5.67	4.87	4.35	3.73
3.375%	9.83	7.09	5.74	4.94	4.42	3.80
3.5%	9.89	7.15	5.80	5.01	4.49	3.87
3.625%	9.95	7.21	5.86	5.07	4.56	3.95

Term of Loan

Rate	10	15	20	25	30	40
3.75%	10.01	7.27	5.93	5.14	4.63	4.03
3.875%	10.07	7.33	5.99	5.21	4.70	4.10
4%	10.12	7.40	6.06	5.28	4.77	4.18
4.125%	10.18	7.46	6.13	5.35	4.85	4.26
4.25%	10.24	7.52	6.19	5.42	4.92	4.34
4.375%	10.30	7.59	6.26	5.49	4.99	4.42
4.5%	10.36	7.65	6.33	5.56	5.07	4.50
4.625%	10.42	7.71	6.39	5.63	5.14	4.58
4.75%	10.48	7.78	6.46	5.70	5.22	4.66
4.875%	10.55	7.84	6.53	5.77	5.29	4.74
5%	10.61	7.91	6.60	5.85	5.37	4.82
5.125%	10.67	7.97	6.67	5.92	5.44	4.91
5.25%	10.73	8.04	6.74	5.99	5.52	4.99
5.375%	10.79	8.10	6.81	6.07	5.60	5.07
5.5	10.85	8.17	6.88	6.14	5.68	5.16
5.625%	10.91	8.24	6.95	6.22	5.76	5.24
5.75%	10.98	8.30	7.02	6.29	5.84	5.33
5.875%	11.04	8.37	7.09	6.37	5.92	5.42
6%	11.10	8.44	7.16	6.44	6.00	5.50
6.125%	11.16	8.51	7.24	6.52	6.08	5.59
6.25%	11.23	8.57	7.31	6.60	6.16	5.68
6.375%	11.29	8.64	7.38	6.67	6.24	5.77
6.5%	11.35	8.71	7.46	6.75	6.32	5.85
6.625%	11.42	8.78	7.53	6.83	6.40	5.94
6.75%	11.48	8.85	7.60	6.91	6.49	6.03
6.875%	11.55	8.92	7.68	6.99	6.57	6.12
7%	11.61	8.99	7.75	7.07	6.65	6.21
7.125%	11.68	9.06	7.83	7.15	6.74	6.31
7.25%	11.74	9.13	7.90	7.23	6.82	6.40
7.375%	11.81	9.20	7.98	7.31	6.91	6.49
7.5%	11.87	9.27	8.06	7.39	6.99	6.58
7.625%	11.94	9.34	8.13	7.47	7.08	6.67
7.75%	12.00	9.41	8.21	7.55	7.16	6.77
7.875%	12.07	9.48	8.29	7.64	7.25	6.86
8%	12.13	9.56	8.36	7.72	7.34	6.95
8.125%	12.20	9.63	8.44	7.80	7.42	7.05
8.25%	12.27	9.70	8.52	7.88	7.51	7.14
8.375%	12.33	9.77	8.60	7.97	7.60	7.24
8.5%	12.40	9.85	8.68	8.05	7.69	7.33

Term of Loan

Rate	10	15	20	25	30	40
8.625%	12.47	9.92	8.76	8.14	7.78	7.43
8.75%	12.53	9.99	8.84	8.22	7.87	7.52
8.875%	12.60	10.07	8.92	8.31	7.96	7.62
9%	12.67	10.17	9.00	8.39	8.05	7.71
9.125%	12.74	10.22	9.08	8.48	8.14	7.81
9.25%	12.80	10.29	9.16	8.56	8.23	7.91
9.375%	12.87	10.37	9.24	8.65	8.32	8.00
9.5%	12.94	10.44	9.32	8.74	8.41	8.10
9.625%	13.01	10.52	9.40	8.82	8.50	8.20
9.75%	13.08	18.59	9.49	8.91	8.59	8.30
9.875%	13.15	10.67	9.57	9.00	8.68	8.39
10%	13.22	10.75	9.65	9.09	8.78	8.49
10.125%	13.28	10.82	9.73	9.18	8.87	8.59
10.25%	13.35	10.90	9.82	9.26	8.96	8.69
10.375%	13.42	10.98	9.90	9.35	9.05	8.79
10.5%	13.49	11.05	9.98	9.44	9.15	8.89
10.625%	13.56	11.13	10.07	9.53	9.24	8.98
10.75%	13.63	11.21	10.15	9.62	9.33	9.08
10.875%	13.70	11.29	10.24	9.71	9.43	9.18
11%	13.78	11.37	10.32	9.80	9.52	9.28
11.125%	13.85	11.44	10.41	9.89	9.62	9.38
11.25%	13.92	11.52	10.49	9.98	9.71	9.48
11.375%	13.99	11.60	10.58	10.07	9.81	9.58
11.5%	14.06	11.68	10.66	10.16	9.90	9.68
11.625%	14.13	11.76	10.75	10.26	10.00	9.78
11.75%	14.20	11.84	10.84	10.35	10.09	9.88
11.875%	14.27	11.92	10.92	10.44	10.19	9.98
12%	14.35	12.00	11.01	10.53	10.29	10.08
12.125%	14.42	12.08	11.10	10.62	10.38	10.19
12.25%	14.49	12.16	11.19	10.72	10.48	10.29
12.375%	14.56	12.24	11.27	10.81	10.58	10.39
12.5%	14.64	12.33	11.36	10.90	10.67	10.49
12.625%	14.71	12.41	11.45	11.00	10.77	10.59
12.75%	14.78	12.49	11.54	11.09	10.87	10.69
12.875%	14.86	12.57	11.63	11.18	10.96	10.79
13%	14.93	12.65	11.72	11.28	11.06	10.90
13.125%	15.00	12.73	11.80	11.37	11.16	11.00
13.25%	15.08	12.82	11.89	11.47	11.26	11.10
13.375%	15.15	12.90	11.98	11.56	11.36	11.20

	Term of Loan					
Rate	10	15	20	25	30	40
13.5%	15.23	12.98	12.07	11.66	11.45	11.30
13.625%	15.30	13.07	12.16	11.75	11.55	11.40
13.75%	15.38	13.15	12.25	11.85	11.65	11.51
13.875%	15.45	13.23	12.34	11.94	11.75	11.61
14%	15.53	13.32	12.44	12.04	11.85	11.71
14.125%	15.60	13.40	12.53	12.13	11.95	11.81
14.25%	15.68	13.49	12.62	12.23	12.05	11.92
14.375%	15.75	13.57	12.71	12.33	12.15	12.02
14.5%	15.83	13.66	12.80	12.42	12.25	12.12
14.625%	15.90	13.74	12.89	12.52	12.35	12.22
14.75%	15.98	13.83	12.98	12.61	12.44	12.33
14.875%	16.06	13.91	13.08	12.71	12.54	12.43
15%	16.13	14.00	13.17	12.81	12.64	12.54

PLANNING AHEAD

SAVING FOR RETIREMENT

How do we begin to **save for retirement**?

The easiest way to begin saving for retirement is through your employer's 401k program. Companies will match the amount that you contribute, up to a certain limit (4% to 6%). The money may appreciate by the combined effect of your bi-weekly contributions, the matching funds provided by your employer, as well as through the growth of your investment choices over a long period of time.

What is a **participant-directed 401k** Plan?

Employer-sponsored plans that are participant-directed permit the employee to choose from a variety of stocks, mutual funds, and bond funds, as well as the company's own stock (if the company is publicly traded), and invest a sum of money before taxes, each pay period.

Do I have to **pay taxes** on my **401k** account?

No, the 401k can grow tax free, until you begin making withdrawals when you retire. At that time, you will pay taxes on the amount of income that you have during your retirement years.

What is the **maximum** that I can **contribute each year**?

The maximum today is $16,500 per year, and may change each year with inflation, in $500 increments. If you are over the age of 50, the 401k program allows employees to make additional catch-up contributions of $5,500 into their account.

187

WHAT IS YOUR FINANCIAL LIFESTYLE?

Check all that apply. If you answer "Yes" to more than half of these questions, you need to re-evaluate your lifestyle because you probably won't have any savings by the time you are ready to retire.

❑ Do you dine out a lot and put the expense on your charge card?

❑ Do you often go out to the movies, even when your checking account is low on funds?

❑ Do you go on vacation out of state two or more times a year?

❑ Do you stay at expensive or trendy resorts when you go on vacation?

❑ Do you make car purchases based on cars that are status symbols?

❑ Do you often purchase clothes, even when you don't need them?

❑ Do you purchase CDs, video games, and software for the fun of it?

❑ Do you ever make major purchases on a whim without budgeting for them first?

❑ Does your closet contain clothing, shoes, and other items that you have not used or worn in over a year?

❑ Do you go out shopping as soon as you receive a paycheck?

❑ Do you tend to NOT put away money in savings and investments once a month?

What if I am **self-employed**, is there a **similar program** for savings for retirement?

Yes, self-employed people may open an individual retirement account (IRA), and contribute up to $5,000 per year if you are under 50, or $6,000 per year if you are over 50. There are several types of IRAs that are described on pages 74 to 75 of this book.

How do I know if I will have **enough money** saved for my **retirement**?

It is important to understand what your financial picture is today, what kind of income will you want to live on in your retirement years, and what other sources of income will you have (like social security, pensions, insurance investments, or other after tax investments). It is equally important to know if you will have any large debts, like mortgages, college tuition payments, or student loans, as that will also impact what your expenses will be. With compounding of investment income, reinvesting dividends, company matches, and getting an early start on investing for retirement, it may be easier to reach your retirement goal than you think.

What is a **retirement calculator**?

Widely available on the Internet, a retirement calculator allows you to input key variables, like your income, how much money you have in retirement savings, and your expected social security income, and see where you would be today if you were to retire, and how much you need to start saving in order to retire and live comfortably. The actual results of your savings plan really depend on how early you start saving, how much you are contributing to your plan, the rate of return of your investment choices, and how long you will live.

How much should I **save for retirement**?

In order to retire by age 65 with enough money to have a comparable standard of living to what you have currently, you will need to save the following amounts.

The sooner you begin planning for retirement, the better off you will be. If you wait too long, you will have to stash away a huge percentage of your income before you retire in order to live comfortably in your golden years.

Savings Goals

Your Age	Percent of Salary to Save from Your Income
20 to 29	10% to 15%
20 to 39	15% to 25%
40 to 44	25% to 35%
45	37%
46	41%
47	44%
48	48%
49	53%
50 and older	58% or more

SAVING FOR EDUCATION

What is a **529 plan**?

A 529 Plan or Qualified Tuition Plan, is a plan designed to make higher education more affordable for families by helping parents save for college or prepay college and university tuition for their children. It is named after section 529 of the Internal Revenue Code.

What types of **529** plans are **available**?

The 529 plans are divided into two types: college savings plan and prepaid tuition plan.

What is a **college savings plan**?

A college savings plan allows people to make contributions into an account, grow the money tax free, and then make withdrawals to pay for their dependent's higher education expenses. Some states also exempt the earnings from 529 accounts from state taxes, as well as allow state tax deductions for contributions.

How does the **college savings plan work**?

You set up an account similar to a retirement account, which may offer you investment choices, and choices as to the amounts you wish to invest and the frequency of those investments. Some people like to fund these accounts with several large payments, whereas others may fund it each month, over many years. When your child begins attending college or university, the money can be withdrawn from the account to be used for room, board, tuition, and books.

May I **change** the name of the **beneficiary** on the account?

Yes, when you set up an account, you must name a beneficiary for the plan, but you may also change beneficiaries later if you choose.

Do I have to **select** a **529 plan** in the **state** that I **live in**?

No, you may choose any state's 529 plan, even if you or your dependents do not reside in that state. As each 529 plan is actually sponsored by the state that you live in, there is some variability in the plans and benefits that each state offers.

Are there any **income restrictions** that I should be aware of?

No, the 529 plan does not restrict who may contribute to a plan by income.

Somewhat like an IRA, a college savings plan can allow you to save money before taxes in order to grow the fund more quickly. Then, when it is time for your son or daughter to move into the dorm, you can start making withdrawals for tuition and other education-related expenses.

What is the **maximum** that I may **contribute**?

States restrict the total amount that you may contribute into the plan, up to a maximum amount of $300,000. At that point, you cannot contribute any more money into the account.

What if I **don't want** to tie up my child's **educational savings** in the **stock market**?

There are many states that offer investment choices that do not invest in the stock market.

Are there any **tax advantages** to having a **529 plan**?

Yes, earnings accumulate tax free while in the account, and no tax is due on a distribution that is used to pay higher education expenses. The beneficiary does not have to include any of the earnings from a 529 in income unless the amount distributed is greater than the beneficiary's higher education expenses. However, contributions made to a 529 are not deductible on your federal tax return. Each state offers different tax incentives, and even matching programs. Check your state's 529 plan Website for more specific state tax benefits to opening a 529 plan.

191

How does the **prepaid tuition plan** work?

Each state has its own method of administering a prepaid tuition plan. Some states allow the parents to make the tuition payments over 4, 7, 10, or 15 years. The money can be spent a college or university in the state, or even in other states, depending on what plan you select. If you do not use the money, it is refunded to you.

How much is **tuition increasing**?

According to the National Center for Education Statistics, in the period from 1980 to 2008, college tuition increased overall on average more than 18% per year. In the period of time from 1997 to 2008, tuition rates increased more than 30% at public universities and 23% at private universities.

Why is **prepaying tuition** such a **great deal**?

Prepaying tuition is a great deal, since you are able to pay for tuition when your earning power is very high, and using today's dollars, you are able to pay for a greatly discounted higher education expense.

CARING FOR AGING PARENTS

What **percentage** of people have **no health insurance**?

According to the U.S. Census Bureau, 15.4% of Americans, or 46.3 million people, have no health insurance.

What **percentage** of people have **Medicaid and Medicare** coverage?

About 14.1%, or 42.6 million people, have Medicaid, and 14.3%, or 43.0 million people, have Medicare.

What **percentage** of all households in America have someone **elderly living with them**?

According to the U.S. Census Bureau's American Community Survey, 31.6% of all households have someone aged 60 and above living with them.

What is the **average credit card debt** of someone aged **65 and older**?

The average amount of credit card debt that the elderly carry is $10,235.

According to the U.S. Census Bureau's American Community Survey, 31.6% of all households have someone aged 60 and above living with them.

How do I begin to **prepare** for **assisting** my **elderly parents**?

You may begin by having a talk with them about their end of life planning. Ask them if they have made a will, do they have a medical or durable power of attorney in place, are all of their financial documents in order and in one place. You may also want to familiarize yourself with their medical insurance.

What if these subjects are **sensitive** for our **parents** to **talk to about**?

It might be a good idea to begin a conversation with what your plans are for yourself, and see if that will help stimulate their thinking, and perhaps disclose to you what plans, if any, have they thought about.

What is **Medicare**?

Medicare is a federal health insurance program that helps to defray many of the medical expenses of most Americans over the age of 65. Medicare has two parts: Part A and Part B.

What is **Medicare Part A**?

Part A-Hospital Insurance helps pay the cost of inpatient hospital care. The number of days in the hospital paid for by Medicare is governed by a system based upon patient diag-

193

Medicare Part A helps pay the cost of inpatient hospital care.

nosis and medical necessity for hospital care. Once it is no longer medically necessary for the person to remain in the hospital, the physician will begin the discharge process. If the person or the family disagrees with this decision, they may appeal to the state's Peer Review Organization.

What is **Medicare Part B**?

Part B-Medical Insurance pays for many medically necessary doctors' services, outpatient services, and some other medical services. Enrollees pay a monthly premium.

Will my parents' **Medicare** policy **cover** any kind of **custodial care** or nursing home care?

No, Medicare does not pay for custodial care or long-term nursing home care. It will, however, cover up to 60 days in a nursing home as part of convalescence after hospitalization.

Can I **claim** my **elderly parent(s)** as a **dependent** on my IRS tax return?

Yes, if certain conditions are met. They must not earn more than $3,650 annually, and must live with you for the full year. You also are required to pay for half of their household expenses. If these conditions are met, there may be certain tax advantages, depending on your situation. And the tax advantages may help defray some of the costs associated with their care.

What is **Medicaid**?

Medicaid is a joint federal–state health care program for people with low incomes. The program is administered by each state and the type of services covered differs from state to state. Medicaid is the major payer of nursing home care.

What if my **parents** have **too much income** to qualify for **Medicaid**?

There are strict income requirements to qualify, which change from time to time, so check with Medicaid to see updated requirements. New Medicaid rules now allow the spouse to keep a monthly income and some assets, including the primary residence, while their husband/wife live in a nursing home or other long-term care facility.

If I am **elderly**, how do I legally let my **wishes be known** to my caregivers or have them act on my behalf?

There are several ways to do this, including giving your principal caregiver (perhaps a sibling, son, or daughter) a power of attorney, doing a living will, or by doing a health care power of attorney.

What is a **power of attorney**?

It allows you to specifically grant the power to someone to act on your behalf in legal or financial matters. The power of attorney may be general or limited, for a definite or indefinite period of time. As long as you remain competent, you

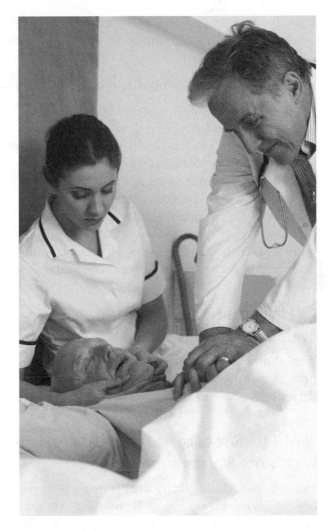

One of the stipulations you may put into a living will is whether or not you wish to be resuscitated or put on indefinite life support.

may change or end the power of attorney at any time. These powers of attorney are effective only as long as the principal is competent.

What is a **living will**?

This is a written statement of wishes regarding the use of specified medical treatments. It is provided to the doctor, hospital, or medical provider, and becomes part of the official medical record. You may specify if you wish to be resuscitated, whether or not you wish to be held on life support indefinitely, or for a period of time, whether you would like to use hospice, instead of prolonging treatment, etc. Each state requires the use of its own form for a living will and many states have other limitations. In some states, living wills apply only to those with Alzheimer's disease, strokes, degenerative disorders, or those in a coma or persistent vegetative state.

What is a health care or **medical power of attorney**?

It allows you to appoint an agent (a very close relative, son, or daughter), who is then legally authorized to make health care decisions for you in the event you are unable to make such decisions. The health care power of attorney can also include a statement of wishes and preferences in specific situations (for example, you may want to forego respirators, but continue nourishment). You can use health care powers of attorney to indicate that you want life-sustaining treatments continued, or to relinquish such treatments. An increasing number of states are enacting statutes that recognize health care powers of attorney and many states provide forms and procedures for creating the document. Without such a document, many health care providers and institutions may make critical decisions for you, not necessarily based on what you would want.

How **important** is it for your parents to have in place a general **durable power of attorney**, and a durable power of attorney for healthcare?

They should have a current power of attorney in place before they have a serious illness. If one of your parents becomes ill, you need to make sure that you have these documents.

What is the **first thing** that you need to do in **caring** for **elderly parents** when you have medical power of attorney?

You have to find out exactly what is wrong with your parent or parents, or other loved one for whom you are caring. By meeting with the doctors, and getting a proper diagnosis and treatment plan, you will be able to help them so that they can proceed on their own, if possible. If they are not able to proceed on their own, then you need to provide a higher level of care.

What is the **best way** to stay **organized** during these medical events?

It is a great idea to keep a journal of names of friends, family contacts, doctors and nurses with phone numbers, the names of the diagnoses, and names of people who would be willing to help out who live nearby.

What about the **spouse** who **may not require care**?

You have to deal with both the parent and the surviving or healthier spouse as well.
And that may mean re-training them on how to live and care for the person who is

When you have medical power of attorney for a loved one, it is vital that you understand fully what kind of care he or she may need. Meet with doctors and openly discuss and learn about the medical conditions that your parent or other relative or spouse may have.

afflicted, from giving them medicine, knowing where the doctors are, scheduling appointments, getting them to the appointments, home services, and tests. You may also have to work with them so that they are able to pay for bills and prepare meals if they have never done so in the past.

What about **insurance coverage** and **helping the parent** understand what to pay, how to pay and **how to resolve issues**?

This is one of the biggest concerns during this critical time. Since many retirees no longer live in the state that provides them their health insurance coverage, your parent may not have coverage in the state that they live in. Make sure that your parent has coverage and that the medical establishment in their city will accept their coverage. This needs to be done immediately, and most likely before your parent has a problem.

Why is it that a **child** of an elderly person **can't sort** out the **parent's insurance issues**?

Because of privacy issues, many medical institutions will not release any information regarding the health case without the written consent of the relative. It is good to make sure that the relative or elderly parent has given the right permissions to the medical doctors and hospitals that they may use and that it is okay to discuss the case with you.

197

Home nursing are home medical care are considered higher levels of care. A well-thought-out plan for the possibility of more intensive care for parents or other elderly people in your family can save you a great deal of stress in later years.

The parent may also feel that your involvement in their medical issues is an infringement on their independence and abilities, so often it is difficult to do these things ahead of time.

What is a **higher level** of **care**?

A higher level of care is needed when both the father and mother are incapacitated. In this case, you need to have home nursing, and perhaps even home medical care, which may be paid for, or partially paid for, by medical insurance. You have to put this in place, and at least investigate this before both parents are incapacitated. It is very important to monitor the health and well-being of both parents to see if this option may work better for you.

What else do you **need to know** about **caring** for **elderly parents** or relatives?

You need to know beforehand who pays the bills and does the finances, and then reorganize it for yourself. In fact, it is a good idea to know this beforehand, so that when something happens you are prepared to help deal with the bills, and can handle it if one parent becomes ill.

How **important** is it for **you** to become **connected** to **their doctors**?

You want to have a professional and peer relationship with the doctors, and hold them accountable for what is happening. Interview the doctors, and don't be afraid to communicate with them. It is good to include in your journal their email addresses or cell phone numbers, and ask whatever questions that you feel that you need to ask.

Is it **important** to be your parent's **patient advocate**?

Yes, you have to be the advocate of the sick parent. This means that you must act on his or her behalf as if it were you in the hospital. It is okay to seek other opinions, and use what you feel are the most experienced and knowledgeable medical professionals that you can find, as you move along the path toward resolving the medical issues.

What is a **patient advocate** service?

It is an organization, sometimes "not for profit" and other times "for profit," which for a fee will develop a whole plan of care with you. There are many such companies in every state. Check with your parents' or relatives' doctors for referrals, and also ask them if any of it can be covered by insurance. Patient advocate services bring an entire team of people on your side that will help in all aspects of your parents' or relatives' care.

What are some of the many **core services** that they provide?

Patient advocate services may provide such services as personal care, homemaker services, companion services, and supervision by registered nurse. This may be a necessary and costly option if your parent or relative is incapacitated and you live out of state. It is very difficult to manage the complexity of medical treatments when you are not physically located where the medical treatment is.

Are **patient advocate** services **free**?

No, they are not free. Depending on what services you contract with the company, it can be quite costly. In some cases, it may be paid for by their Medicare policy or other health insurance policy.

Long-Term Care Costs in 2009*

State	Average Daily Nursing Home Private Rate	Average Daily Nursing Home Semi-Private Rate	Average Monthly Cost in Assisted Living Facility	Home Health Aide Average Hourly Rate	Homemaker Services Average Hourly Rate	Adult Day Services Daily Rate
Alabama						
Birmingham	$169	$162	$2,675	$14	$14	$35
Montgomery	$196	$186	$2,649	$17	$16	$27
Rest of State	$164	$155	$2,244	$23	$22	$31

State	Average Daily Nursing Home Private Rate	Average Daily Nursing Home Semi-Private Rate	Average Monthly Cost in Assisted Living Facility	Home Health Aide Average Hourly Rate	Homemaker Services Average Hourly Rate	Adult Day Services Daily Rate
Alaska	$584	$618	$4,315	$25	$23	$74
Arizona						
Phoenix	$212	$169	$2,595	$28	$25	$100
Tucson	$221	$170	$3,156	$19	$18	$83
Rest of State	$215	$173	$3,009	$23	$21	$83
State Avg.	$216	$171	$2,942	$23	$21	$84
Arkansas						
Little Rock	$158	$144	$2,701	$17	$16	$76
Rest of State	$145	$121	$2,042	$15	$14	$78
State Avg.	$150	$128	$2,194	$15	$15	$77
California						
Los Angeles	$240	$192	$2,347	$18	$17	$77
San Diego	$264	$200	$3,031	$21	$20	$82
San Francisco	$432	$275	$3,311	$24	$24	$71
Rest of State	$236	$194	$3,412	$21	$18	$73
State Avg.	$286	$214	$3,085	$21	$19	$75
Colorado						
Colorado Springs	$211	$188	$2,828	$23	$18	$72
Denver	$212	$191	$2,361	$23	$20	$61
Rest of State	$200	$184	$3,269	$24	$19	$62
State Avg.	$206	$187	$2,872	$23	$19	$64
Connecticut						
Hartford	$354	$331	$4,321	$22	$18	$77
Stamford Area	$411	$376	$5,139	$26	$22	$77
Rest of State	$360	$326	$4,453	$28	$19	$72
State Avg.	4372	$340	$4,591	$26	$19	$74
Delaware						
Wilmington	$257	$222	$5,219	$19	$18	$74
Rest of State	$255	$239	$4,079	$26	$20	$65
State Avg.	$255	$233	$4,839	$23	$19	$70
Florida						
Jacksonville	$198	$186	$2,479	$20	$16	$67
Miami	$235	$216	$3,220	$16	$15	$49
Orlando	$221	$207	$2,611	$17	$17	$64
Rest of State	$236	$207	$2,820	$18	$17	$61
State Avg.	$223	$204	$2,768	$18	$16	$61

State	Average Daily Nursing Home Private Rate	Average Daily Nursing Home Semi-Private Rate	Average Monthly Cost in Assisted Living Facility	Home Health Aide Average Hourly Rate	Homemaker Services Average Hourly Rate	Adult Day Services Daily Rate
Georgia						
Atlanta	$188	$168	$2,713	$20	$17	$50
Marietta Area	$182	$168	$2,931	$17	$16	$83
Rest of State	$158	$151	$2,810	$18	$17	$65
State Avg.	$171	$160	$2,818	$18	$17	$65
Hawaii	$360	$316	$4,575	$23	$20	$59
Idaho	$202	$188	$2,624	$17	$17	$73
Illinois						
Chicago	$164	$159	$2,802	$20	$19	$53
Des Plaines Area	$268	$212	$4,228	$24	$23	$67
Peoria	$225	$152	$2,308	$18	$17	$71
Rest of State	$183	$153	$3,178	$21	$19	$65
State Avg.	$206	$167	$3,250	$21	$19	$63
Indiana						
Fort Wayne	$213	$168	$2,552	$23	$19	$62
Indianapolis	$195	$165	$2,612	$22	$18	$82
Rest of State	$199	$159	$2,876	$25	$19	$77
State Avg.	$201	$163	$2,717	$24	$19	$76
Iowa						
Des Moines	$167	$158	$2,915	$27	$23	$46
Rest of State	$140	$131	$2,598	$27	$22	$50
State Avg.	$148	$140	$2,756	$27	$23	$49
Kansas						
Wichita	$158	$142	$2,541	$17	$15	$70
Rest of State	$146	$136	$2,931	$19	$16	$117
State Avg.	$150	$138	$2,807	$18	$16	$111
Kentucky						
Lexington	$197	$177	$2,425	$19	$18	$68
Louisville	$213	$181	$3,304	$17	$16	$63
Rest of State	$174	$161	$2,370	$20	$19	$60
State Avg.	$190	$170	$2,700	$19	$18	$62
Louisiana						
Baton Rouge	$136	$129	$2,628	$16	$15	$50
Shreveport Area	$136	$135	$2,345	$13	$13	$45

201

State	Average Daily Nursing Home Private Rate	Average Daily Nursing Home Semi-Private Rate	Average Monthly Cost in Assisted Living Facility	Home Health Aide Average Hourly Rate	Homemaker Services Average Hourly Rate	Adult Day Services Daily Rate
Rest of State	$132	$128	$2,643	$18	$15	$59
State Avg.	$134	$130	$2,568	$16	$14	$53
Maine	$270	$244	$4,365	$21	$19	$98
Maryland						
Baltimore	$256	$233	$3,346	$22	$20	$74
Silver Spring	$262	$237	$3,552	$18	$18	$76
Rest of State	$258	$235	$4,150	$21	$16	$74
State Avg.	$258	$235	$3,873	$20	$18	$75
Massachusetts						
Boston	$327	$293	$4,034	$29	$23	$61
Worcester	$308	$294	$4,611	$21	$20	$71
Rest of State	$315	$293	$4,195	$25	$21	$54
State Avg.	$316	$293	$4,259	$25	$21	$59
Michigan						
Detroit	$177	$173	$2,923	$16	$16	477
Grand Rapids	$248	$221	$2,736	$19	$18	$117
Rest of State	$215	$204	$2,788	$19	$19	$68
State Avg.	$212	$201	$2,816	$19	$18	$74
Minnesota						
Minneapolis/ St. Paul	$172	$148	$2,493	$27	$23	$74
Rochester Area	$136	$121	$2,865	$30	$25	$50
Rest of State	$147	$130	$2,598	$29	$21	$63
State Avg.	$150	$132	$2,664	$29	$22	$64
Mississippi						
Jackson	$179	$171	$2,686	$15	$14	$53
Rest of State	$192	$184	$2,258	$20	$17	$60
State Avg.	$189	$180	$2,525	$18	$15	$57
Missouri						
Kansas City	$149	$136	$2,921	$18	$17	$69
Saint Louis	$176	$147	$3,527	$18	$17	$65
Rest of State	$138	$126	$2,844	$20	$18	$68
State Avg.	$151	$134	$3,034	$19	$17	$67

State	Average Daily Nursing Home Private Rate	Average Daily Nursing Home Semi-Private Rate	Average Monthly Cost in Assisted Living Facility	Home Health Aide Average Hourly Rate	Homemaker Services Average Hourly Rate	Adult Day Services Daily Rate
Montana						
Billings	$176	$162	$2,575	$23	$20	$76
Rest of State	$183	$168	$2780	$21	$19	$101
State Avg.	$181	$167	$2,701	$22	$20	$94
Nebraska						
Omaha	$202	$170	$2,837	$20	$17	$31
Rest of State	$147	$134	$2,393	$22	$19	$56
State Avg.	$163	$146	$2,655	$22	$18	$52
Nevada						
Las Vegas	$226	$198	$2,655	$21	$20	$65
Rest of State	$210	$195	$3,551	$20	$19	$80
State Avg.	$215	$196	$,2991	$21	$19	$72
New Hampshire	$276	$256	$4,347	$25	$21	$59
New Jersey						
Bridgewater Area	$302	$278	$4,354	$20	$18	$86
Cherry Hill Area	$315	$289	$3,681	$20	$18	$81
Rest of State	$290	$255	$4,429	$24	$21	$82
State Avg.	$299	$269	$4,212	$22	$18	$83
New Mexico						
Albuquerque	$201	$181	$2,752	$19	$17	$70
Rest of State	$176	$159	$2,382	$19	$15	$48
State Avg.	$185	$166	$2,667	$19	$16	$57
New York						
New York City	$373	$352	$4,602	$16	$17	$128
Rochester	$322	$309	$2,968	$23	$20	$67
Syracuse	$302	$297	$3,468	$20	$19	$76
Rest of State	$312	$302	$3,806	$25	$24	$99
State Avg.	$335	$323	$3,741	$22	$21	$98
North Carolina						
Charlotte	$205	$189	$3,301	$17	$15	$50
Raleigh/Durham	$203	$175	$3,542	$17	$15	$54
Rest of State	$189	$172	$3,061	$18	$17	$38
State Avg.	$197	$177	$3,224	$18	$16	$45

State	Average Daily Nursing Home Private Rate	Average Daily Nursing Home Semi-Private Rate	Average Monthly Cost in Assisted Living Facility	Home Health Aide Average Hourly Rate	Homemaker Services Average Hourly Rate	Adult Day Services Daily Rate
North Dakota	$156	$143	$2,041	$24	$22	$86
Ohio						
Cincinnati	$233	$193	$3,067	$19	$18	$64
Cleveland	$216	$188	$3,233	$19	$17	$55
Columbus	$207	$190	$3,370	$21	$18	$55
Rest of State	$199	$180	$2,646	$18	$17	$49
State Avg.	$209	$186	$3,031	$19	$18	$54
Oklahoma						
Oklahoma City	$168	$131	$2,288	$19	$17	$45
Tulsa	$168	$135	$3,150	$19	$16	$39
Rest of State	$145	$125	$2,237	$19	$14	$53
State Avg.	$156	$129	$2,503	$19	$16	$48
Oregon						
Eugene	$221	$214	$2,796	$17	$16	$117
Portland	$230	$216	$3,226	$21	$19	$72
Rest of State	$225	$205	$2,672	$28	$20	$86
State Avg.	$226	$210	$2,904	$21	$18	$90
Pennsylvania						
Philadelphia	$269	$252	$2,933	$18	$18	$64
Pittsburgh	$274	$255	$3,085	$20	$18	$52
Scranton	$226	$221	$2,630	$21	$18	$73
Rest of State	$238	$223	$3,140	$20	$19	$60
State Avg.	$248	$235	$2,986	$20	$18	$61
Rhode Island	$254	$233	$3,157	$25	$21	$63
South Carolina						
Charleston	$187	$173	$3,017	$18	$18	$48
Columbia	$190	$174	$2,641	$17	$16	$49
Rest of State	$185	$166	$2,697	$21	$17	$47
State Avg.	$186	$170	$2,797	$19	$17	$47
South Dakota	$175	$158	$2,309	$20	$19	$70
Tennessee						
Memphis	$173	$158	$2,897	$18	$15	$33
Nashville	$201	$179	$3,083	$23	$17	$41

State	Average Daily Nursing Home Private Rate	Average Daily Nursing Home Semi-Private Rate	Average Monthly Cost in Assisted Living Facility	Home Health Aide Average Hourly Rate	Homemaker Services Average Hourly Rate	Adult Day Services Daily Rate
Rest of State	$168	$155	$2,590	$21	$19	$55
State Avg.	$178	$162	$2,840	$21	$17	$49
Texas						
Austin	$182	$133	$3,271	$19	$18	$29
Dallas/Ft. Worth	$200	$130	$3,050	$16	$16	$44
Houston	$215	$131	$3,142	$20	$16	$43
Rest of State	$171	$128	$2,757	$19	$18	$38
State Avg.	$187	$130	$2,991	$19	$17	$40
Utah						
Salt Lake City	$204	$162	$2,917	$25	$21	$50
Rest of State	$170	$147	$2,558	$25	$23	$95
State Avg.	$183	$152	$2,698	$25	$22	$59
Vermont	$254	$235	$4,167	$24	$20	$150
Virginia						
Alexandria Area	$269	$236	$4,566	$19	$18	$83
Richmond Area	$208	$189	$3,147	$20	$18	$59
Rest of State	$158	$170	$3,567	$18	$16	$60
State Avg.	$207	$189	$3,768	$18	$17	$62
Washington						
Seattle	$281	$247	$3,053	$23	$22	$72
Spokane	$243	$224	$2,635	$21	$21	$54
Rest of State	$231	$215	$2,887	$22	$20	$91
State Avg.	$246	$225	$2,870	$22	$21	$69
West Virginia	$215	$205	$3,073	$15	$16	$59
Wisconsin						
Madison Area	$236	$213	$3,707	$29	$25	$56
Milwaukee	$252	$216	$3,436	$21	$17	$52
Rest of State	$204	$191	$2,965	$23	$18	$62
State Avg.	$225	$201	$3,261	$24	$19	$58
Wyoming	$193	$178	$3,039	$22	$22	$67
U.S. Avg.	$198	$219	$3,131	$21	$19	$67

*Source: longtermcare.gov

205

SURVIVING FINANCIAL CRISES

OVERVIEW

What is a **major life crisis**?

A major life crisis can be job loss, divorce, death of a spouse, or serious illness or disability of an immediate family member or of oneself. Each of these events could have long-term financial implications for the family.

Why does a **life crisis** pose such a **financial challenge** to people?

Because of the unpredictable nature of these types of crises, people are vulnerable, emotional, and tend to not be prepared for the crisis, and therefore they make poor decisions during these times. Some people choose to take no action at all, and this lack of decision may actually make the outcome financially worse.

What two **crises** seem to have the **worst long-term effect** on our finances?

According to a survey by the AARP (American Association of Retired Persons), 60% surveyed said that long-term unemployment had the greatest effect on their finances, while 47% said that illness and disability seem to have the most effect on our finances.

Why do **women experience more** of the **consequences** of life crises than men?

Women live longer than men, and therefore will have to deal with more of these situations than men. Since women tend to be the caregivers to their family, they tend to focus more on the emotional and logistical aspects of the crises, with little time or energy left for understanding the financial aspects of the crises.

Unemployment can—and usually does—hit you unexpectedly. In recent years, long-term unemployment has been the worst since records were first kept in 1948. Many Americans have been unemployed for nine or more months. Worse still, studies show that employers are reluctant to hire people who have been out of work.

Where do **women** turn to for **financial advice** in times of **crisis**?

In the AARP survey cited above, the majority of respondents said that they look to family members and friends for financial advice, many of whom are not qualified to give financial advice.

After experiencing a life crisis, what **percentage of women** were **unhappy** with the **financial advice** that they received?

About 45% of those who had experienced a life crisis said it was hard to trust the financial information that they were receiving from friends and family members.

For those people who **sought professional financial advice** after a crisis, how many were **satisfied** with the advice?

Approximately 66% of people surveyed were very satisfied with the advice, and a further 24% were somewhat satisfied with the professional financial guidance they received.

IDENTITY THEFT

What is **identity theft**?

Identity theft is the stealing of personal identifying information from someone, and using this information to commit fraudulent and criminal acts. It may include acquiring credit using another person's identity, accessing bank accounts, obtaining and using credit cards, redirecting various private or government benefits like pensions and social security checks to the criminal's address or accounts, or accessing email and various online accounts using stolen information.

How many people are victims of identity theft?

In a survey released in 2010, using data gathered most recently in 2008, 11.7 million people experienced identity theft during a two year period, up 12% from the year before.

What percentage of the U.S. population does this represent?

About 5% of all people aged 16 and older have been identity theft victims.

What is the most prevalent type of identity theft?

The most prevalent type of identity theft, involving 6.2 million victims in the United States, is the attempt to steal, or the stealing of, credit card numbers.

What percentage of our population has had someone steal or attempt to steal and use their credit card?

Approximately 3% of all persons 16 and older have had someone try to steal their credit card information.

What is true identity theft?

The U.S. Justice Department divides these statistics into two categories: identity theft and true identity theft. In identity theft, a person may obtain one's credit card number or bank account number and make purchases, until it is noticed. In true identity theft, someone obtains a victim's social security number, and other identifiable information, and then attempts to assume that identity for the purposes of obtaining credit cards. They then make huge purchases over a long period of time, going undetected for months or even years.

How much money is lost due to identity theft?

Each year, identity theft costs more than $17.3 billion.

How does true identity theft go undetected for so long?

It happens because the victim does not review his/her credit report on a regular basis to see if anyone is generating inquiries into the credit report for the purposes of

Over six million Americans have been victims of identity theft as a result of their credit card numbers being stolen.

obtaining credit. The credit report will also pick up new addresses that perhaps the criminal is using under your name.

How many **cases** of **true identity theft** are there?

Of the 11.7 million cases of identity theft surveyed by the Justice Department in 2008, 1.6 million were true identity theft cases.

What **percentage** of **identity theft** cases involved lost or **stolen wallets, checkbooks** and **credit/debit cards**?

In the cases where the method of access to one's personal data was known, 43% of all cases could be traced to a lost or stolen wallet or purse containing cash, cards, or checks.

How many **people reported** the **misuse** of **personal information** in order to commit other crimes?

About 619,000 people reported that someone used their personal information to fraudulently obtain health care or government benefits, or to provide false information to law enforcement using during a criminal act or routine traffic stop.

What **percentage** of identity theft **victims suffered** some sort of **financial loss**, as a result of the crime?

Approximately 23% of all victims lost some money as a result.

What is the **average out of pocket loss** reported by victims of identity theft?

The average reported loss was $1,870. Half of all victims lose $200 or less.

What **percentage** of identity theft **victims know** how their personal **information was obtained** by the criminal?

About 40% of victims seemed to know how someone obtained their personal information. And of those people, 30% thought that the theft occurred after a recent transaction, 20% thought that the information was stolen from a wallet or checkbook, and 14% believed that the information was obtained from personnel or other files at the office.

What **percentage** of victims **reported the crime** to a **law enforcement** agency?

Only 17% officially reported the crime to their local police.

What **percentage** of victims **reported the crime** to their **bank or credit card companies**?

About 68% of all victims reported the crime to their local banks and credit card companies.

How long on average do **victims spend resolving issues** with identity theft?

Approximately 42% of all victims spent one day solving the identity theft issue with their creditors and 27% spent more than one month trying to resolve all of the problems caused by the theft.

Who is more likely to be a **victim of identity theft**, men or women?

In the survey, men and women are victims in the same proportion.

Are **older people** more likely to be **victims** than younger people?

People aged 16 to 24 fell victim to identity theft 6% of the time, while people aged 65 or older fell victim only 3.7% of the time.

What are the **ways** that people can **protect** themselves from **identity theft** using the **mail**?

Do not use your home mailbox to send mail. Always either use a U.S. Post Office mailbox or go to the post office itself to send your outgoing mail, since a favorite way of obtaining credit card numbers and bank account numbers is by stealing outgoing mail from people's houses. Keep track of your incoming mail. If you find that you are not receiving mail, check with your post office to make sure no one has filed a change of address form for your address. Also, reduce your incoming mail by using more of the online, paperless billing offered by most of your service providers, like your credit cards and utility bills. When you send checks for your bills, make sure the check is hidden, so that the account information on the check is concealed in the envelope.

What about **mail** that I receive that **poses as coming from** a U.S. **government agency**?

The U.S. government and its agencies are rarely sending direct mail advertising to your home. So it is safe to destroy this mail and not respond. This includes offers to reduce your taxes, refinance your mortgage, find you a high-paying job, or offers for health and life insurance. These may very well be scams, and this mail should be destroyed.

Should I use a **shredder** at home to **destroy** copies of receipts and other **sensitive information**?

Yes, one of the favorite ways that identity thieves get your personal information is by "dumpster diving," actually stealing your garbage and going through it to find such information that you threw away. A shredder will help conceal the sensitive data.

What about **"pre-approved"** credit card applications which **contain blank checks**?

You can quickly destroy these by shredding them.

How do I **get my name off** of credit card applications and blank check **offers**?

Go the Direct Marketing Association Website (www.the-dma.org), and put your name on the "do not mail" lists, so that credit card companies will not send such offers to you.

What can I **do about** a **theft** of my **wallet or purse**?

Never carry your social security card with you, for any reason. It should be kept in a safe, secure place, hidden from an obvious place where a burglar might find it. Also, only carry a minimum number of credit cards with you at any time. Cancel and destroy the cards that you do not use or need. Keep a list of the customer service numbers for each of your cards and the account numbers in your house, in case you do lose your purse or wallet, so that you may immediately cancel these cards if anything should happen.

How can obtaining my **credit report** help **prevent identity theft**?

You should run a credit report at least once per year, for yourself, and for any dependent children, since a favorite scheme of identity thieves is to steal the social security

Another way that people fall victim to identity theft is when their mail is stolen, usually straight out of their mailbox. Paying bills online is one of a number of ways you can reduce this risk.

numbers of children and open credit cards in their names using a false address. If you run the credit reports on your social security number and those of your children, you will be able to spot any potential problems much sooner.

How often may I get a free credit report?

You can actually get one free credit report every year, from each of the major credit reporting companies, by applying on their Websites. You can do it more than once per year for a nominal fee.

Who are the biggest credit reporting companies?

The biggest companies that track your credit history are Equifax, TransUnion, and Experian.

How can I order my free credit report?

Copies of a credit report can be obtained from one of the following sources: (1) Experian (formerly TRW), http://experian.com; (2) Equifax, http://equifax.com; (3) Trans Union, http://tuc.com or through the Federal Trade Commission's authorized Website www.annualcreditreport.com.

What do they **know** about **me**?

Credit reporting companies know all of your debts, credit card balances, available lines of credit, mortgage amounts and balances, checking and savings balances, bankruptcies, wage information, job history, all addresses both current and previous, car loans, liens on property, history of credit applications, both denials and acceptances, child support payments and of course your credit score.

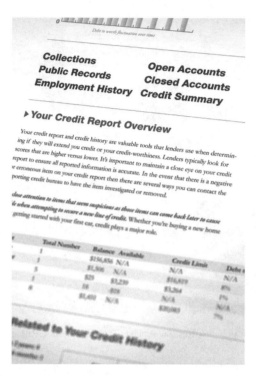

Check your credit report once a year to make sure that there is no unusual activity attributed to you, including opened accounts that you know you did not open yourself. You can obtain a free credit report annually by contacting the companies Equifax, TransUnion, or Experian.

What should I do **when people ask** me for my **social security number**?

In places like pharmacies, an assistant may ask you for your social security number in order to open up the computer record of your visit. Always decline when asked to provide your social security number. You may ask the person if it is okay to use the last four digits of the social security number. If they insist, you may write it down for them, or tell it to them, as long as there are no others standing nearby. Legitimate companies that you do business with will never call you requesting any personal information of any kind. So if you receive any phone calls from a representative of a company requesting your social security or other personal identification numbers, hang up immediately. If you must give out a number to access an account like a bank, or credit card for security purposes, always ask if you can just use the last four digits of your social security number.

How can I **protect myself** from **identity theft** on the **Internet**?

Although rare, victims have reported identity theft by using the Internet. Read reviews of unfamiliar online stores before making purchases. Check to see if the site is legitimate by reading a bit about the company before deciding to make a purchase.

How can I use my **credit card** to **prevent identity theft**?

You may contact your credit card company to place daily or monthly limits on how much can be spent on the card. Use a separate credit card for these transactions. Your credit card company may also offer alerts when your daily spending exceeds a certain limit that you decide to place on the card, and they will email you whenever that limit is reached. This way, you will know long before you receive your statement if there are any fraudulent charges.

What is **another great way** to add **protection** to your **credit card**?

Some cards offer a signature box on the back, where, instead of writing your signature, you can write the words "Check I.D." Clerks will then ask for ID whenever your card is used.

What **other tactics** can I use to **prevent theft** of my credit **card number**?

Always save each and every receipt whenever you make a charge on your card, no matter how small. Although many companies are only printing a few digits of the number on the actual receipt, if you leave your receipt at the gas pump or register, someone can obtain some information from the receipt. Make sure that you reconcile or check each receipt against your monthly statement.

So if I notice that someone has **stolen my identity** what should I **do**?

Immediately contact each credit card company that you use, and each bank account, and immediately put a "hold" or "fraud alert" on the account. You may completely close your bank account and open a new one with a new account number, so that you may still have access to cash. You can call the three credit reporting companies (Equifax, Experian, and TransUnion) and alert them that you have been a victim of identity theft, and ask them to put a hold on all activity, and credit applications that may be received. You may challenge any item on your credit report that you think is false. Also, file a police report at your local police department, so that they may open an investigation, and perhaps catch the criminal who stole and used your information.

Should I **tell my employer** about credit card theft?

Yes, especially if you are having your employer automatically deposit checks in your account. Put a hold on that account and ask your employer to pay you with normal paper checks during this time, until the issue is closed.

What if I **know** someone has **stolen** my **social security number**?

Immediately call the credit reporting agencies, as well as the Social Security Administration and report it. They will put a freeze on any benefits, and monitor your account for any suspicious activity.

215

PROTECTING YOUR PRIVACY
ON THE INTERNET

What is a **data aggregator**?

A data aggregator is a company that culls the Internet looking for personal identifying information such as your name, address, mortgage information, legal information, phone numbers, past addresses, names of children, or your age, and ties this information together in order to sell the information to marketers and the general public.

How can this **information** be used for **fraud**?

Because the information about you is taken from many sources, or aggregated, the information can be used to build a pretty accurate record of who you are and where you live, and therefore makes it easy for someone to steal your identity.

Who are some of the **biggest data aggregators**?

Anywho, Switchboard, Yahoo People Search, Internet Address Finder, US Search, Intelius, Acxiom, Spokeo, Whitepages.com, Rapleaf, and Pipl are the biggest. There are perhaps hundreds or thousands of such companies, but since many feed off the same primary aggregators, if you get yourself off the primary companies, you will slowly remove yourself from all others.

How can I **remove my name** from such aggregators?

You may contact some of the biggest offenders directly through their Websites, and ask to be put on their name removal or opt-out list.

What else can I do to **protect my privacy** while **online**?

Never click on or open up forwarded jokes, poems, and patriotic emails from friends. They are the source of viruses and may direct you to identity theft sites. Never give any credit card information to any site, without first verifying that the site itself is what it claims to be. Check to make sure you are typing the Website properly, as many fake Websites prey upon people who misspell the Website, and make a fake site that looks EXACTLY like the site that you wish to go to. These sites move around frequently, and are difficult to trace, so be careful when you enter a Website name. Never enter a social security number in a site, and never use a social security number or a variant as a password, for any reason. Never open up any spam or even an email, if you do not personally know the sender, no matter how enticing the offer. Delete these emails immediately.

SIGNS OF CREDIT CARD THEFT

❏ You see charges on your card for items you did not purchase.

❏ You have been called about charges you did not make.

❏ You received mail about credit cards or other lines of credit for which you did not apply.

❏ You are not receiving bills that you expected in the mail (they may have been stolen).

How is my **privacy protected** when using **social networking sites**, like Facebook or Twitter?

Your privacy is barely protected. These sites make it very difficult for a novice user to find the settings that allow users to hide their profiles from the public web. This means that if you leave all of the settings alone, your initial profile is readily visible to anyone anywhere in the world. If you use your real name, or maiden name if you are or were married, you are telling the world, "Here is my maiden name." And maiden names are often used as security questions for credit cards and banks. So go into the settings and hide your profile from being displayed on the public web.

Should I **post questions** on **Websites** in hopes of **finding answers**?

No, you should not. Millions of people post questions on the Internet, hoping to find answers. Trouble is, these sites readily post any information that you input, so if you give them your real email address, or name, it becomes permanently embedded in the Internet, making it very difficult to remove. So it is best to never post questions, and if you do, use a fake email address, if prompted.

BANKRUPTCY

How many people filed for personal bankruptcy in 2010?

More than 1.5 million Americans filed for personal bankruptcy in 2010, increasing 9% over the year 2009.

How many people have filed for bankruptcy in the period 2008 to 2010?

About 4 million people filed for bankruptcy during this three year period.

Why are there so **many bankruptcies** lately?

Among many factors, the most often cited are long-term joblessness, unavailability of credit, and a depressed real estate market which makes it difficult for people to get any equity from their house by trading down and selling their more expensive house in order to buy a smaller, more affordable house during tough economic times.

What parts of the United States were **hardest hit** and filed the most personal bankruptcies?

The Pacific Southwest and the Southeast in the United States were hit the hardest.

Which states' **bankruptcy** filings **grew the most** from **2009 to 2010**?

Hawaii was up 28.9%, California up 25%, with Arizona and Utah up 24.4%.

What are the **two types of bankruptcy** filings?

Chapter 7 and Chapter 13.

What is a **Chapter 13 bankruptcy** filing?

Chapter 13 is a reorganization of your debts, where you are partially paying off your debts. Debtors work out a payment plan with the court to ensure that all of the debt is eventually paid. If you have equity in your house, or a paying job, or some other assets, you may have to partially pay back your debts. The only way to save your house from foreclosure is to file Chapter 13, which protects your house from being sold to pay off creditors. You also pay your normal secured debts (things like a house and car). For the unsecured things, you have a plan to pay off approximately 10% of what you owe (depending on your income), over a period of time.

What is a **Chapter 7 bankruptcy** filing?

Chapter 7 filers forfeit most of their assets and most of their debts are forgiven. It is a total discharge of most of your debts.

Why should I **file** for **bankruptcy**?

If someone has huge medical bills with no possibility of paying them off, these charges can be discharged when someone files for bankruptcy.

After I file for bankruptcy, can **creditors contact me**?

No, creditors and collections agencies are not allowed to contact someone after they have filed for bankruptcy. Every creditor gets a notice of your bankruptcy from the court after you file.

What happens when I **first visit** a **bankruptcy attorney**?

You fill out a form that lists all of your assets, all of your income, and all of your expenses and debt. Then there is a formula that attorneys use to determine if you should file for Chapter 13 or 7.

What if during my interview with my attorney, we determine that **I make enough to pay off my debts**, with a few corrections in my personal spending habits?

If this is the case, the attorney will not recommend filing for bankruptcy.

Your social security number is one of your most precious forms of identity and should be carefully guarded. *Never* give your social security number over the telephone. No law-abiding, responsible company will ever as you for your SSN while talking to you on the phone. Your social security number is one of your most precious forms of identity and should be carefully guarded. *Never* give your social security number over the telephone. No law-abiding, responsible company will ever as you for your SSN while talking to you on the phone.

What happened under the **bankruptcy law** before it was **rewritten in 2005**?

So many people were filing for Chapter 7 bankruptcy, walking away from huge debts, that Congress decided to rewrite the law to make it much more difficult for people to completely discharge their debts under Chapter 7. Creditors lobbied hard to have Congress change the law.

What is **fresh start**?

Fresh start is when you discharge all of your debts under Chapter 7 and start your financial life again.

Isn't **bankruptcy** going to **ruin** my **credit rating**?

If you are sitting in bankruptcy attorney's office, more than likely your credit scores have already been ruined, since you have been behind in payments over a long period

Bankruptcy filings have been up dramatically in the United States since 2008. Many people have lost their jobs and their homes.

of time. So, actually, when you file for bankruptcy, you are already on your way to good credit scores because under Chapter 13 you have created a payment plan, and under Chapter 7 your debts are already discharged, and companies are more likely to begin to extend credit to you. Since the accounts are older than your filing date, they will be removed prior to the seven year period that it takes for the court filing to expire within the credit reporting company's system. If the accounts were not delinquent when you filed for bankruptcy, they will be discharged in seven years.

What is **worse** for my **credit rating**, Chapter 13 or Chapter 7?

Chapter 7 is worse because you are defaulting on all of your debt, and to a creditor, this makes you a much more risky potential client than someone who is making a good faith effort to pay off their reorganized debts under Chapter 13.

How many **years** does a **bankruptcy** stay on your **credit report**?

A Chapter 13 bankruptcy will remain on your credit report for seven years from the filing date. This is the actual public record item that is in the court record, which typical credit reporting companies pick up when they create a file on you. The actual debts themselves will remain in your file for seven years from when the problem occurred and was first reported to the credit company. If the debts were not delinquent at the time of filing, they will also be removed from your credit profile. However, the public record is removed in seven years. Under Chapter 7 bankruptcy filing,

After you declare bankruptcy, creditors and collection agencies are no longer allowed to contact you, and they certainly are not allowed to do so in person.

the accounts will be removed after seven years, but the public record item will be removed after ten years.

Do I have to **sell my furniture** when I file for **bankruptcy**?

The court gives you a certain allowance for things like furniture. If you purchased the furniture from a store that extended credit to you, the store will try to make a deal on the value of the furniture.

Must I use a **credit counselor** in order to **file for bankruptcy**?

The Bankruptcy Abuse Prevention and Consumer Protection Act of 2005 requires that most people, with some exceptions, get credit counseling 180 days before they file for bankruptcy. A debtor's education course is also required.

What will my **bankruptcy attorney** actually **do**, when I file?

They interview you, prepare the petition, and file the paperwork in the court. In about two weeks you get a notice to appear in court for a creditors' hearing.

What is a **creditors' hearing**?

It is when the bankruptcy trustee conducts a brief hearing, where the client is sworn in, and can then answer questions from either the trustee, or the creditors regarding your

Don't worry about your credit rating when you declare bankruptcy. That is the time to cut up your credit cards and start over to rebuild your credit worthiness.

petition, which they have received ahead of time. At the end of the hearing in Chapter 7, the trustee approves your petition, and the client receives a discharge of all debt. Under Chapter 13, the trustee will approve your plan of payment.

Under **Chapter 13**, where my debt has been reorganized, and I am now paying off a portion of what I owed, **how do I** actually **make the payments**?

The filer doesn't actually make the payment. The filer writes one check per month to the court, and the court then pays each of the creditors, according to the pre-approved plan.

What **happens** after I **pay off** my final plan?

The filer than receives a Chapter 13 discharge, and can begin rebuilding their credit history again.

What if while I am in bankruptcy under **Chapter 13**, I wish to **buy a car**?

You must get approval from the court for any purchases involving credit.

What if I am married, does my **spouse also file** for bankruptcy **with me**?

You can, if you have joint debts, like joint mortgages or car payments, both file for bankruptcy. If you have no joint debts, then only one person needs to file, the person who is responsible for the debt.

How do I **rebuild** my **credit history** after bankruptcy?

Try to establish credit in small amounts, and pay off these amounts every month. And make a commitment to never spend more on your credit cards than you can afford to pay off entirely each month. If your issue was overspending, begin now learning how to create and live within a budget. If your central issue was large medical expenses for you or your family, consider getting a job that offers medical insurance at subsidized rates. If your issue was not having adequate savings to ride through economic down turns, work hard to save enough for six months to one year of expenses, and do not touch these savings, no matter what happens.

What does it **cost** to **file** for **bankruptcy**?

The costs vary, depending on where you live and which attorney you choose. In Chapter 13, the attorney fee is set by the court and the attorney is paid by the financial plan through the court. In Chapter 7, you pay your attorney a fee up front, which varies from $400 to $2,000.

What **debts** survive bankruptcy and **cannot be discharged**?

Income taxes due, government loans, any secured purchase, and any fraudulent purchases cannot be discharged.

What are **fraudulent transactions**?

Fraudulent transactions are when a client knowingly, with malice, opens many credit cards, knowing that he or she can never pay them off. During the interview with your attorney, they will ask a series of questions that will determine if there is any kind of fraudulent use of credit. If there is, the creditor may object to the payment plan in Chapter 13. Under Chapter 7, if a creditor objects to the full discharge of the debt, a separate hearing to cover these items will be held, and the trustee will make the final decision.

What is a **secured purchase**?

Any purchase where credit is given in exchange for a lien against that purchase, like a house, car, or furnishings, is a secured purchase. After the loan is paid the lien is removed.

How long does a bankruptcy **hearing last**?

Each filer is given a one-hour time block at the federal court house in their state at which many filers are petitioning the court. The average time is 5 to 10 minutes per filer, once your name is called.

When I select a **bankruptcy attorney**, whom should I **avoid**?

You should avoid any attorney who offers or advertises a "too good to be true" price. You also may want to avoid attorneys who only send their assistants to meet with you. If you call the attorney, and cannot get a return phone call, it is best to consider someone else. Find an attorney who is recommended or referred, and one that only specializes in personal bankruptcy.

What are some of the **negative consequences** of filing for **bankruptcy**?

It is very difficult for people who have filed for bankruptcy to get mortgages to buy a house. You most likely will need a co-signer on the loan in order to do so for many

Watch out for bankruptcy attorneys who offer amazingly low fees or who send their assistants to meet with you instead of talking to you directly.

years after the filing. You will also require a co-signer in order to obtain credit, and even credit cards. And credit card interest rates will be much higher than for people with good credit scores. If a potential employer runs a credit check, they may react negatively to a bankruptcy. You will also have to have a high interest rate secured credit card, which means a lien is placed on some asset for the amount of credit you wish to use. Apartment rental companies will oftentimes run credit checks and look at a bankruptcy as a significant risk when considering your application. So a bankruptcy can have some pretty negative consequences as well.

How long must I **wait** if I filed for **bankruptcy once before**?

It depends on how you filed the first time. Under Chapter 7, eight years must have passed before you can re-file. Under Chapter 13 after a Chapter 7, you must wait four years. If you had filed a Chapter 13 bankruptcy, and wish to file again, two years must pass.

DIVORCE

What **percentage** of all married people **get divorced**?

According to National Healthy Marriage Resource Center, using data from the U.S. Census Bureau, about 1.94% of married couples become divorced each year.

What parts of the United States have **divorce rates above the national average**?

The South, extending from Texas to Florida, has above-average divorce rates.

What parts of the United States have **divorce rates lower than the national average**?

Lower divorce rates occur in the Northeast, from Pennsylvania to Massachusetts.

What is the **median annual family income** of **married-couple** families with children under 18?

The median annual family income with children under 18 is $79,015.

What is the **median annual family income** of **single parent** (female headed) families with **children under 18**?

The median annual family income of single parent (female headed) families with children under 18 is $23,011.

Why should we **consider** the **financial consequences** when considering a **divorce**?

Because the two separated parents must manage two different financial lives (rent, mortgage, food, etc.) on the same income with which they were previously living, representing a large increase in their overall expenses.

Who gets **more money for college**, children from **divorced families** or those with **married** parents?

Data from the National Postsecondary Student Aid Study suggest that children from divorced families must shoulder more of the burden to pay for their college education. Where children of married parents must pay 23%, children of divorced families must pay on average 58% for their college education. Children from parents who remarried still must pay upwards of 47% for their education.

And **why** do **divorced parents pay more** of the **children's education**?

The overall income of divorced parents is lower than that of married couples. With the added expenses of living in two households, this may have a significant effect on parents' ability to contribute more.

225

What about some of the **hidden costs** of **divorce**, such as child care?

The costs of child care must be considered, as a newly divorced single parent will have to pay for child care, if they enter or remain in the workforce, and have young children at home.

What is the **average cost** of **childcare** in the United States?

It may range anywhere from $2,000 to $18,000 per year, per child, depending on where you live and the age of the child.

Is it **expensive** to file for **divorce**?

Depending on where you live, the complexity and size of your financial picture, whether or not you have children, and how easy both parties wish to make the dissolution of their marriage, it can

Many spouses going through a divorce forget to consider unexpected costs, such as paying for child care.

cost anywhere from a few hundred dollars to many thousands of dollars in attorneys' fees to end a marriage. In California, an average divorce costs between $5,000 and $15,000, and may take anywhere from six months to one year before it is concluded in the courts.

Why is it so **expensive** to go to **court** for a **divorce**?

It's expensive because your attorney is charging you by the hour, and one must wait many hours before the court can hear your case, while you are being charged for each hour of waiting time.

How can I **decrease the fees** that I must **pay an attorney** when dealing with a divorce?

One of the easiest ways is to have your entire financial situation known and documented, so that your attorney will not have to spend the time (and your money) organizing and understanding this. Attorneys charge in 15 minute increments, so a five minute phone call could be very expensive.

Can using a **mediator** help **lower the costs** of a divorce?

Yes, mediators usually are lawyers, who will listen to the case, make recommendations and work out a settlement with your spouse's attorney, before any court hearing. The court appearance would be to file the divorce in the public record, saving thousands of dollars.

What types of **information** will I **need to bring** to a typical meeting with a **divorce attorney**?

Be prepared to bring statements that show your net worth, and those of your spouse, including your 401k plan statements, recent paycheck stub, copies of tax returns, bank and checking account statements, statements verifying stocks or mutual fund holdings, mortgage agreements, and balances on loans.

What are some **steps** that you should take **before a divorce** to prepare for these financial consequences?

It is very important for you to build up a savings or emergency fund that will get you through the tough times that may be ahead. If you are not in the work force, consider updating a resume, and perhaps even applying for jobs, so that you do have some safety net. If you will be keeping your house, you may consider taking on a housemate to help defray the costs of living alone. You may also want to establish your own credit cards separately from your soon-to-be ex-spouse.

DEATH OF A SPOUSE

What is the **first thing** that you should do if a **spouse dies**?

It is very important to get at least 5 to 10 certified copies of the death certificate, as you will need this to transfer assets to the surviving spouse. Most financial accounts, where there is only one account holder named, will require the death certificate in order to effect the transfer.

227

If my **spouse dies**, and he or she is the sole bread winner in the family, do the **assets automatically transfer** to me?

If all of your assets are jointly owned, all of these assets pass directly to the surviving spouse. Normally, cars are not jointly owned, but the department of motor vehicles in your state should easily transfer the title to your name without your having to go to probate court.

What is **probate court**?

It is where the county administers an estate in the name of one person. Depending on the size of your estate, it can be classified as a "small estate," and can be adjudicated by yourself, without an attorney, depending on where you live. Larger, more complex estates require more assistance, which an attorney can provide. A probate judge or clerk will then decide how the estate should be divided.

What if my **spouse has a will**?

If there is a will, the will is filed with the probate court, and is considered when dividing up the assets.

What about **life insurance** policies, **401k** accounts, or **pensions**?

Any assets with a beneficiary named do not go in to probate, and are immediately disbursed after presenting a death certificate to each of the plan administrators. Check to make sure that each of your accounts has a beneficiary named.

If I was **covered** under my deceased **spouse's health insurance** through their employer, will my **coverage continue**?

It is very important to contact the spouse's employer within 30 days after the death to find find out how you and your dependents, if any, may be eligible for continued medical insurance benefits under COBRA (Continuation Coverage Assistance Under the Recovery and Reinvestment Act). Depending on the size of the employer, you may be entitled to up to 36 months of continued insurance coverage.

What about **social security** survivor's benefits?

In order to get survivor's benefits for social security, merely present the death certificate at your local Social Security Administration office, fill out the form, and they will file the necessary papers.

The death of a spouse is one of the most difficult life experiences you can imagine, which makes it even harder to think about the practical tasks that must be accomplished, such as obtaining death certificates and going through probate court.

Could I be **entitled** to any **other survivor's benefits** through my **spouse's employer**?

It is important to immediately check with their employer to see if there are any benefits due you, including union pensions, professional organization insurance, vacation pay, etc.

When it comes to a death of a spouse, what is the **best thing** that we can do to **make the financial transition easier**?

The most important thing to do is to have all of the financial documents and statements up to date and organized so that they are easily accessible and understandable to the survivors. This means you should have recorded somewhere all account names and numbers, passwords (if they are using online statements), updated balances, and toll-free customer service numbers for every account.

WILLS AND TRUSTS

Why should we have a **last will and testament** written before we die?

It is used so that you can choose where your assets go, and if you have children, to indicate who will be the guardian of and raise your children, rather than having the court decide this.

229

What is **included** in a **will**?

A will includes the name of the person that you wish to execute your will to carry out your wants (personal representative), it names the guardian to your children, and who will then be responsible for their finances, and finally, it describes how you want your estate to be given to your heirs.

What is the **difference** between a **will** and a **trust**?

You will always want to have a will even if you have a trust. It is not an either/or proposition. A trust allows the deceased to pass on to their heirs their assets without having to go through probate court. Unless you have millions of dollars in assets, you most likely do not need to protect your portfolio inside a trust, as setting up the trust can be very expensive, depending on its size and complexity. A will is a statement of a few specific wishes. If you have a will and a trust, the will names your personal representative, the guardian of your children, and then states that all assets will go into your trust and be distributed pursuant to the terms of the trust.

How **important** is it that the **will is current**?

The will, however old, is still enforceable, but it is a good idea if you have elderly parents that you encourage them to update it. Often, elderly parents will have one will/trust and then redo the will without informing the executor.

What should I do about my **deceased spouse's debts**?

If the debts are joint, the surviving spouse must continue to pay for them. But if the debts are small individual debts, sometimes the creditors may forgive them. In general, the estate is responsible for those debts, and the names of all debts/creditors should be reported to the probate court. Contact all credit card companies and let them know of the death. Cancel all cards unless you're named on the account and wish to retain the card.

What should I do about my **deceased spouse's taxes**?

The surviving spouse must file a tax return as normal, indicating on it the death of a spouse. You may be responsible for any taxes due.

What if I **cannot pay** for the **current bills** after my spouse dies?

If you have a lot of joint debts that cannot be paid off, you may have to consider filing for bankruptcy. You can negotiate a payment plan with some of your creditors to see if they can lower your monthly payments. If the debts are loans for such things as a car or a house, you may have to immediately consider selling the assets.

Wills do more than just name beneficiaries; they also direct who should handle the deceased's estate, who will become the guardian for any young children, and other specific wishes.

What about the **deceased spouse's health care bills** that continue to come to me?

You may ask for debt forgiveness from the medical hospital or doctors' offices. Otherwise, it must be paid for out of the estate.

What if my **deceased spouse** owned a company or had a **financial interest in a company**?

Check to see if there are any buy–sell agreements under which his or her interest must be sold, or if the ownership can transfer directly to the surviving spouse, so that you may continue to earn income from these holdings.

GETTING OUT OF DEBT

How can I **get out** of **debt**?

The most important step to getting out of debt is to understand what behaviors or circumstances caused the debt to begin with, and then focus on changing those behaviors first. This means that if you have incurred a lot of credit card debt because of

231

When trying to pay off high credit card bills, always tackle those with the highest balances first.

undisciplined spending habits, you must immediately attack the root cause of the debt, in order to reduce your debt. If you incurred a debt because you obtained a mortgage for more house than you can afford, you must find a way to sell the house without incurring a loss, and purchase a smaller, more affordable house.

What is the **second most important step** to getting out of **debt**?

The second step is by saving what money you used to pay off loans and credit cards, and pay special attention to not taking on any more debt going forward. In other words, take the money that you used to pay for your monthly credit card bill or car loan, and put that money directly into a savings account, and spend nothing on your credit card going forward. And remember to pay yourself first.

Is there any **priority** that I should think about when **paying down debt**?

Yes, you should pay off the highest interest loans or credit obligations that you have. High interest credit obligations like credit cards carry the highest interest rate. So, you should pay as much as possible on your credit card balance, plus the interest on the balance, each month until the balance becomes zero. If you plan it out, and pay a certain amount each month, without taking on any new debt, you will see the light at the end of the tunnel. Pay a consistent amount each month—as much as you can afford. If you think that you can pay off more, because of a wage raise or pay increase at work, use the extra cash that you are earning to reduce your debt.

How much **debt** can I **afford**?

It depends roughly on your front end and back end ratios or debt-to-income ratio. Although the use of the ratios differs from lender to lender, on average your front end ratio should never exceed 28% and your back end ratio should never exceed 36%.

What if my **debt-to-income ratios** are **higher than average**? Will a lender still **give me a loan**?

Just because a lender qualifies you for a loan does not mean that you should take the loan. The lender may not care about your long-term financial success. Having worse than average debt income ratios means trouble on the horizon if not corrected, and should signal action on your part to reduce the debt.

What is the **average percentage** of typical Americans' **gross income** used for **mortgage and consumer debt payments** each month?

According to the Federal Reserve, Americans spend about 11.89% of their monthly gross income on mortgage and consumer debt payments. Homeowners (those with mortgages) spend about 15.27% of their gross income on monthly payments for their loans and credit card debt.

Can **adding** just a few hundred dollars **to my mortgage payment** help in **reducing my debt**?

Yes, some people choose to add an additional sum to their normal monthly mortgage payment, so that they may pay down their principal. The effect can shave several years off your mortgage, and save you thousands of dollars in interest payments, depending on your loan size, your interest rate, and how many months you have remaining on your mortgage.

RETAINING
FINANCIAL RECORDS

What are a few **reasons why** I should **retain** my **financial records**?

One saves financial records in order to backup or prove a tax issue with the IRS, provide some information about a purchase, reconcile a monthly statement from a credit card company, and obtain warranty coverage or return an item for a refund.

How long should I keep my personal financial records?

You need to keep records of your finances for several years. The IRS has guidelines for several different cases, but it is easiest to remember, just to be safe, to keep all tax records for at least seven years.

It really varies. The IRS requires that we retain any proof of any income, deductions or credit claimed for at least three years from the date of a return. The IRS also requires that we keep six years' of records in case we fail to report income that is more than 25% of our gross income in any tax year. If you have ever failed to file a tax return, or filed fraudulently, the IRS can go back as far as they would like, in order to collect what is properly owed. That said, most people agree that keeping six to seven years' of important financial information, like tax returns, W-2s, 1099s, year-end financial account statements showing income earned, and paychecks, is prudent.

BUDGETING EXPENSES

LIVING WITHIN YOUR MEANS

What does "**living within your means**" mean?

It means given the amount of income that you take in, minus all taxes that you must pay, you spend enough money in order to live without putting yourself in financial risk by spending more than what you make.

What is "**living beneath** your **means**"?

Living beneath your means suggests that given all of your income that you make in a year, less your taxes, your total expenses are less or far less than what you actually can afford.

Why is this so **important** in the **creation** of wealth and **financial success**?

Because if you are good at managing your expenses, spending less than what you bring in, you will find money left over each month, which can be directed to savings or investing. Certainly, living beneath your means is one of the most important keys to financial success.

What must we do in order to **live beneath** our **means**?

The answer to this is found within our attitudes about money and material goods, and our ability to postpone or do without certain items now in expectation of getting some future payback as a result of our frugality. For example, we must decide that having a stress-free financial life by driving a paid-for, ten-year-old car, actually feels better than the stress created by having to pay off a $20,000 loan for the smell of a brand new car.

CREATING A BUDGET

Why create an **expense budget**?

We create an expense budget so that we may attain some financial goal in the future, such as to save a certain amount of money for a future purchase, like a house down payment, educational expense, perhaps a vacation or large appliance, or even to pay down debt.

How **important** is having a **goal** in mind when we decide to create an **expense budget**?

It is very important to have a goal in mind, because by visualizing the goal it makes it much easier to check our progress toward that goal and measure our progress, both positive and negative. Having the end prize in mind, whether it is an amount or the actual physical item that you would like to purchase, makes the goal more tangible and, in the end, more easily attainable.

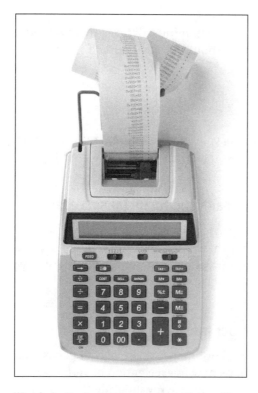

When budgeting for your expenses, have a fixed goal in mind, including income limitations and how much you are trying to set aside for savings.

What is a **budget**?

A budget is the established limit of the amount of expected expenses during a defined future period.

What is **zero-based budgeting**?

This is a method of budgeting where one accounts for the spending of every dollar of income from all sources. If any one category must be revised upward, another must be revised downward so the effect is zero on the total amount that is spent during the budgeting period. This way, our expenses can never exceed our income if we stick to our budget.

What are some **typical** family **budget categories**?

Food (groceries, restaurants) housing (mortgage/rent, property taxes, insurance, utilities, repairs), clothing, transportation (public, fuel, insurance, lease payments, car loan, rental), health care, entertainment, personal care, education, communications (land line, cell phone, Internet, cable), computers/technology, income taxes, pensions/401k, after tax investments/savings, charity, life insurance, entertainment, lawn care, credit card debt, other loan payments, hair/salon, medical (co-pays, insurance), and travel.

What are some **steps** in using a **budget**?

The steps in using a budget are goal setting, budgeting, analysis, monitoring actual expenses, improving the budget, and adjusting behavior.

How do I **create a goal**?

You may create a goal around nearly anything that you can imagine. It is very important that you focus on attainable goals, goals that are easily manageable. that are easily manageable.

Why should our **goals** be easily **manageable**?

This is important because as you make these life changes, you will want to see results and reward yourself many times in order to reinforce the changes in behavior and attitudes that financial success requires.

What are some **examples** of **financial goals**?

Some financial goals might be: reduce debt by 20%; save 10% of what I earn; save $20,000 to pay for house down payment; reduce my credit card debt to $1,000; save $10,000 per year for my children's education; or reduce my heating expenses by 25%.

How does my **budget help** attain my **goal**?

Your budget is a map of your current and future expenses, and is a guide that

There are many creative ways to save on gasoline. For instance, if you often make short commutes, you might like to purchase a gas-saving scooter. Even better, get a bicycle and get some exercise while you are at it!

BUDGETING

Income (monthly)

Salary(ies): _____

Investment Income: _____

Inheritance income: _____

Government-related income: _____

TOTAL INCOME: _____

Outgo (monthly)

Mortgage or Rent: _____

Car payments: _____

Car maintenance: _____

Utilities

Heat (Gas/Oil) : _____

Electric: _____

Water/Sewer: _____

Phone: _____

Cable: _____

Internet: _____

Insurance

Home: _____

Medical: _____

Life: _____

Auto: _____

Business: _____

Other Monthly Expenses

Groceries: _____

Dining: _____

Gasoline: _____

Tolls/Parking: _____

Subway/Bus: _____

Other Transportation: _____

Clothing: _____

Subscriptions: _____

Dry cleaning: _____

Other services (e.g. lawn care) : _____

Entertainment: _____

Incidentals: _____

Monthly Maintenance (est.)

Home: _____

Auto: _____

Taxes

Federal: _____

State: _____

Local: _____

Property Taxes (if not already in escrow): _____

TOTAL OUTGO: _____

INCOME MINUS OUTGO: _____

describes in pretty good detail, where you are headed financially. It allows you to make changes in each item or category in order for you to redirect that money to attain your goal.

Over what period of time do we **set up expense budgets**?

Expense budgets will describe all expenses that we have each month for a year. Sometimes, people will create expense budgets based upon weeks, depending on how much time they wish to spend inputting, tracking, and analyzing.

What will a **budget tell you**?

After a while of using a budget, we can learn many things about our spending, and immediately see what areas we need to change to stick to our budget. We may see that we actually spend too much in entertainment, eating out in restaurants, or attending sports events with high ticket prices. We may also see, for the first time, that we are spending more in our loan payments than we probably should be, and perhaps we need to change the loans or pay them off in order to improve our financial picture.

How do we **create a budget**?

In order to create a budget, we must record all of our sources of income. This may include all the income that we make from our jobs, as well as income that we may make each month from savings and investments. It is important to gather all of your investment and financial statements, which will show this income on them. Next, we look at all of our expenses, and record each one in a column that we pay regularly. You may want to look at all checks that you have written over the past few months, as well as credit card expenses, and try to group them all into various categories.

How far back should we **analyze** our **spending patterns**?

The more data you use, the more accurate your budget will be. And the key is to be as accurate as you can. So it's best to use at least one month of expenses, but at least six months is preferable. Write down how you are spending your money no matter how small the purchase.

Is there any easy way of using **credit card purchase statements** in order to **get this information**?

Yes, many credit card companies will send you an annual statement at the end of December, which itemizes all of your charges and groups them in different categories for the year, much the same as we described for your budget.

SAVE ON GASOLINE

Use the following checklist to insure you are saving as much as possible on gas expenses.

❏ Buy a fuel-efficient car.

❏ If you can walk, ride a bike, or take public transportation, do so.

❏ Keep your tires properly inflated.

❏ Keep your car not too warm, not too cold. If you have a garage, park it there in the winter, and if it is a hot, sunny day, park in the shade. This keeps you from running the air conditioning and heater more than needed.

❏ Keep your car in good running condition. Tune it up according to manufacturer guidelines; change air filters regularly; and use oil that says "energy conserving" on the API performance label.

❏ Keep the trunk as empty as possible to lighten the weight, and don't leave a roof rack on the car when not in use.

❏ Do not sit and idle your car's engine.

❏ Plan your routes to avoid doubling back or making multiple trips to destinations that are close to each other.

❏ Don't circle the parking lot looking for a space. You're better off walking and getting a little exercise anyway.

❏ Don't speed. Running a car between 45 and 70 mph is more efficient than going above 70 mph.

❏ If you have cruise control, use it. Running a car at a constant speed is much more efficient.

❏ Buy low-octane fuel. Regular gasoline works just fine in all but the most high-performance vehicles.

❏ Use a gas card to receive discounts.

❏ Buy gas at wholesale clubs like Sam's.

❏ Use a price-watch service such as www.gasbuddy.com to find where gas prices are the lowest in your area. You can usually access these on the Internet and as phone apps.

❏ Try not to use air conditioning in your car; it uses up fuel.

❏ Keep your tank over one-third full, but don't fill it to the top, either. Below one-third full the engine might not receive a steady supply of fuel, making its operation less efficient, but when you fill the tank even after the automatic shut-off of the pump, you risk releasing gas vapors or spilling fuel.

❏ Keep the gas cap on tight. A loose cap allows vapors to be released.

❏ Use other forms of transportation when you can, including fuel-efficient motorcycles and scooters, bicycles, or taking public transportation.

Impulse buying is the best way to blow your budget out of the water. Before you make a purchase, pause for a minute and think to yourself: "Do I really need this?"

After we have a **history of expenses**, what should we **do** with this **information**?

At this point, you want to take the average of each group of your expenses, and put them in each of the categories. Add up each monthly expense, like your electric bills, and divide it by the number of months that you are using (6 or 12), and that is the average. Use this number for your budget. In the case of an expense that is fixed, like a rent check or mortgage payment, just use that number as your monthly budget number for that category.

Why do you choose to include **savings** as a **budgeted category**?

We include savings as a budgeted category because we must plan for and have a goal of setting aside money, however small, into savings each and every month in order to attain our financial goals. Savings is not something that happens after you pay your bills. It is something that happens before you pay your bills.

What is the concept of "**paying yourself first**"?

As part of your overall expense budget, it is very important for you to get in the habit of paying yourself first, above all else, no matter how small. It teaches you the discipline of allotting the first dollars that you earn to your future financial goals.

FINANCIAL GOALS

Keep track of your financial goals using this simple worksheet.

Goal	Cost	Target Date	Monthly Cost

But if I **pay myself first**, will I have **any left for something else**, like new clothes or an evening at my favorite restaurant?

Again, it is a personal choice that we all must make, but once you decide that it actually feels better knowing that you have a lot of money saved, rather than getting into more debt and not saving, the decision becomes rather easy.

So once I have created a budget, **what is the next step**?

The next step after we have created a budget is to analyze and see if there are any obvious warning signs or immediate problems.

What types of **immediate problems** can one see?

One of the most critical problems would be that the person's expenses exceeded their income. Other problems could be that the amount of money used to pay back loans is far higher than what we can comfortably afford. We may also see individual problems, like discretionary expenses are too high.

What is a **discretionary expense**?

A discretionary expense means an expense that we incur at our discretion or by our own choice. Much of our financial problems involve these expenses.

Why do so many of our **financial problems** involve **discretionary expenses**?

Because these are the expenses that are more impulsive, unplanned, or immediate. They are also expenses that we normally put on a credit card, which, if not paid in full each month, means that we will pay interest on these charges. And over time, all of these charges can add up to many thousands of dollars in financial problems.

Why is it **important** to study my budget, and **memorize each category** name and **how much** I spend in **each category**?

One of the most interesting things about changing our behavior is that just by the act alone of monitoring our behavior, seeing our budget, seeing how the decisions we make on a daily basis affects our budget, we begin to see a decrease in our spending. Our attention to it already begins to alter the way that we think about money, and paves the way for many great, positive changes up ahead.

After I have my budget set up, **what** types of things should I now **look for** when **analyzing my expenses**?

You should look at each item, and see which ones you can actually control, or decrease, and which ones are fixed. Monthly payments like mortgages or loans are more difficult to decrease, than say, credit card purchases for lunches and dinners, or clothes. Look to see which ones you can immediately decrease.

CUTTING EXPENSES

After I found through my analysis that my **big problem** is my **discretionary purchases** what should I **do about it**?

Begin to alter some of the things that are contributing to this. If you find yourself spending a lot in some area like entertainment/restaurants, try bringing a lunch every other day, at first, and gradually wean yourself off that expense. If you find that you are spending too much money on a car payment, try seeing if you could sell your car for the amount of what you owe on it, and use some savings to purchase a perfectly good used car for cash instead. You will immediately begin to see that you can accumulate the amount that you used to pay for a car loan in your savings account. Do this for each item, keeping in mind that you want to attack the expenses that are causing the most problems.

What can I do about expenses like **heating and electricity**?

Many energy companies offer tools online that provide you with an analysis of your past bills and energy usage in order to help you see if you are spending too much each month compared to previous bills. Then, you can begin to make little changes, like turning off lights more regularly, not using exterior lights all night, turning down the heating temperature at night, or keeping the temperature a little

The government has been urging consumers to save electricity by purchasing energy-efficient appliances and LED or CFL light bulbs.

higher in the summer cooling months in order to save money on your utility bills. You may turn down the temperature on your water heater slightly to save on your monthly gas or electric bill.

Does using **big appliances** at **night** actually **save** money on my **electric bill**?

Yes, electric companies charge lower rates in the evening than during the day for using electricity off peak hours. The savings over a year can be substantial.

How much does **dialing down** my **thermostat save** me?

Each degree that you permanently set your thermostat below 72 degrees will reduce your heating costs by 3%.

How much **impact** do my **lights** have on my **electric bills**?

Lighting accounts for about 20% of your total electric bill. So we may find ways of saving by turning off lights in rooms that we do not use, installing lower wattage lights in rooms where we can, and also using low wattage compact fluorescent bulbs for big savings on our electric bills.

Why do **Compact Fluorescent Lights** (CFLs) help **save energy**?

They are four times more efficient than regular bulbs, use about 75% less energy, and last ten times longer than incandescent bulbs.

What is an **AFUE rating**?

It is the Annual Fuel Utilization Efficiency rating, which measures the overall performance of a heating boiler or furnace. A furnace with an AFUE of 92% means that 92% of your heating expense is actually heating your house, while 8% is escaping out the chimney or through some other exit.

Why is **AFUE important**?

We want to replace our older, less efficient appliances like furnaces, water heaters or boilers, which have AFUE values in the 70s or 80s, with newer models, which are far more energy efficient and waste far less energy each month.

What **incentives** are there available to **replace old appliances**?

Check with your local electric or gas provider to see the list of appliances that may qualify for a rebate. Rebates are often given by either the manufacturers or by the state that you live in to replace older, less efficient appliances.

How can I **save** on items like **food expenses**?

The easiest way to save is to see how much you are really spending on eating out. Just an $8 lunch three times per week is more than $120/month that you can save. A $5 cup of coffee at your favorite café every morning can cost you more than $100 per month in added expenses. Stop buying lattes and coffees at your favorite café. It doesn't make sense to spend $5 to $10 every morning, when it costs pennies to have it at home. Try drinking filtered tap water, rather than spending $2 for bottled water. Bring your lunch to work, instead of going out. This act alone will save you between $5 and $20 per day. Over the course of a month, you can bank nearly $400.

You can save a ton of cash by "brown bagging it" at work. Fix lunch at home and take it to the office, rather than buying from a restaurant. Even cheap fast food is more expensive—and less healthy—than a meal you can prepare in your kitchen.

What are some **easy ways** to **cut** hundreds of dollars from my **monthly communications expenses**?

Cut off your cable television, or at least scale back on what premium packages you may have subscribed to. Cable television can cost upwards of $50 to $150/month, and since there is so much free media available on the Internet today, it is easily replaceable. Try cutting your home land line phone. Aside from saying good bye to telemarketers forever, you can easily save $100/month doing without a second line. We all use cell phones, and in some families, multiple cell phones, so the need for a land line is unnecessary. Make sure you have a cell phone plan as closely matched to your usage as possible, and never go over on the number of minutes that your plan allows, as it can cost you hundreds of dollars. If this does happen, or you see yourself approaching the maximum during a billing month, you can call your provider and change the plan and ask for a credit for the overage, which they will provide, without changing the term of your agreement.

What **other ways** are there to **save** on **monthly expenses**?

Kicking the cigarette habit can easily shave hundreds of dollars from a pack-a-day smoker's budget. At over $8 a pack, it represents $240 a month in savings. Resist the impulse to buy a new car, or even to change cars. It is a lot cheaper to change your oil and have it cleaned than to buy a new car.

SAVING ON YOUR FOOD BILL

Gasoline prices and other factors are causing food prices to soar as well. You can fight back and cut your budget by using this checklist. Check Yes or No as to which strategies you are following, then try and move those No answers to the Yes column!

Yes   No

❑   ❑   Eat at home instead of dining out

❑   ❑   Bring a lunch to work instead of buying lunch

❑   ❑   Brew coffee at home and take it with you in a thermos

❑   ❑   Take a pass on vending machines

❑   ❑   Do not buy coffee at specialty coffee shops

❑   ❑   Buy food in bulk

❑   ❑   Store bulk and other foods properly so they will not spoil and go to waste

❑   ❑   Buy store brand foods instead of brand names

❑   ❑   Buy fresh foods rather than canned or frozen

❑   ❑   Buy foods from local growers

❑   ❑   Start a vegetable or fruit garden

❑   ❑   Go hunting or fishing, storing food when there is too much to eat immediately

❑   ❑   Drink tap water (use a filter, if it helps) instead of bottled

❑   ❑   Make a grocery list before going to the story and stick to it!

❑   ❑   Plan meals a week or more in advance to prevent last-minute trips to fast food restaurants

❑   ❑   Don't take the kids to the grocery store. They tend to pressure adults into buying expensive and unhealthy items

❑   ❑   Clip and use coupons

❑   ❑   Buy day-old bread and other baked goods

❑   ❑   Check price labels carefully; it is not always true that large-sized containers are cheaper per unit of weight

❑   ❑   Shop at discount food stores

❑   ❑   Shop after eating so you don't buy foods not on your list because you're hungry

❑   ❑   Get non-food items at places other than grocery stores because they tend to be cheaper at discount stores

❑   ❑   If you are going to more than one store, plan your trips so that you don't waste gas on multiple drives for groceries

❑   ❑   Organize your neighbors to share coupons with one another

How can I use the **Internet** to help **compare prices**?

Before you buy anything new, compare prices on such sites as Nextag.com, Amazon.com, and Ebay.com. Even if you include the price of shipping, it still may be cheaper to buy over the Web, than at your local store.

Can I **buy used items** using the **Internet**?

Yes, in fact you can save from 50% to 90% of the price of the same item purchased new if you buy from someone advertising on your local Craigslist.org site. The beauty of Craigslist is that it is

Cigarettes have become increasingly expensive, especially as governments add taxes to tobacco. Do your lungs and pocketbook a favor, and quit the habit today.

run by a not-for-profit organization, charges nothing to post ads, and has nearly anything that you could want available within a short car ride away. It is a giant classified advertising marketplace/garage sale.

TEACHING OUR CHILDREN ABOUT FINANCES

Why is it **important** to **teach** our **children** the **value of money**?

It is important because financial literacy and values toward money are greatly influenced by what we observe of our parents from the time that we are very young all the way into adulthood.

What is the **first step** in **teaching** our **children about money**?

Perhaps the first step is that you and your spouse share similar attitudes about money, common goals about saving and investing for the future. Children need to see parents speaking with one voice, with little conflict, on financial matters.

Why must we be **positive and neutral**, as opposed to negative and emotional, when it comes to **speaking about money** with our kids?

You want to be positive because you want your children to associate saving money with something positive, so that they can have these feelings in their adulthood. You

249

want to be balanced in your outlook and explanation so that they may approach financial talks from a neutral rather than an emotional point of view.

What is the **next step** to **teaching a child** about **money**?

Begin rewarding them in some small way for chores done around the house, and encourage them to save by opening up a bank account in their name in which to make deposits. This will greatly boost their self-esteem, even if they are only depositing a few dollars. Each deposit will help the child to think positively about saving, and this may last a lifetime.

What else can I do to **teach** my **child about money**?

It is important to teach a child the value of delaying purchases for things, not impulsively buying just because someone wants it. Show your children that you are saving every week for a vacation, or a car. Let them see that when you are in a store, you may look at things to buy, but since you don't need it right now, you decide not to buy it. Children learn by observation, and if you believe in delaying purchases, and do not pull out the credit card to buy something that you do not have the cash to pay for, your children will begin to do the same.

What is **another way** to **encourage children** to save?

Like your employer's matching program for your 401k retirement plan, you can also match what your children put in to their account. Some have suggested making this match for a long-term goal, like the purchase of some new game or clothes. The match will allow the child to see how fast the money has grown, and will really boost self-esteem, as well.

As my children grow, how can I **encourage** them to **continue learning** about money and **finances**?

Encourage them to get their first job, whether it is babysitting, cutting lawns, or working in a restaurant, and encourage them to have some goals in mind for what they wish to save for. Be interested in their pursuit, always encouraging them, no matter how small their success. Success breeds more success when it comes to creating wealth, and it begins at a very young age.

What is the **minimum age** for a child to **open a bank account**?

There are no minimum age requirements for opening a bank account. Some banks will allow a child to open a direct account in his or her own name, and others allow someone to open a custodial account for that child.

It might be surprising to find out that most parents do not take the time to teach their children basic skills in handling money. A few basic lessons can go a long way toward helping your children manage their income wisely.

What is a **custodial account**?

A custodial account is an account that is in the name of the child, but the main signatory and responsible party on the account is the child's custodian, normally a parent.

What is the **Uniform Transfers to Minors Act**?

It is an act created in 1986, and adopted by most states, and in keeping with the IRS code, it allows for the transfer of funds to one's child or children up to an annual limit of $13,000 tax free.

When can my **child** have **access** to **this account**?

Most states allow for a child to begin drawing from this account at age 21, although some states allow for children who reach the age of 18 before transferring ownership of the account. Some states even require the child to be between 18 and 25 to use the funds in the account.

What does the term **irrevocable account** mean?

This means that a custodial account cannot be changed. The person for whom you originally created the account must remain the same, and cannot be reversed.

251

Can I **give money** to my children **without incurring** any **tax liability**?

Yes, although the tax code changes from time to time, you may give your child any amount less than $13,000 in any year without your child having to pay taxes on this income.

What if my **bank doesn't allow accounts** for kids?

Shop around until you find one. Ask the right questions at each of the banks, like what is the minimum age, what is the interest rate, and what is the minimum deposit to open the account.

INTERESTING FACTS AND TRENDS

Are things **more expensive today** than they were **in 1984**?

According to a report issued by Businessweek.com, the average household spent $49,067 on such things as housing, transportation, food and entertainment in 2009. This is up $3,692 (in 2009 dollars) from 1984, or 7.5%, which is a small percentage of growth.

What **categories** have **increased** the **most**?

The advent of the Internet, and the related products and services that we buy, on average represent more than $1,000 per person/per year, according to a study in the *New York Times*. College tuition plus room and board have increased more than 500% since 1980 to $20,435 according to the National Center for Education Statistics. Health insurance has more than doubled between 1984 and 2009, to $5,049 per single insured person.

Have **food prices** increased or decreased **since 1984**?

Food as a percentage of our annual total expenditures dropped 2% since 1984, from 15% of our annual income to 13% in 2009, according to the Bureau of Labor Statistics. And the prices for items like ground beef fell more than 30%, while coffee fell more than 55%. Even high-priced items like computers have seen incredible decreases in prices, where a PC in 1981 on average cost $3,693 and today costs about $700, a decline of more than 80%.

What **percentage** of online **economic Internet** users uses the Internet for **price comparisons**?

About 67% of users use the Internet to comparison shop, allowing them to save hundreds to thousands of dollars on purchases.

Online sites such as Groupon.com offer coupons and discounts you can use for merchants in your specific area.

What **percentage** of online **consumers** use the Internet to find **coupons**?

Approximately 40% of people on the Internet use it for daily or weekly savings using the myriad of sites that provide online coupons.

What types of **online activities** can we use during tough financial times to **help us succeed**?

Compare prices online to find the lowest possible price; find a new job, find second jobs or create second incomes; find online coupons; find information on protecting our finances; online learning and training to improve job skills; sell personal items to recycle and earn extra income; find out and obtain unemployment benefits, etc.

What **other** types of **activities** on the **Internet** can we use to **help us succeed**?

Finding house values; lowering prices of insurance; managing our health insurance; comparison of interest rates; comparison of credit card fees; ranking and comparisons of mutual funds and stocks; comparison of online brokers; obtaining information on getting a loan or refinancing a loan; comparison shopping for appliances; and vacation ideas.

What **percentage** of online **economic users** uses the Internet for **job searches**?

About 41% of all economic users use the Web to find information on new jobs.

253

CREDIT CARDS

What is the **average amount of** credit card debt **that a typical American family has?**

Approximately $15,788.

How many credit cards are out there right now?

There are 609.8 million cards being used in the United States.

How many **credit card holders** are there in the **United States** and how much has this **number grown**?

In the year 2000, there were 159 million card holders, in 2006 nearly 173 million card holders, and in 2010 there were 181 million card holders, according to the U.S. Census Bureau. Since the year 2000, the number of users has grown 13.8%.

What is the **average number** of **cards** that a **person has**?

The average number of cards that people carry is 3.5.

Can I ask the card company to **decrease my credit allowance**, so that I may not overspend on the card?

Yes, credit card companies also allow for consumers to establish spending limits on the cards, so that your purchases in any given period must be less than this amount in order for the charge to go through.

IMPROVING YOUR CREDIT SCORE

If your credit score has fallen below 720, or, worse, below 600, there are steps you can take to rectify the problem. Use the following checklist to work on improving your credit score.

❏ **Get a credit card**

If you don't have a credit card, this can actually be a problem when it comes to credit scores. This doesn't mean you have to carry a big balance—not at all! No, instead, get one or two major credit cards and carry a small balance on each.

❏ **Get an installment loan**

Having a loan with regular payments and showing that you can responsibly meet those payment requirements shows that you are a competent money manager and can dramatically improve your score. This includes home mortgage, home equity, car, boat, and student loans, or most any other personal loans.

❏ **Start using an older card**

The older and more established your line of credit, the better. If you have a credit card account that you have been using for many years successfully, this will dramatically benefit your score. Sometimes, though, we allow older cards that we have paid off to become inactive. And when this happens, the creditor may decide to close the account. Rather than let this happen, if you have an older card, start using it again. Just don't do so exorbitantly.

❏ **Check your credit limits**

Ironically, sometimes credit card companies report lower limits on your card than you actually have. Having a higher limit available can help your scores, so if you think that is the case you can contact your credit lender, who will more often than not gladly correct the disparity.

American Express cards, of course, need to be paid off each month, so this is not an issue in this case. However, if you have a card with ìno preset spending limit,î it can appear as if you are maxing out your card each month. With these cards, it is probably best to pay off the balance.

How many credit cards should I have?

It's probably a good idea to have not more than two cards, in case you absolutely need to use one, and have one as a back-up card in case your primary card does not work.

What is the **average interest rate** being charged to consumers for balances?

In 2010 credit card companies charged consumers an average interest rate on balances of 14.48%.

❑ **Pay off revolving credit accounts**

Using credit cards wisely is really a one-two punch. It's good to have credit cards with small balances, but paying off a credit card also shows you are a trustworthy borrower, and a low risk.

It is important to keep your balances below 50% of your credit limit (anything higher can hurt your score), and it helps to keep them below 30%. In an ideal world, you should have balances on your credit cards of no more than about 10% of your credit limit.

Therefore, work on paying those cards that have the biggest balances, whether or not they have higher interest rates than your other cards. If you're in a financial pinch, consider moving some of what you owe from one card to another. HOWEVER, don't play the shell game and

❑ **Clean up a slightly flawed account**

If you have a credit card with just one late payment in its history, you might try contacting your credit lender and seeing if you can have that one mishap expunged from the record. Ask if you can have the card "re-aged." If the company does not agree right away, ask if they will erase the incident from your record after you have made 12 or more on-time payments. Credit companies will usually be amenable to this if you have been a good customer otherwise.

❑ **Get errors corrected**

Having problems with a charge on your card? If you have charges for which you believe you are not responsible, and the billing company will not resolve them, you can dispute these charges as "not mine" with your credit card issuer. In many cases, credit card companies will either remove the charge or, in the possible case of credit card theft, hold you liable for no more than $50.00 of the total bill. It's a great idea to clear these erroneous charges off your record as soon as possible.

What **percentage** of the total U.S. **revolving debt** is made up of **credit card debt**?

About 98% of all the revolving debt is credit card debt.

What is the **total amount** of U.S. **revolving debt**?

The amount of revolving debt in the United States is $852.6 billion.

What is the **total** amount of **consumer debt** in the United States?

The total amount of consumer debt is $2.42 trillion.

The problem with credit cards is that they are too tempting to use. It doesn't seem like you are actually spending money when you swipe a card through a reader. Try to use cash for purchases instead, but when you do use your card pay off the balance each month.

What **percentage** of card holders **default** on their **cards**, meaning they decide that they cannot or will not pay off the card balances due?

Roughly 13% of card holders eventually default on their credit card terms, and cannot pay off the balances due.

Why use credit **cards**?

Credit cards give you access to cash immediately so that you may pay for many different expenses, from food to utility bills, without having to carry large amounts of cash. Consumers only have to write one check each month to cover many monthly expenses. Some credit cards allow consumers to earn points for using the card, which are later redeemable for products or services.

What is the **first rule** of using **credit cards**?

Do not use a credit card unless you can pay off the balance in full each month.

Why **pay off** the **balance** each month?

You want to pay off your balance each month so that you can avoid paying the interest rate on your balances, which can be exorbitant depending on your credit history and interest rate calculation.

BAD PRACTICES THAT LOWER YOUR CREDIT SCORE

❑ Making late payments. Depending on your current score, late payments can lower scores by 100 or more points.

❑ Applying for more credit when you do not need the funds.

❑ Consolidating credit card accounts, resulting in one or two cards with high balances, rather than several cards with lower balances. It's generally best to keep your balances lower than half the limit and, even better, lower than one-third of your credit limit.

❑ Lowering your credit limits by contacting creditors. As noted above, it is better to have more credit available rather than less.

❑ Having too many in-store credit cards. Department and other stores try to lure consumers into opening accounts by offering initial discounts off merchandise or services, but opening a number of accounts such as these makes you look like a bigger credit risk.

❑ Fines such as for traffic violations and even overdue library books can cause you problems if they go unpaid. Local governments are contacting collection agencies to collect delinquent fines, and such activity can hurt your credit score.

What does my **credit history** have to do with the **credit card interest rate**?

Card issuers look at our credit history to see what kind of a risk we might be to them, what the chances are that we will default, and how much debt we could handle. Depending on this, the card issuers decide on an interest rate that will cover the costs of defaulting accounts, fraud, and profit, and this number is the rate which they then charge the consumer.

So if I have a **great credit rating**, I might get access to a **better card**?

Yes, if you are less of a risk, have a higher steady income, and other assets, you will be approved for a lower interest rate card.

What **other convenience** do credit cards bring **to the consumer**?

They allow the consumer to spread payments for more expensive items over a period of weeks or months, depending on how long they wish to pay off the balance.

CREDIT REPORT ERRORS YOU SHOULD FIX

Fixing a credit score can be a time-consuming process. There are some errors on a credit report, therefore, that you really don't need to worry about correcting, and others that you should. Don't worry about the following errors:

- Typos, misspellings, even when they are misspellings of your name.

- Incorrect or outdated address information (unless you strongly suspect identity theft).

- Employers incorrectly listed as current or as not current.

- Accounts listed as open that you have closed, or accounts listed as closed that do not say "closed by consumer."

- Inquiries about your credit.

Do, however, correct the following:

- ❑ If you have declared bankruptcy, all accounts that were included in the bankruptcy should be listed as paid. If they are not, you need to correct these errors.

- ❑ Also, if you declared bankruptcy, negative items older than ten years should be removed.

- ❑ Negative items over seven years old should be eliminated in all other non-bankruptcy cases.

- ❑ Any reports of late payments, collections, or charge-offs that are not yours.

- ❑ Check that all credit limits are correct.

- ❑ For accounts you know you paid on time, these should be listed as "paid as agreed" or "current," but NOT "paid derogatory," "paid charge-off," or "settled."

FINANCE RATES, INTEREST RATES, INTRODUCTORY RATES

What if I am **offered a credit card** with an **interest rate** that is still **too high**?

You may shop around until you find one that is acceptable to you.

What if I am **already using a credit card**, and think that my **rate is too high**?

Depending on how well you have made payments on the card, and what programs are available, they may be able to reduce your interest rate.

Do I have to have **large balances** on my credit card in order to **establish credit**, or **improve** my **credit rating**?

No, you don't have to have large balances or many credit cards in order to establish or improve your credit rating. What you do need is a consistent history of paying the balances off in full, each month.

What is an **introductory offer** from a credit card company?

An introductory offer, sometimes called a teaser rate, is offered by credit card companies as a way of getting you to sign up with their card by offering a very low interest rate. What most people don't know is that the rate is only temporary, and eventually the rate will go up, as soon as you begin using the card, or after you transfer the balance from your old card to the new card. So, be skeptical when presented with these offers and read the fine print. If you are still curious, call and speak to a representative.

What **percentage** of card issuers will **raise** your **promotional rate** if you are **late or miss** a monthly **payment**?

According to a Pew Research Survey on credit cards in 2009, 72% of all card issuers will raise the promotional rates because of a late or missed payment.

How do credit card companies **calculate** my **finance charges** (fees and interest) on my balance?

Finance charges are calculated by applying a periodic interest rate, the annual interest rate that you see on your statement, divided by 12 monthly periods, to the outstanding balance of your account, multiplied by the balance that you have on your card on the closing date of the statement. Many credit card companies calculate your balance differently, so read the fine print about your card before deciding which card to use.

How do I **choose** a **credit card**?

You want to choose a credit card that offers the lowest interest rate, and the least amount of fees associated with using it, with access to the line of credit that you need or would like to have.

What is an **affinity card**?

An affinity card is a credit card associated with a brand or service that the card member likes and provides rewards for using the card. Many brands, like airlines, hotel

261

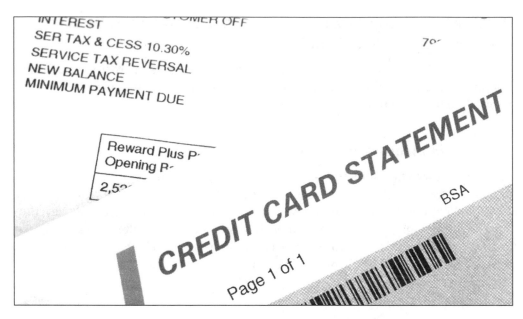

INTEREST
SER TAX & CESS 10.30%
SERVICE TAX REVERSAL
NEW BALANCE
MINIMUM PAYMENT DUE

Reward Plus P
Opening B

2,5

CREDIT CARD STATEMENT

BSA

Page 1 of 1

Many consumers never bother to check their credit card statements and just pay the bill. This is a mistake. Mistakes and erroneous charges do sometimes occur, and when they do you need to know about it so that you can dispute the charge with your credit card company. This is also a key clue to protecting against identity theft!

chains, and gas stations, offer credit cards that allow consumers to earn points, which are redeemable for products or services.

What should I do with my monthly **credit card statements**?

As you use a credit card, you should keep copies of each and every receipt, no matter how small, so that you may compare with the actual monthly statements. This prevents fraud, and allows you to make sure that what you thought you spent is the same as what you are charged.

How do I **dispute a charge**?

You can call the toll-free number for your card, and after entering some information, you can navigate your way to a representative, who will set aside the charge temporarily, while your dispute is investigated, so that you do not have to pay the disputed amount that month. Then, after a period of time, 30 to 60 days, if the card company agrees with your dispute a permanent credit will be issued back to you for the charge.

What are some **other ways** of **preventing fraud**?

You may set up your account to alert you if you spend more than $100 in a day or $1,000 in a week. The alert can be sent to your cell phone or email, so if for some reason someone does get your number, you will be alerted and can put a hold on the card immediately.

How long does it take to **resolve** a **credit card issue**?

According to a survey by Javelin Research, the average time to resolve a credit card fraud issue dropped 30% to 21 hours.

What are the **best credit cards**?

According to a 2010 J.D. Powers Survey of card holders, the best cards in terms of overall customer satisfaction are: American Express, Discover, US Bank, Wells Fargo, Chase, Barclaycard, Bank of America, Capital One, Citi, and HSBC.

If I have a balance of only $1,000 on my credit card, with a 15% interest rate, and I only made the **minimum payment** of $15 each month, **how long** would it take for me to **pay off the balance** and **how much** will it really **cost** me in the end?

It would take about 12 years, and end up costing you more than $2,000.

ELIMINATING CREDIT CARD DEBT

What is the **first step** to **eliminating credit card debt**?

The first step to eliminating credit card debt is to destroy the cards. This will prevent you from adding further debt onto the card.

How FICO Scores Are Calculated

Percent Weighed	Description
35%	Payment History (how reliable you are in making payments on credit cards and long-term loans)
30%	Debt, including total owed, number of accounts with balances, percentage of available credit
15%	Length of Credit History. Generally, a longer credit history improves your score
10%	New Accounts, including those recently opened and those for which you are in the process of applying
10%	Other. FICO considers other minor factor, such as whether you have a diverse range of loans, including auto, home, and credit cards. Generally, it is better to have a range of loans rather than several of one type.

263

MY CREDIT CARDS AND BALANCES

Use the sheet below to list your credit cards, your current balance, and to plan how you can pay off your balance by a specific date. By planning for a goal, you are much more likely to be successful in paying off credit cards. List your cards from those with the highest interest rate to those with the lowest, and try to pay off the higher rate cards first.

Credit Card Name	Balance	Monthly Payment	Planned Pay-off Date

What are **additional steps** that I can take?

The next step is to analyze how much you can afford to pay each month, and make it a priority to pay both the monthly payment and a piece of the balance each month, so that you may reduce the balance that is accruing interest and fees as fast as possible. Do not ever believe that you may get out of debt by paying the minimum monthly payment on the credit card.

How can I calculate **how much credit card debt** I can afford?

The easiest answer to this is zero. Credit cards should not be used as a way of financing the purchase of anything, because the interest rate and finance charges are too high to ever justify it. If you were to use a card to buy an expensive television, it would end up costing you twice the original price if you use a credit card and pay the minimum monthly payment and "finance" the purchase. Credit cards should only be used to make purchases for an amount that you can pay off entirely each month.

What **percentage** of card holders are **more than 60 days delinquent** on their credit cards?

Nearly 4.27% of all card holders are more than 60 days past due on their credit card payments.

DEBIT CARDS, ATM CARDS AND PRE-PAID CREDIT CARDS

What is a **debit card**?

A debit card is a plastic card, issued by your bank, which allows the user to withdraw funds or purchase goods and services by immediately debiting the card holder's bank account for the purchase.

What is the **difference** between a **debit card** and a **credit card**?

A credit card allows the users to borrow money from the card issuer in exchange for paying in full in exchange for paying in full for the good or service. the good or service. The card user must pay off the balance of the purchase in full plus any interest or fees charged during the statement balance period. A debit card deducts money immediately from the account, and therefore incurs no interest payments. The bank then sends the card holder a statement showing all transactions cleared for the month on the debit card.

265

ATM cards are different from debit cards in that the former shows up on your statement as a direct withdrawal from your account, while purchases with the latter will show up in a separate statement.

What is the **difference** between an **ATM card** and a **debit card**?

Before the advent of debit cards, ATM cards gave account holders at banks access to cash withdrawals from ATM machines, up to certain limits imposed by banks. Later, merchants began offering purchasers the option of using their ATM card to make purchases for everyday items and services in the same way as debit cards. But for the ATM cards the transactions are shown as withdrawals on the bank's monthly statement, rather than a separate statement, as in the case of a debit card. Today, many banks offer both debit and ATM cards, while some banks offer only debit cards as an option.

Do **debit cards replace checks**?

There has been a fundamental shift in the way that we pay for goods and services. For the most part, checks have now been replaced by debit cards and other non-cash payment types. Many people use paper checks for goods and services that do not offer any electronic method of clearing non-cash payments.

Why use a **debit card**?

Debit cards are attractive because the consumer immediately makes a withdrawal from their primary bank account for the purchase.

What **percentage** of all transactions in 2009 were **electronic, non-cash transactions**?

In a study by the Federal Reserve, released in December 2010, nearly 75% of all transactions cleared were using some form of electronic payments, either debit cards, credit cards, or bank-to-provider-bank transactions for the payment of goods and services. The study does not include bank wire transfers. In 2006, nearly 66% of all transactions were non-cash or electronic.

What is the **growth of electronic payments** since 2007?

The use of electronic payments has grown 9.3% per year since 2007.

From the period 2006 to 2009, how much did **check usage decline** in the United States?

The number of checks paid fell by about 6 billion or 7.2% over the same period, while the number of checks written fell by about 5.7 billion, an average of 6.1% per year.

267

How many payments were made in 2009 using debit cards?

About 37.9 billion in payments were made using Americans debit cards, growing 14.8% annually. The use of debit cards exceeds all other forms of non-cash payments and, by the number of payments, represents nearly 35% of total non-cash payments used in the United States.

What is a pre-paid credit card?

A pre-paid credit card allows consumers to purchase a credit card, and "charge it" with a small sum of money, and then use the card to pay for goods and services. When the balance is zero, the consumer can recharge the card, and begin using it again.

Why use a prepaid card?

A prepaid card is good if you wish to be on a budget and want to control the amount of money that you spend each month on a card without the inconvenience of using cash and without the hassles of trying to get approved for a credit card.

How many transactions of prepaid cards were there in 2009?

About 6 billion transactions were cleared by the Federal Reserve for pre-paid credit cards.

What is the fastest category of non-cash transactions in the United States?

The fastest growing non-cash payment instrument is the prepaid credit card, which grew at an annual rate of 21.5% from 2006 to 2009.

CREDIT COUNSELING

What is a credit counselor?

A credit counselor is a person employed by a credit counseling agency whose job is to help clients understand how their spending and misuse of credit has created their debt, and guiding them to solutions to reduce their debt and improve their overall financial situation.

How can I tell a legitimate credit counselor from a fraudulent credit counselor?

If the credit counselor charges an up-front fee for assisting you, this could be a sign of fraud. A legitimate counselor is affiliated with some national body, like the National

---

QUESTIONS TO ASK A POTENTIAL CREDIT COUNSELOR

❏ Is your agency accredited by the National Foundation for Credit Counselors?

❏ Is your agency a nonprofit organization? (the answer should be "Yes")

❏ Are your counselors certified by the NFCC?

❏ What, if any, fees do you charge?

❏ How do you handle the funds that you collect from me?

❏ How quickly are funds disbursed to creditors once you receive money from me?

❏ Are your services confidential?

❏ Can I have a payment plan tailored to my specific needs?

Foundation for Credit Counseling (NFCC). It should also be accredited by some accrediting body. Most legitimate credit counseling service providers are 501 (c) (3) nonprofit community organizations. This means they are not attempting to profit from your situation, and are "more" legitimate than for-profit providers. Also, look out for providers who say their fees are "voluntary". This could be a sign of a scam.

How much does typical credit counseling cost?

Most credit counselors charge fees of less than $50/month.

Should my counselor be certified?

Legitimate counselors are certified by the National Foundation for Credit Counseling, and counselors that have gone through the rigorous tests and coursework are called Certified Consumer Credit Counselors. You should avoid un-certified counselors.

DEBT CONSOLIDATION

What is debt consolidation?

Debt consolidation is the act of taking out a loan in order to pay off several other loans. Assume that you have credit card debt carrying interest rates as high as 20%, and you have a home mortgage, with some equity in your house, with an interest rate of 5% for 30 years. In a consolidation, you take out a home equity loan, which charges

269

a smaller interest rate, for the value of your high interest credit card debt, and then make payments on your equity loan until the debt is paid off.

What are the **advantages** of using **home equity to pay off** your **debt**?

The advantage is that in most cases the interest on this loan is tax deductible, whereas the interest on the credit cards is not deductible. You also immediately get a rather large savings from paying off the debt at a much lower interest rate.

What are the main **disadvantages of debt consolidation** through the use of a **home equity loan**?

The biggest downside risk is that of default in paying this loan off and losing your house as a result. In debt consolidation, you are trading an unsecured debt (your credit cards) for a secured debt (your house). If you default on that payment, you could lose your house to foreclosure.

What is a **debt consolidator**?

A debt consolidator provides a service where they look at your debt situation and create strategies designed to pay off the debt, in exchange for a fee.

What is the **trouble** with **debt consolidators**?

It is a largely an unregulated business, and many companies that promise unsuspecting families assistance end up taking fees and leaving town. They may promise to work with banks to arrange for your loans, and in the end may take what little money that you do have.

How do we **check** the **credibility** of the **debt consolidator** company?

It is important to check with your state's attorney general's office, as well as the Better Business Bureau. You may also search the Internet for any negative comments or stories written about the company. Check the company's references to see if they are legitimate. Also, contact the local chamber of commerce in the city where they are located to see if there are any complaints about the company. If you sense that there is any time pressure from a pushy debt consolidation representative, find another company to use. This is a sign that the business may not be legitimate.

If I have a much **lower interest rate** for my **old credit card debt**, by using my home equity, **what else** could be **wrong** with debt consolidation?

Because the debt is now spread out over a long period of time, if you make the minimum payments each month, you may pay much more to retire the debt.

How might I find out the name of a **legitimate debt consolidator**?

Go to the National Foundation for Credit Counseling Website at www.nfcc.org to identify and meet with a credit counselor who can perhaps direct you to a debt consolidator if it is recommended as a strategy.

Appendix I: Real Estate Tips

When you buy a home you are making a bet. As in the case of any investment, you are taking somewhat of a risk. And the risk is that if you put a substantial amount of money in the form of a down payment, perhaps greater than 25% of the negotiated price of the house, and get a loan for the rest, you are betting that your home value will increase over time, that interest rates will increase higher than what you are paying (which means the money is becoming more valuable), and that should you sell it you would get back the value of your loan, the down payment, and any other appreciation. Optimally, if you put money into the house to renovate it over the years you want to also get this money back, as well. This has historically been the trend, until the last few years, when city governments, hoping to recoup income in the form of property taxes, allowed developers to build more than the usual number of houses, flooding the market.

Banks and mortgage investors were also culpable because they created new investment vehicles for financing and investing in these mortgages, making loans freely available to people who otherwise could not afford to make the payments. When all of these homes and mortgages hit the market, the prices fell and continue to fall in most areas of the United States. Even given this information, the market corrects itself, and buyers are now able to purchase homes at historically low prices. Therefore, over the long term, these homes may appreciate in value.

Investment Rental Property

When you think of buying a real estate property as a rental, there are several factors to consider. It may not be such a bad idea to practice, if you are just starting out, to buy a property and try your hand (and time) at being a landlord. Do you enjoy chasing rent checks, interviewing potential renters, doing background checks, rehabbing the house, and providing maintenance services, etc.? These are just some of the real considerations. If you still intend to invest in rental real estate or purchase a rental property, make sure it is near to where you live because you will have to deal with this property and its renters. If you choose to have someone else manage your property for you, and are willing to part with 20% to 30% of your gross rent, that is an option, too. But you stand to lose that amount of money each month in exchange for outsourcing these services. Some people suggest that you may want to consider buying a duplex or a two-family house, since it may in one sense reduce your risk. This may be achieved if you buy it and can afford to make the mortgage, interest, taxes, and insurance payments with only one unit rented (50% occupancy). If that is possible, you will still have the same or more work to do than with a single family house, but part of your risk will be reduced.

Another consideration is the quality of the tenants. Some tenants may be low income, welfare recipients who may not be able to regularly make payments to you. Or they may be underemployed or chronically unemployed people. You must factor this in when deciding to buy a rental house, no matter what the appreciation might be. Even when renting to high income families or individuals, there still is a considerable amount of risk that the tenant may not keep his or her job. You might think, "Well, I can just get a new tenant." In some states, however, it is very difficult to evict a tenant without a lot of cost and time for the landlord, who may not have much of either if he or she is working as a landlord on the side. Even if your tenants stop paying, it may take months to evict a tenant while you are still paying on the mortgage, interest, taxes, and insurance. You might also get squatters, who may take up residence in your unoccupied rental and will not leave or pay the rent, making it nearly impossible for you to rehabilitate the house or find new tenants.

Condominiums

People like to buy condominiums because of a perceived ease of maintenance, flexibility, more free time, and common amenities like swimming pools or exercise facilities. Are condos good investments? Condominiums are usually not as good as single family homes when you are thinking of investment value. There are many factors to consider, including no possibility to enlarge a condominium; monthly condo fees and dealing with strict condo association rules; you may not like your new neighbor with whom you have to share a wall (unless it is a detached condo); and your complex neighbors might be going into default on their mortgages, which will affect your home's price. You also have to consider that there may be additional assessments for capital improvements of the complex, including the pool, roads, roofs, and other things like exterior paint by the condo association, which controls the common areas and exteriors. There used to be a working capital requirement of condo associations which the buyer would then be credited with upon purchase, but this convention is still only used in a few condo associations. So check with your realtor before buying.

Home Ownership for Personal Wealth

How does home ownership—both of your principle residence or rental property—create personal wealth? If you buy your own home, on your net worth sheet you get to show that you have a big debt (your loan amount, or the balance remaining on your loan) as a liability, as well as what the house's market value is (if you could sell it today) as an asset. The difference between these two numbers represents the amount of wealth that you now have because of your ownership. If you owe more than the loan, you will have to make some pretty important decisions, namely, should you stay and ride it out or cut your losses and sell? Can you make money in the end? Can you sell your house, downsize, and lower your monthly payments and buy a relatively less expensive place that will appreciate better than your current house? Depending on your strategy, you can make a difficult financial situation into a real win financially. Most people buy houses because the alternative is to pay rent, which is money down the drain. Purchasing a home is an investment.

Preparing to Buy or Sell

How do you avoid "going underwater on a mortgage"? When your house value drops to below the value of what you owe, it is said to be "underwater." There are many ways of avoiding this, all within your control. One key point is to not over-improve your home in relation to the other homes nearby. If the other homes in your neighborhood do not have granite kitchen countertops, stainless steel appliances, grand master baths, swimming pools, entertainment rooms, and tens of thousands of dollars "invested" in landscaping, it is probably a good idea to avoid these improvements. They may be over and above what people are willing to pay for houses with such features in that area. It is also a good idea to avoid using equity in your home to make such improvements, no matter how tempting the offer or the interest rate. Each additional line of equity must eventually be repaid, either now or when you sell the house, and you may end up spending thousands more in interest payments because of creative financing products that banks and mortgage lenders create and offer to clients.

People commonly misunderstand the difference between the interest rate and the annual percentage rate (APR). The annual percentage rate is the actual finance charge for a loan, including all points and loan fees, in addition to the stated interest rate. So even though you sign up for a low interest rate loan to purchase a house, you may end up having to pay more for the actual annual percentage rate. All of these fees are disclosed before you sign for the loan, but it is something that should concern all potential buyers.

A note about appraisals and inspections: appraisals are usually done by lenders and buyers to ensure that the price asked by the seller is in keeping with the prices that real buyers have currently paid for houses nearby. Of course, buyers want to make sure that they are getting somewhat of a deal, hoping that the house appraises out for more than what they must pay for the house. Sellers usually don't do appraisals for a variety of reasons. The city in which the seller resides does an appraisal of every house each year, and the real estate person who assists the seller in bringing potential buyers to the table will do comparables to show the seller what the real market value is. These comps (as they are known) represent similar houses that have recently sold nearby and help the real estate person to accurately price the house for the market. In fact, one reason houses do not sell quickly is that the sellers refuse to accept that the "real" value of the house is less than what they expected, given the new market realities, and they hold out for more money, no matter how long the house is on the market.

On the other hand, buyers may order a home inspection before they decide to enter into a purchase agreement to see if there are any major flaws that they should be aware of before purchasing a home. This inspection may uncover serious deficiencies, which allows the potential buyer to adjust his or her offer, perhaps even including in the purchase agreement a contingency that states that the problem must be corrected in order for the seller to get the offering price. Sometimes potential buyers will use this information to reduce the price of the house by that amount in order to get a good deal on the house price, as well. The home inspection is very important to a potential buyer, as the inspection itself yields a highly detailed analysis of all aspects of the physical house and property itself, describing every problem and what needs to be done to correct it. Perhaps the house has electrical issues, or water issues that may cost many thousands of dollars to correct. The home inspection will describe these, so that both the potential buyer and the seller may know the basis for the offer. Sometimes, just the information alone may be enough for the seller to either reduce the price or fix the issue for the potential buyer before the home is transferred.

FSBO vs. Traditional Realtor

Why should you use a real estate person to sell a house? People who use real estate professionals in order to find a house are very serious about buying. In some states, buyers may have a pre-approved letter from a lender showing that they can actually afford to see the house that you are offering. So, in effect, by using a real estate professional, a seller is getting a pretty well-defined market audience of interested buyers.

This is in direct contrast with buyers of houses listed for sale by owner (FSBO). People who are trying to sell their homes themselves do not have the benefit of screening potential buyers, since they are coming into contact with people who are not pre-approved for any loan and who may not show up for appointments. These are the sort of people who are surfing the Web on their lunch breaks in order to find homes, who may not be able to afford the house in the first place, nor be able to obtain financing. Although the market of potential buyers for an FSBO home might be larger, the quality of the potential buyers is relatively lacking. As a potential buyer, when you deal with an FSBO home, sellers might not be able to produce a proper or legal contract; they might be eccentric and decide at the last minute not to sell, or they might think they can get out of a legal contract at the very last minute.

When we sell a house through a real estate company, a commission of between 5% and 10% is collected from the seller. It does not go directly to the real estate professional who has been working with you for many weeks or months. This commission is divided between the selling agency and the listing agency. A listing agency is the real estate company that actually draws up the listing that goes out on the electronic multi-listing service (MLS), and this commission covers all of those costs, as well as the costs of advertising and maintaining the real estate offices and services. Both the selling and buying agent get a portion of this commission, because they brought the buyer to the house, they did the searches, and they know how to draft a real estate contract.

Your real estate professional does not earn a commission directly from the seller. The realtors receive their commissions from the agency for which they work. The percentage amount of the commission is decided at the time when the realtor initially joins a real estate company or agency. There are plenty of companies that make offers to sell your home for less than the usual 5% to 10%, but these companies must still give a portion of the commission to the other realtor.

How important is experience when selecting a real estate professional? A seasoned realtor can save a buyer and a seller time. For buyers, an experienced real estate professional can zero in on just the right areas that are appropriate for the buyer, since they may have been decades of experience. Currently, because of the widespread use of Internet-based real estate databases like the MLS and other real estate Websites, many new realtors may not even live in the area that you wish to buy, or sell, and therefore will be less likely to succeed, since they truly do not know or live in the area. For sellers, this is an important consideration because one would want a real estate professional who is more familiar with the area, has more local leads and contacts who are interested in changing houses, and may have more connections to people who are transferring from out of town, people who may not go on the Internet to find a house. Inexperienced realtors may not know or have enough experience in understanding the nuances of legal contracts, or the character of the neighborhood in which the buyer may be interested.

House Hunting and Websites

There are many great Websites to use to explore real estate for sale or rent (see below). But today most large local and national chains such as Century 21 offer access to your local states' listings so that you can at least become familiar with the prices for homes in your area. Generally speaking, people who are buying high-end homes, who are more defined in their objectives, simply do not have the time to search the Internet and tend to only use real estate professionals in their home searches.

What can potential buyers do to improve chances of getting the houses they want? Write down what your major objectives are in terms of size, location, schools, features of the house, number of bedrooms, number of floors, noise levels, community services, sidewalks, city services, property taxes, and so on. A couple who are house hunting should be in agreement about what they want before the search, rather than fighting it out after every viewing.

What about people who don't like the color of the paint in a room in a potential house and use this as a reason not to purchase? It is probably one of the more ridiculous excuses for not buying a home because changing paint color is really a minimal expense. However, it is a good idea to evaluate the defects of a potential house in terms of how much it might cost to fix, and then go back to the seller and ask for a reduction in price or money to repair the major defects discovered by an inspector.

What about mortgage companies that give loans for more than people can afford? Never assume that just because a bank or mortgage lender is willing to give you a loan for a substantial amount that it necessarily means you can afford to live in that home. You should buy less house than you can afford so that you can stick with your financial plan to increase your savings, even after you have purchased the house. The reason for this is that you should not direct too much of your income into your house as one of many different investments that you can and will make. Remember that part of your portfolio should be in real estate, part in cash, part in stocks, etc. But if your home payment is large you will not be able to diversify your investments, and depending on how long you stay in the house, you might not be able to get any return on your investment.

There are thousands of Websites that enable users to search for homes. Many real estate companies are using software that includes Google maps, enabling users to see the homes, nearby parks and neighborhoods, or even see the prices of all houses for sale on a map. This is making it much easier for sellers to properly price their houses, and for buyers to have the proper expectation as to the market price of all houses in a specific area.

The sites below consistently rank very high according to usage. The data supporting the following list is taken from a Experian Company's Hitwise study, which uses monthly, sophisticated sampling data to support its conclusions and rankings.

- Yahoo Real Estate
- Realtor.com
- Zillow.com
- Front Door Real Estate
- Trulia
- Rent.com
- MSN Real Estate
- Homes.com
- Zip Realty
- Mynewplace.com

Appendix II:
Starting a Business Plan

One thing to understand and focus on when starting a business is the importance of controlling of costs. Although the expense side of business is covered in several places within the business plan, perhaps a separate section would be helpful, since the cost, or expense side, of the business is one of the most critical areas to look at when evaluating a plan.

What types of problems do we see when looking at business plans? Many business plans overestimate revenues and underestimate costs. It's best to do just the opposite. By doing this you will eliminate possible sources of funding. But in the end, you will be happier for it, as you will be able to hit goals that you have set, which is most important. Always think about the business in terms of high, medium, and low risk; and do separate planning for each of these scenarios. This shows that you have the analytical skill to be realistic about your business. People who may invest in the idea have heard and seen every type of entrepreneur imaginable: from the very positive to the incredibly cynical.

Many times, entrepreneurs are looking for money, but have "no skin in the game," which means they have no cash themselves and are looking for other people to provide the start-up cash, whether it is an individual, a group of private investors, or some other source like a bank, equity fund, etc. The most glaring negative indicator is if the company founder is bad at managing his or her own personal finances. If so, you would be wise to request a larger percent (equity) share of the business, or undervalue the company, or demand a much larger return over a shorter period of time. Potential investors will want to know this information about the company founders and, if they lack confidence in them, may not invest. So, personal finance matters, even if you are starting a new, small business.

If you already own and operate a small business, all of the above is still relevant. Cash and expense management is the key to success, and having enough cash to ride out months or years of economic downturns is a prudent way to manage the business. Of course, by doing so you may not have the cash available for other kinds of expansion, but you will have enough to survive major problems in the economy or in your particular market. Control your costs and you will survive.

Scale your costs to changing business climates and markets, too. This means that if you are planning on shrinking your business, just adjust your costs to match this change.

But you need to do this either as it is happening—and know that it is happening—or plan on making the changes before the market causes you to have to make these types of changes. The opposite is true for market expansion. Perhaps you need some extra cash to fuel investment in some new market. You use the business plan to present your case to a group of investors from another company, perhaps a competitor. You must scale your costs and make use of this investment capital to give you, your business, and the investors the biggest return on the money that you (and the markets that you serve) can bear.

Remember that there are many different types of investors in a business. Some are willing to restructure the business or combine it with another business that they hold a position in or are shopping for. In order to make this happen, your business must be sound, well run, and have a history of making the right decisions in support of your plan.

Think about it like this: "I want to be here, by this date, and here is how I planned it, and here is what happened." The investors may want to hold onto part of your business for three years, five years, or even fifty years. It really depends on who your business attracts, how good of a job you have done in making it an attractive, profitable business, and how adept you are at marketing and selling the concept to investors. You could be the greatest manager ever, but a poor communicator, which could hurt your chances. So pay attention to the planning, and begin to introduce some form of it in your business if you haven't already done so.

Some investors may be looking to get their initial cash investment back inside of three years, while others might like to recover their initial investment, and double it, inside of three years, and still others are happy getting their investment back every three years for the next fifty years. It all depends, and this is a good question to ask yourself about what your vision is for the business, and then find investors who share your vision. Maybe your vision is too restrictive, too personal, too myopic. Broaden it so that your business can be attractive, even if you don't intend to sell it. The more attractive the business, the more valuable it is, and the more valuable it is the more valuable your equity becomes. Your equity in the business (what it would actually sell for today, times what percentage you actually own) creates your wealth (at least on paper).

The template below comes to us from the Small Business Administration, an extraordinary, free resource provided by the U.S. government.

Template for Writing a Business Plan

What goes into a business plan? There is no single formula for developing a business plan, but some elements are consistent throughout all business plans. Your plan should include an executive summary, a description of the business, a plan for how you will market and manage your business, financial projections, and the appropriate supporting documents. To help you get started in writing your business plan, the essential elements are summarized in the following outline.

1. Cover sheet
2. Executive summary (statement of the business's purpose)
3. Table of contents
4. Body of the document
    a. Business
        i. Description of business
        ii. Marketing
        iii. Competition
        iv. Operating procedures
        v. Personnel
        vi. Business insurance
    b. Financial data
        i. Loan applications
        ii. Capital equipment and supply list
        iii. Balance sheet
        iv. Break-even analysis
        v. Profit-and-loss statements
        vi. Three-year summary
        vii. Detail by month, first year
        viii. Detail by quarters, second and third year
        ix. Assumptions upon which projections were based
        x. Pro-forma cash flow
    c. Supporting documents
        i. Tax returns of principals (partners in the business) for last three years, personal financial statements (all banks have these forms)
        ii. Copy of franchise contract and all supporting documents provided by the franchisor (for franchise businesses)
        iii. Copy of proposed lease or purchase agreement for building space
        iv. Copy of licenses and other legal documents
        v. Copy of resumes of all principals
        vi. Copies of letters of intent from suppliers, etc.

Appendix III:
College Costs Trends

We all know that the price of products and services are increasing, but few products or services seem to increase faster than college and university tuition. The numbers do not even reflect the price increase in textbooks (which seem to be averaging approximately $100.00 per book), rent and utilities (room), or food (board), or even gas to get around campus or to commute to school. Coupled with additional expenses like spending money, clothing, travel, health and car insurance, and many other incidental expenses, the cost of college is becoming one of life's largest expenses.

At least when you purchase a house, you can do so and only have to pay 10% to 20% in initial cash for the down payment, obtaining a loan for the rest. But when one finances a college or university education, the up-front cash expenses can be in the tens of thousands of dollars.

Luckily, as described previously in this book, one can prepay at today's dollars the cost of tuition for one's child many years from now. In effect, you may buy tuition at today's prices, saving the amount of the increase, which has averaged more than 30% per year since the 1980s. Such advance savings plans appear to be a very good deal for people capable of saving for the future by doing without something today.

The data below comes from the National Center for Education Statistics, an arm of the U.S. Department of Education.

For the 2008–2009 academic year, annual prices for undergraduate tuition, room, and board were estimated to be $12,283 at public institutions and $31,233 at private institutions. Between 1998 and 2009, prices for undergraduate tuition, room, and board at public institutions rose 32%, and prices at private institutions rose 24%, after adjusting for inflation.

More statistics are available online at http://nces.ed.gov/.

Total tuition, room, and board rates charged for full-time students in degree-granting institutions, by type of institution: Selected years, 1980–81 to 2008–09.

Year	All Insitutions*	4-Yr Schools	2-Yr Schools
All Institutions			
1980–81	$3,101	$3,499	$2,230
1990–91	$6,562	$7,602	$3,930
2000–01	$10,818	$12,922	$5,460
2001–02	$11,380	$13,639	$5,718
2002–03	$12,014	$14,439	$6,252
2003–04	$12,953	$15,505	$6,705
2004–05	$13,792	$16,509	$7,086
2005–06	$14,629	$17,447	$7,231
2006–07	$15,483	$18,471	$7,466
2007–08	$16,159	$19,323	$7,637
2008–09	$17,143	$20,435	$8,230
Public Institutions			
1980–81	$2,373	$2,550	$2,027
1990–91	$4,757	$5,243	$3,467
2000–01	$7,586	$8,653	$4,839
2001–02	$8,022	$9,196	$5,137
2002–03	$8,502	$9,787	$5,601
2003–04	$9,247	$10,674	$6,012
2004–05	$9,864	$11,426	$6,375
2005–06	$10,454	$12,108	$6,492
2006–07	$11,049	$12,797	$6,815
2007–08	$11,573	$13,429	$6,975
2008–09	$12,283	$14,256	$7,567
Private Institutions			
1980–81	$5,470	$5,594	$4,303
1990–91	$12,910	$13,237	$9,302
2000–01	$21,368	$21,856	$14,788
2001–02	$22,413	$22,896	$15,825
2002–03	$23,340	$23,787	$17,753
2003–04	$24,624	$25,069	$19,558
2004–05	$25,810	$26,257	$20,093
2005–06	$26,889	$27,317	$21,170
2006–07	$28,439	$28,919	$20,284
2007–08	$30,258	$30,778	$21,685
2008–09	$31,233	$31,704	$22,742

*Costs are calculated in 2009 dollars. Data are for the entire academic year and are average total charges for full-time attendance. SOURCE: U.S. Department of Education, National Center for Education Statistics. (2010). Digest of Education Statistics, 2009 (NCES 2010-013), Table 334.

Appendix IV: Government Sources

The U.S. government, through its clearinghouse of information the Federal Citizens Information Center, offers many free publications in personal finance and small business, and for a nominal fee of $2 you can download PDFs. You may find them directly on the internet at http://www.pueblo.gsa.gov/cic_shop/cicshop.htm or by calling the toll-free number 1-888-8-PUEBLO (1-888-878-3256) to order a copy.

Money

51 Ways to Save Hundreds on Loans and Credit Cards
(http://www.fdic.gov/consumers/consumer/news/cnsum07/index.html)

Simple strategies for cutting costs any time, plus specific tips for saving money when you use credit cards and apply for home, auto, small emergency, student, and small business loans. (PDF file at http://www.fdic.gov/consumers/consumer/news/cnsum07/summer07color.pdf).

Affinity Fraud
(http://www.investor.gov/node/441)

Affinity fraud refers to investment scams that prey upon members of identifiable groups—often religious or ethnic communities. The fraudsters who promote affinity scams frequently are—or pretend to be—members of the group.

Bankruptcy Basics
(http://www.uscourts.gov/bankruptcycourts/bankruptcybasics.html)

There are five basic types of bankruptcy cases used to obtain relief from debt. Learn the differences in debts discharged, assets kept, forms needed, where to file, and more.

Before Disaster Strikes
(http://www.fema.gov/areyouready/)

Suggests ways to be financially prepared to deal with a natural disaster. Provides information on buying insurance, preparing a household inventory, filling an evacuation box, and more.

Building Wealth PDF

(http://www.dallasfed.org/educate/pubs/lessons.pdf)

Building Wealth is a personal finance education resource that can be used individually or in the classroom to help young people develop a plan for building personal wealth. It contains information about budgeting, saving and investing, controlling debt, and protecting wealth with insurance.

Certificates of Deposit: Tips for Investors

(http://www.pueblo.gsa.gov/cic_text/money/cert-deposit/cert-deposit.htm)

Learn how CDs work, how to purchase them, and questions to ask before buying.

Choosing a Credit Card

(http://www.pueblo.gsa.gov/cic_text/money/choosecard/cards.htm)

Compare the features and costs, and learn your liability limits when using a credit card. Covers what to do if there is a billing error or another problem with your credit card.

Cold Calling

(http://www.sec.gov/investor/pubs/coldcall.htm)

How can you stop sellers from calling, what are the signs of a scam or fraud, and who can you contact for help?

Consumer Handbook to Credit Protection Laws

(http://www.federalreserve.gov/creditcard/regs.html)

This guide explains how consumer credit laws can help and protect you.

Consumer's Guide to Disability Income Insurance

(http://www.ahip.org/content/default.aspx?bc=41%7C329%7C352)

This booklet covers the significant chances of becoming disabled during one's career, how a disability can affect one's finances, potential sources of disability income, what disability insurance covers, and what to look for in an insurance plan. (PDF file at http://www.ahip.org/content/default.aspx?bc=41%7C329%7C19531).

Credit and Divorce

(http://www.ftc.gov/bcp/edu/pubs/consumer/credit/cre08.shtm)

Compares the benefits and disadvantages of individual, joint and "user" accounts. Includes steps to take if you divorce or separate. (PDF file at http://www.ftc.gov/bcp /edu/pubs/consumer/credit/cre08.pdf).

Credit Card Repayment Calculator

(http://www.federalreserve.gov/creditcardcalculator/)

The Federal Reserve Board has put on their Website an easy "calculator" to estimate how long it will take to pay off credit card debt.

Credit Repair: How to Help Yourself

(http://www.ftc.gov/bcp/edu/pubs/consumer/credit/cre13.shtm)

You see the advertisements in newspapers, on TV, and on the Internet. You hear them on the radio. You get fliers in the mail, and maybe even calls offering credit repair ser-

vices. Use this free guide, instead, before you hire someone. (PDF file at http://www.ftc
.gov/bcp/edu/pubs/consumer/credit/cre13.pdf).

Credit Reporting 101 PDF

(http://www.ncua.gov/NewsPublications/Publications/PDF/brochures/Financial
Education/Cr-Reporting.pdf)

When was the last time you checked your credit report for accuracy? How do you
obtain your credit score? What does your credit report mean to those who lend you
money and credit? Not only does your credit report affect your financial life, but it can
also affect your career, education, and the interest rates that lenders offer you. By periodically reviewing your credit report, you can see your payment history, understand
how your credit is rated, prevent errors from going undetected, and know how to wait
until you need an accurate credit report the most.

Electronic Banking

(http://www.ftc.gov/bcp/edu/pubs/consumer/credit/cre14.shtm)

Learn more about electronic transactions, such as debit cards and online account
access, including how transactions are processed, their timing, security, and legal protections. (PDF file at http://www.ftc.gov/bcp/edu/pubs/consumer/credit/cre14.pdf).

Employment Background Checks and Credit Reports

(http://www.ftc.gov/bcp/edu/pubs/consumer/credit/cre36.shtm)

Credit reporting companies and other businesses that provide background information sell your file to employers that, in turn, use it to evaluate your applications for
employment. Employers also are allowed to use these reports to consider you for
retention, promotion, or reassignment.

Finding a Lost Pension PDF

(http://www.pbgc.gov/docs/Finding_A_Lost_Pension.pdf)

Here's how to find out if you have an unclaimed pension, where to search, documents
you'll need, and what to do when you find your pension fund.

Fiscal Fitness: Choosing a Credit Counselor

(http://www.ftc.gov/bcp/edu/pubs/consumer/credit/cre26.shtm)

Credit counselors offer a variety of services that can help you put your financial life
back in order. Use this guide to choose the credit counselor that is right for you.

How the SEC Handles Your Complaint

(http://www.sec.gov/investor/pubs/howoiea.htm)

Information on how and when to file an investor complaint with the SEC.

How to Resolve a Complaint against a Thrift Institution or Savings Association PDF
(http://files.ots.treas.gov/4809245.pdf)

Information on how the Office of Thrift Supervision of the U.S. Department of Treasury may be able to help.

iBonds Investor's Guide

(http://www.savingsbonds.gov/indiv/research/indepth/ibonds/res_ibonds.htm)

Follow this easy-to-read Q&A format to find out if iBonds are a good way for you to save and invest money.

Identity Crisis ... What to Do If Your Identity Is Stolen

(http://www.ftc.gov/bcp/edu/pubs/consumer/idtheft/idt07.shtm)

It sounds like something out of a spy movie, but it can happen. Thieves can get your bank, credit, debit, charge, and Social Security card numbers. Find out how to protect yourself. (PDF file at http://www.ftc.gov/bcp/edu/pubs/consumer/idtheft/idt07.pdf).

Invest Wisely

(http://www.sec.gov/investor/pubs/inws.htm)

Basic tips to help you select a brokerage firm and representative, and make and monitor an investment. Identifies questions to ask and warning signs to look for to avoid problems.

Investors' Bill of Rights

(http://www.pueblo.gsa.gov/cic_text/money/investor-bill/investor.htm)

What you should know about investments and what information you are entitled to before investing. (PDF file at http://www.pueblo.gsa.gov/cic_text/money/investor-bill/investor.pdf).

IRS Guide to Free Tax Services

(http://www.irs.gov/pub/irs-pdf/p910.pdf)

The IRS provides this booklet to help you with taxes. Publication 910, IRS Guide to Free Tax Services, lists and explains the many tools, information, and services that the IRS provides to help you meet your tax obligations. It also covers recorded tax information and automated information about your refund. Most of these resources are available for free.

Money & Mobility: For Military Personnel and Families

(http://www.saveandinvest.org/microsites/moneymobility/000100.asp)

A comprehensive resource to help you prepare for deployments and duty station changes. Focuses on a wide variety of financial issues and the concerns of service members with children. Discusses money traps and scams; gives tips on investing and saving.

Money Tips for All Ages: Your Finances at Different Stages of Life

(http://www.fdic.gov/consumers/consumer/news/cnspr08/)

Practical help for teens, young adults, newlyweds, people at midlife, parents, retirees, and financial caregivers. Also for those dealing with a medical emergency, job loss or other major life events. (PDF file at http://www.fdic.gov/consumers/consumer/news/cnspr08/spring_08_bw.pdf).

Need a Loan? Think Twice about Using Your Home as Collateral
(http://www.ftc.gov/bcp/edu/pubs/consumer/homes/rea01.shtm)
> Useful tips to help you protect your home and equity when applying for a loan. (PDF file at http://www.ftc.gov/bcp/edu/pubs/consumer/homes/rea01.pdf).

New Consumer Protections for Credit Cards and Mortgages
(http://www.fdic.gov/CONSUMERS/CONSUMER/news/cnsum09/index.html)
> A new law that went into effect in 2010 protects consumers from surprise fees, rate increases and other credit card penalties. New rules effective in 2009 and 2010 prohibit many of the unfair and deceptive mortgage lending practices that led some borrowers to unaffordable home loans. This booklet details the eagerly-awaited changes. (PDF file at http://www.fdic.gov/CONSUMERS/CONSUMER/news/cnsum09/Summer09 Color.pdf).

New Credit Card Rules Effective August 22, 2010
(http://www.federalreserve.gov/consumerinfo/wyntk_creditcardrules2.htm)
> More new rules from the Federal Reserve mean more new credit card protections for you. Here are some key changes you should expect from your credit card company that went into effect on August 22, 2010.

Reverse Mortgages: Are They for You?
(http://www.occ.gov/news-issuances/consumer-advisories/2009/consumer-advisory-2009-2.html)
> Reverse mortgages generally are available to consumers who are 62 or older, and they can be used to supplement retirement income or meet health care or other financial needs. But beware—reverse mortgages are complex loans and are secured by your home.

Settling Your Credit Card Debts
(http://www.ftc.gov/bcp/edu/pubs/consumer/credit/cre02.shtm)
> Many different kinds of services claim to help people with debt problems. Among them are "debt settlement" companies that negotiate with your creditors to reduce the amount you owe. But there is no guarantee that debt settlement companies can persuade a credit card company to accept partial payment of a legitimate debt. (PDF file at http://www.ftc.gov/bcp/edu/pubs/consumer/credit/cre02.pdf).

Shopping with Your ATM Card
(http://www.pueblo.gsa.gov/cic_text/money/shopwith-atmcard/shop-atm.htm)
> Describes the new and expanded ways you can use an ATM card. Also provides safety precautions and a listing of ATM networks and affiliated shopping services by state.

Start Smart: Money Management for Teens
(http://www.fdic.gov/consumers/consumer/news/cnsum06/index.html)
> Teens have access to more money than ever before, thanks to allowances and gifts and, for many, income from chores, summer jobs or part-time jobs. Teens also are becoming more responsible for handling money and making decisions—for everything from

small, everyday purchases to bigger-ticket items (such as a bike or a camera) to saving for college. If you consistently make smart decisions about your money, you can have more of it for what you truly need.

Taking Control of Your Finances
(http://www.fdic.gov/consumers/consumer/news/cnspr05/index.html)
A handy guide geared toward young adults—from those still in school to just starting a career or a family. Learn the right ways to save and manage money and how to avoid some common mistakes people make with their money. (PDF file at http://www.fdic.gov/consumers/consumer/news/cnspr05/spring_05_color.pdf).

Ten Questions to Ask When Choosing a Financial Planner
(http://www.pueblo.gsa.gov/cic_text/money/financial-planner/10questions.html)
Covers credentials, costs, services, an interview checklist, and resources to contact for more information. (PDF file at http://www.pueblo.gsa.gov/cic_text/money/financial-planner/10questions.pdf).

Trading in Cash Accounts: Beware of the 90-Day Freeze under Regulation T
(http://www.sec.gov/investor/alerts/cashaccounts.pdf)
The SEC's Office of Investor Education and Advocacy issued an investor bulletin to help educate investors regarding the rules that apply to trading securities in cash accounts and to highlight the 90-day account freeze that may arise with certain trading activities in these type of accounts.

What You Need to Know: New Overdraft Rules for Debit and ATM Cards
(http://www.federalreserve.gov/consumerinfo/wyntk_overdraft.htm)
Bank account overdraft fees can be a source of unexpected costs for consumers. Understand the rules that provide additional protection when a debit card or automated teller machine (ATM) transaction causes an account to be overdrawn. It contains basic information about types and typical costs of overdraft services and defines common terms consumers may encounter in communications from their bank about overdrafts.

What You Need to Know: New Rules about Credit Decisions and Notices
(http://federalreserve.gov/consumerinfo/wyntk_notices.htm)
Describes the types of notices consumer may receive and provides links to sample notices. It includes information about what consumers should do if they receive a notice, including instructions on how to dispute credit report errors.

What You Need to Know: New Rules for Gift Cards
(http://www.federalreserve.gov/consumerinfo/wyntk_giftcards.htm)
New Federal Reserve rules provide important protections when you purchase or use gift cards. This publication describes the types of cards that are covered under gift card rules released last month and highlights key protections, including new limits on expiration dates, requirements for clear fee disclosures, and fee restrictions. These key changes apply to gift cards sold on or after August 22, 2010.

What You Should Know about Financial Planning
(http://www.pueblo.gsa.gov/cic_text/money/aboutfinan-planning/aboutfpbroc.html)
Discusses the benefits of financial planning for life-changing events, such as buying a home or retirement. (PDF file at http://www.pueblo.gsa.gov/cic_text/money/aboutfinan-planning/aboutfpbroc.pdf).

You Have the Power to Stop Identity Theft PDF
(http://files.ots.treas.gov/4820291.pdf)
There is a type of identity theft using the Internet called "phishing." Pronounced "fishing," that's exactly what thieves are doing: fishing for your personal financial information. They want your account numbers, passwords, Social Security numbers, and other confidential information so they can use your financial accounts or run up bills on your credit cards. If you understand how phishing works and how to protect yourself, you can help stop this crime.

Your Credit Scores
(http://www.pueblo.gsa.gov/cic_text/money/creditscores/your.htm)
Your credit score is a number based on the information in your credit file that rates how much of a risk you are. Learn why your credit score matters, what good and bad scores are, the elements of your FICO credit score, and how you can raise your score. (PDF file at http://www.pueblo.gsa.gov/cic_text/money/creditscores/your.pdf).

Your Investments
(http://www.fdic.gov/deposit/investments/investments/index.html)
Consumer facts about investments that are not deposits and are not insured by the FDIC.

Your New, Higher FDIC Insurance Coverage
(http://www.fdic.gov/consumers/consumer/news/cnfall08/)
Up to $250,000 of your money is now protected in FDIC-insured banks. Learn about expanded protection of certain trust and checking accounts, how to qualify for more than $250,000 at one bank, why and how to use the FDIC's deposit insurance calculator, plus common misconceptions and tips for avoiding costly errors. (PDF file at http://www.fdic.gov/consumers/consumer/news/cnfall08/fall_08_color.pdf).

Your Rights as a Financial Planning Client
(http://www.pueblo.gsa.gov/cic_text/money/fprights/fprights.htm)
Here's a checklist of your rights, what to expect from your financial planner, and what to do if you have a problem. (PDF file at http://www.pueblo.gsa.gov/cic_text/money/fprights/fprights.pdf)

Small Business

Avoiding Office Supply Scams
(http://business.ftc.gov/documents/bus24-avoiding-office-supply-scams)
Learn the most common office scams and tips to avoid receiving overpriced or unordered merchandise. (PDF file at http://www.ftc.gov/bcp/edu/pubs/business/fraud/bus24.pdf)

Consumer Guide to Buying a Franchise

(http://business.ftc.gov/documents/inv05-buying-franchise-consumer-guide)

Want to start your own business? Find out about the benefits of franchise ownership, the limitations, choosing the best franchise for you, and investigating franchise offerings. (PDF file at http://www.ftc.gov/bcp/edu/pubs/consumer/invest/inv05.pdf).

Copier Data Security: A Guide for Businesses

(http://business.ftc.gov/documents/bus43-copier-data-security)

Your information security plans should cover the digital copiers your company uses. If the data on your copiers gets into the wrong hands, it could lead to fraud and identity theft. (PDF File at http://business.ftc.gov/sites/default/files/pdf/bus43-copier-data-security.pdf)

Copyright Basics

(http://www.copyright.gov/circs/circ01.pdf)

Covers what can be copyrighted, who can apply, registration procedures, filing fees, what forms to use, and more. (PDF file at http://www.copyright.gov/circs/circ01.pdf).

Diversifying Your Workforce

(http://www.dol.gov/odep/pubs/20100727.pdf)

Resourceful and flexible, people with disabilities make excellent employees. But not all employers know how to recruit, hire, and retain them. This quick reference guide outlines the advantages of hiring people with disabilities and gives four simple steps to help you accomplish this goal. (PDF file at http://www.dol.gov/odep/pubs/20100727.pdf).

General Information Concerning Patents

(http://www.uspto.gov/patents/resources/general_info_concerning_patents.jsp)

Learn about patent laws, application procedures, costs, and more in this revision. Includes application form with instructions.

Guide to Business Credit for Women, Minorities, and Small Businesses

(http://www.federalreserve.gov/pubs/buscredit/default3.htm)

Find out what loans are available, the credit approval process, and your legal rights.

Introduction to Federal Taxes for Small Business/Self-Employed

(http://www.irs.gov/businesses/small/index.html)

Explains what you need to document expenses and deductions and file federal taxes.

Is Your Business Cybersecure?

(http://www.staysafeonline.org/for-business)

Tips for small businesses to help keep their information systems safe.

Q's & A's for Small Business Employers

(http://www.osha.gov/Publications/OSHA3163/osha3163.html)

Use this guide to develop an effective safety and health program, identify safety hazards, reduce injuries, and more. (PDF file at http://www.osha.gov/Publications/osha3163.pdf).

Small Business Resource Guide
(http://www.osha.gov/Publications/OSHA3163/osha3163.html)
Helpful CD-ROM contains business tax forms, instructions, and publications, plus guidance on preparing a business plan, financing your business, and more.

Using Credit Reports: What Employers Need to Know
(http://business.ftc.gov/documents/bus08-using-consumer-reports-what-employers-need-know)
Explains the legal steps you must take when using credit reports to hire or evaluate employees. (PDF file at http://www.ftc.gov/bcp/edu/pubs/business/credit/bus08.pdf)

Virtual Small Business Tax Workshop
(http://www.irs.gov/businesses/small/article/0,,id=200274,00.html)
Covers a variety of small business tax issues including payroll taxes, electronic filing, and the latest tax law changes that may affect the small business owner.

Glossary

401(k) Plan: a corporate retirement plan that allows employees to set aside a certain percentage of their income, tax deferred, up to a limit, and to withdraw from this account when they retire.

403(b) Plan: similar to a 401(k) retirement plan, except it is open to public education employees and employees of certain types of nonprofit organizations.

529 Plan: a plan designed to make higher education more affordable for families by helping parents save for college or prepay college and university tuition for their children. Also called a Qualified Tuition Plan.

adjustable rate mortgage: a loan that offers a fixed rate of interest for a short period of time—usually three, five, or seven years. At that point, the interest rate may change up or down, depending on what index the interest rate is tied to.

AFUE Rating: the Annual Fuel Utilization Efficiency Rating measures the overall performance of a heating boiler or furnace. A furnace with an AFUE of 92% means that 92% of your heating expense heats your house, while 8% escapes out the chimney or through some other exit.

amortize: to pay down or gradually eliminate a debt or loan (e.g., a mortgage or auto loan) by regular installment payments or transfers each period, with payments covering the principal and interest of the loan.

appraisal: when your bank or mortgage company inspects the house to see if the amount of money that they wish to loan equals what they see as the value of the house.

assets: tangible or intangible economic resource, which when given a monetary value, has the potential to produce value for the company.

295

back-end ratio: your total monthly housing cost plus all other debts divided by your monthly gross income.

balloon payment: the final payment at a date in the future, when the remaining loan balance (mortgage, commercial loan, or any other amortized loan) of principal and interest is paid in order to satisfy the loan repayment terms of a lender. Usually used when the full value of a loan is not amortized over the life of a loan; the borrower may then secure another loan at current interest rates after the balloon payment is made.

bank: a financial institution that is licensed by the government that provides a variety of financial services such as accounts in which to save, including savings accounts, retirement accounts like IRA's and 401k's, certificates of deposit, spending accounts like checking accounts, and debit and ATM cards to make transactions.

bear market: a period of time when the prevailing stock prices are trending downward by more than 20% for two months or more.

blue chip stock: stocks that are nationally recognized as coming from stable, profitable companies capable of weathering financial downturns.

bond: a financial instrument or debt security, which is issued by governments, both local, state and federal, as well as corporations, large and small, that offer fixed interest payments over a period of time greater than one year.

budget: the established limit of the amount of expected expenses during a defined future period.

bull market: a period of time when there are more buyers than sellers of stocks, causing overall stock prices to rise, and in which investor confidence is trending higher in anticipation of rising prices that will increase their investment values over time.

capital gain/loss: the difference between your cost basis, or what you paid for an asset, and what you sold it for. If the difference is positive, meaning its value increased, it is called a capital gain; if the price decreases from the time of purchase, then it is called a capital loss.

Chapter 7: bankruptcy filers forfeit all of their assets and their debts are forgiven.

Chapter 13: bankruptcy filers work out a payment plan with the court to ensure that all or part of the debt is eventually paid.

close-ended mutual fund: a type of mutual fund that offers a fixed number of shares on a public exchange during its initial public offering and then is listed on an exchange with the price of the shares determined by the supply and demand for shares in that fund, as well as the underlying value of the stocks in the portfolio of the fund.

comparables: houses that are physically similar to your house that are in a specific radius of distance from your target house and have sold in the recent past. It indicates the "market price" of the house, the price at which the comparable house actually sold for.

co-pay: a short form of the word co-payment, an expense that the insured must pay whenever medical services are rendered.

corporate bonds: corporations issue bonds in order to raise capital to fund projects instead of issuing new stock to raise capital. Corporate bonds come in several forms, depending on the maturity: short term (less than five years), intermediate term (five to twelve years), and long term (over twelve years).

correction: occurrence in the stock markets when the trends of indexes show a decline in the prices of 10% to 20% over a short period of time, usually one day to less than two months.

cost basis: the amount of money that you use to purchase an item that you own.

CPA: a certified public accountant who has passed the CPA examination, administered by the American Institute of Certified Public Accountants, and has been certified by his or her state to practice accounting.

credit card: a card issued by a company that allows users to borrow money from the card issuer in exchange for paying the provider in full for the good or service.

credit counselor: a person employed by a credit counseling agency whose job is to help the client understand how spending and misuse of credit has created debt; the counselor guides people to solutions to reduce their debt and improve their overall financial situation.

credit union: a credit union is a nonprofit institution that provides many of the same financial services of traditional banks, including allowing members to hold deposits and clear checks against checking account deposits, and it provides members with credit in the form of loans.

curb appeal: the impression that your house makes to buyers when driving by, or as they first approach your house on the way in.

custodial account: an account that is in the name of the child, but the main signatory and responsible party on the account is the child's custodian, usually a parent.

data aggregator: a company that culls the Internet, looking for personal identifying information such as your name, address, mortgage information, legal information, phone numbers, past addresses, names of children, and your age, and ties this information together in order to sell the information to marketers and the general public.

debit card: a card issued by a bank that allows the user to withdraw funds or purchase goods and services by immediately debiting the card holder's bank account for the purchase.

debt consolidation: the act of taking out a loan in order to pay off several other debt obligations.

deductible: the amount of money that one must pay toward a loss in order to collect on a claim.

depreciating asset: something that loses value over time.

DIF score: an abbreviation for the IRS's Discriminate Information Function system average, which uses an analytical formula to allow the IRS to see which returns are falling outside the norm in terms of income, deductions, credits, etc. The IRS then targets those returns for audits to see if they can collect back taxes that are due.

discretionary expense: an expense that we incur at our discretion or by our own choice. Many of our financial problems involve these expenses.

diversification: the act of making investments in different categories with the hope and expectation that the risk of losing money is spread out, or diversified, within the portfolio, thus reducing the overall risk of losing money on the whole portfolio.

dollar cost averaging: a simple timing strategy of investing in which an investor buys the same dollar amount of a stock at regular intervals.

Dow Jones Industrial Average: a price-weighted average of thirty blue chip stocks that are traded on the New York Stock Exchange; the Dow is often considered a barometer for the health of the American economy.

down payment: the amount that you pay in cash for the initial purchase of the house, usually a percentage ranging from three to twenty percent of the home's total purchase price.

educational grant: money given to a student that does not need to be repaid.

equalized value: the value of your property after an assessment, which is then adjusted so that all similar properties are equally and uniformly assessed.

expense ratio: the amount of expenses divided by the average net asset value of the portfolio of stocks, expressed as a percentage.

FAFSA: the Free Application for Federal Student Aid, which covers all types of student aid, from grants, loans, and work study to non-federal aid; all college and university undergraduate students must fill out a FAFSA order to apply for financial aid.

FDIC: The Federal Deposit Insurance Corporation, which was set up during the Great Depression in 1933 to fight the effects of the thousands of bank failures that happened in the preceding years. It protects depositors up to $250,000 per account holder at each institution and guarantees this amount for every depositor at every FDIC-insured institution in the United States.

fiduciary: when your adviser will put you, the client's interest first, above his own, the firm, or the investment companies that he or she may represent.

fixed-rate mortgage: a mortgage that has a fixed interest rate for the period of the loan and allows the purchaser to pay off the loan over a period of time, usually ten, fifteen, twenty, thirty, or even forty to fifty years.

flexible-spending account: this allows consumers to set aside money in an account to be used for medical expenses during the plan year, plus two and a half months, all free from payroll taxes.

forced savings: a method of saving in which an individual puts aside a certain amount of money each week that is not used for consumer expenses during the year.

front-end ratio: your total monthly housing cost divided by your gross monthly income.

fundamental analysis: the analysis of the effects of various economic indicators and financial statements that have influenced and may influence the prices of stocks in financial markets.

government bonds: treasury bills, which mature in less than one year; treasury notes, which mature in one to ten years; and treasury bonds, which mature in more than ten years.

health savings account: a medical savings account, which offers consumers a tax advantage since they pay no federal income taxes at the time of deposit for the funds that are deposited. The money can be used to pay for health expenses, including any out-of-pocket expenses related to your medical care.

home equity: the current market value of your home, minus any mortgages or liens on the home.

identity theft: the stealing of personal identifying information from someone and using this information to commit fraudulent and criminal acts.

individual investor: each individual person who directly or indirectly purchases stocks or bonds and invests in the market on his or her own account.

insider trading: when corporate insiders (officers, directors, and employees) buy and sell stock in their own companies; the law requires them to report their trades to the SEC.

institutional investor: large organizations that pool money together from other large organizations and individuals and invest this money in companies, both private and public.

intangible assets: nonphysical assets, such as patents that have been applied for, the name of the company and its brand identity and logos, trademarks, or the experience of the people on staff.

interest-only loan: a loan that allows a person to pay only the interest on a loan for a period of time. At the end of this period, the borrower must make a balloon payment of the value of the entire loan, or refinance the loan into a conventional loan.

investing: the act of using money to buy a financial product with the expectation of making more money than what you used to initially buy the financial product over a period of time.

IPO: an initial public offering is when a company offers the public shares for the first time in the company in the hope of raising capital.

IRA: An individual retirement account gives individuals who do not have access to an employer-sponsored retirement plan the means to having one; IRAs give individuals the ability to preserve a tax advantages and the growth opportunities of having a retirement plan when they leave their job.

irrevocable: an account that cannot be changed.

life insurance: a policy in which the insurance company will pay out the value of the insurance policy to one or more beneficiaries when the insured dies.

living will: a written statement of wishes regarding the use of specific medical treatments. It is provided to the doctor, hospital, or medical provider and becomes part of the official medical record.

loaded funds: mutual funds that charge a fee for purchasing or selling shares in the fund. They typically have the highest expenses associated with them and are offered by brokers who may then get paid commissions on transactions.

loan origination fee: see "points."

loan-to-value ratio: the loan amount divided by the selling price of a house.

marginal tax rate or bracket: see "progressive tax rate."

matching program: employers match a percentage of what you put into your 401(k), as long as you set aside a certain minimum amount each year, with a limit on the amount per year.

medical deductible: the amount of expenses that the medically insured must pay before the insurance company will pay for the covered services.

medical power of attorney: allows you to appoint an agent (usually a close relative), who is then legally authorized to make health care decisions for you in the event you are unable to make such decisions.

Medicare: the U.S. government's medical insurance, which is available to people of retirement age.

millage: the number of tax dollars that property owners must pay per $1,000 dollars of taxable value of their property. Also called a tax rate.

MLS: a multi-list service is an electronic database of every property for sale nation-wide.

mortgage: the amount of money loaned from a bank, which is the price of the house that is purchased and financed by the bank in the form of a loan to the buyer, less any down payment and closing costs at the closing of the transaction.

multiple: a company with a P/E ratio of 15 is also called "trading at a multiple of 15," meaning that someone who buys this stock is willing to pay fifteen dollars for every dollar of earnings, or a multiple of earnings.

municipal bonds: When a city government needs capital to fund the building of a water system, improve roads, or build a new school, etc., they typically fund this activity through the issuance of a bond.

mutual fund: a professionally managed investment vehicle that pools the funds from many investors and collectively invests these funds in stocks, bonds, cash instruments, commodities, other mutual funds, real estate, and many other types of investment instruments, which enable the investors to gain or lose from the performance of the fund.

no-load mutual funds: funds that do not charge any fee for either purchasing or selling shares of that fund.

open-ended fund: a mutual fund that has no restrictions on the number of shares it issues to the public and is continuously buying and selling shares of its portfolio of stocks to both new and current investors.

overdraft: when we write a check or make a withdrawal from our account for an amount in excess of what our current balance is and a fee is charged.

participant directed: an employee can choose from a variety of stocks, mutual funds, and bond funds, as well as the company's own stock (if the company is publicly traded), and invest a sum of money before taxes each pay period for his or her retirement.

P/E ratio: the price-earnings ratio is the current price of a stock divided by the amount of earnings per share.

personal capital asset: Nearly everything that you have purchased and own for personal purposes is a capital asset. It could be an individual stock, the value of your rental house, etc.

personal finance: the management of our income, expenses and investments in order for us to realize our personal financial goals.

phishing: when a spammer sends out an email with content that makes the recipient think that it is a legitimate site for the purpose of obtaining personal information.

points: fees that lenders typically charge for a fixed-fee mortgage, with one point usually being one percent of the loan amount. Also called loan origination fees.

portfolio: a mixture of investments of different types and risks that individuals or institutions may own in hopes of making more money over time.

power of attorney: allows you to specifically grant someone the legal power to act on your behalf in legal or financial matters; it may be "general" or "limited" for a definite or indefinite period of time.

pre-approved: a lender has already investigated the client's credit worthiness and has established that the client can borrow up to a certain amount from the lender.

premiums: the amount that you pay each month for your insurance coverage.

pre-paid credit card: a card that allows consumers to purchase a credit card with a small sum of money deposited, and then use the card to pay for goods and services.

pre-qualified: the bank or mortgage company has looked at a potential borrower's income and debt to determine the approximate amount of the loan. It does not mean that the borrower has been approved for a loan yet.

principal: the face value of the loan or bond, the original loan amount that is what is used to calculate interest payments. The principal and the interest is what an investor receives when a bond is due or matures.

probate court: where the county administers an estate in the name of one person

progressive tax rate: a tax rate that changes depending on the amount of income earned in a year. As someone earns more income, the percentage of that income to be paid in taxes increases. The higher the income you make, the more able you are to pay the tax. It is also known as marginal tax rate or marginal tax bracket.

property tax: a general term referring to the taxes levied on the value of one's principle residence, with the proceeds going to financing of local services, education, operational costs for the city and county that you live in, and the financing of special projects such as sewers, streets, and parks, depending on what state you live in and what state services are provided.

Qualified Tuition Plan: see "529 Plan."

renter's insurance: a policy that covers the loss incurred by the tenants in a building for their possessions.

residual value: the amount of money that the finance company says a car is worth at the end of a lease period.

ROI : the return on the investment, usually expressed as a percentage, meaning how much more money will you make or earn over a period of time as a result of buying the investment.

sales tax: a tax levied by states on the sale of goods and services.

Schedule A: a tax form used—in conjunction with form 1040—that enables you to report all of your itemized deductions for the tax year, including medical and dental expenses, taxes paid to state authorities, city taxes, interest paid on loans, like mortgage interest, and charitable gifts, etc.

SEC: the U.S. Securities and Exchange Commission, an arm of the federal government, provides protection to investors, maintains fair, orderly, and efficient markets, and facilitates capital formation. It consists of five president-appointed commissioners, who serve five-year terms, and has eleven regional offices. It interprets and enforces federal security laws and issues rules ands amendments pertaining to these laws, which investment firms must then follow, inspects the investment firm community, oversees private regulatory organizations, and assists in the coordination of U.S. securities regulation with federal, state, and foreign authorities.

shadow inventory: the inventory of houses that most likely will move into foreclosure, thus increasing the supply of houses and depressing house prices.

Small Business Administration: The SBA provides many financial assistance programs (loans, grants, venture capital and bonds) to help small business owners to become successful.

staging: the act of changing the furnishings, either by buying, renting, or rearranging the layout of each room, in order to present your house for sale in the best possible manner.

standard deduction: The IRS gives all tax filers a standard deduction, depending on their filing status.

Statement of Benefits: a document generated each time you have a medical treatment or consultation; it describes exactly the service that was performed, what the cost was, what the insurance company thinks the cost should be, what your co-pay, if any, was for the service, and what you owe the service provider.

stock market: a place, whether a physical building or an online virtual environment, where stocks are bought and sold.

stocks: a way of owning the assets and earnings of a company. Companies that offer the opportunity for investors to own stock in the company place a value in the shares, or pieces, of the company based upon the value of all of the assets of the company and the value of the past, current, and future earnings of the company. A stock can be purchased, sold, or traded.

tangible assets: physical buildings, property, factories, stock of products sitting in a warehouse, stocks, or cash sitting in a bank.

tax credit: an item that allows you to reduce the taxes that you must pay; it is generally more valuable to you than a tax deduction.

tax deduction: an item that reduces your taxable income, which is then used to help compute the amount of taxes that you owe at the end of the year.

tax-exempt bonds: bonds issued by a municipal, county, or state government, with interest payments that are not subject to any state, local, or sometimes federal taxes, depending on what bonds you buy and in which state or municipality you reside.

tax preparer: someone who, for a fee, may prepare your tax filings. Preparers usually have had some sort of formal training, may have their own practice, or work at one of the nationwide chains.

tax rate: see "millage."

tax refund: a check from the U.S. Treasury, after taking into consideration income tax, withholdings, tax deductions, or credits and other factors; it represents the amount of money that you overpaid in taxes during that year.

tax schedule: a rate sheet used by individual taxpayers to approximate their estimated taxes due. It is also a term used to describe the addendum worksheets that accompany the IRS Form 1040, including schedules A (itemized deductions), B (dividend & interest income), C (business profit or loss), and D (capital gains).

technical analysis: a method of understanding the patterns and trends of the price of stocks, and which uses this information in order to profit in the future from those trends.

ticker symbol: a unique series of characters, sometimes as many as four or more characters long, that identify the name of the investment actively traded on an exchange.

timing the market: the act of using economic, fundamental, and technical indicators to predict future performance and time one's decisions to enter or exit a stock position based upon this information.

total return: the percent at which your investment grows over time, including all interest, dividends, and capital appreciation, less any fees or commissions.

trust: a trust allows the deceased to pass on assets to heirs without having to go through probate court.

turnover rate: a measurement of the funds trading activity and what percentage of the total portfolio is traded each period.

underwater: when sellers owe more on the balance of their home mortgages than they can make when they sell the house.

Uniform Transfers to Minors Act: an act created in 1986—and adopted by most states and in keeping with the IRS code—that allows for the transfer of funds to one's child or children up to an annual limit of $13,000, tax free.

vesting: after working for a defined period of time, the employee is able to own and keep whatever retirement account balances and employer-matching funds have been deposited into one's "vested" account.

virtual bank: an online bank with no physical branch locations. It exists completely on the Internet.

volatility: the relative rate that the price of a stock or market index moves both up and down. If a price moves up and down over short periods of time, it is said to be highly volatile; if the price doesn't move very much it has low volatility.

will: a legal document that includes the name of the person that you wish to execute your will and to carry out your wants (personal representative), names the guardian to your children who will then be responsible for their finances, and describes how you want your estate to be distributed to your heirs.

zero-based budgeting: a method of budgeting in which one accounts for the spending of every dollar of income from all sources. If any one category must be revised upward, another must be revised downward so the net effect is zero on the total amount that is spent during the budgeting period.

Index

(ill.) indicates photos and illustrations.

311

314

315